CRISIS IN LUTHERAN THEOLOGY

The Validity and Relevance of Historic Lutheranism vs. Its Contemporary Rivals

Volume II

An Anthology Edited by
John Warwick Montgomery

BOOKS
NEW REFORMATION
PUBLICATIONS

An imprint of 1517 the Legacy Project

Crisis in Lutheran Theology: The Validity and Relevance of Historic Lutheranism vs. Its Contemporary Rivals. Volume 2: An Anthology Edited by John Warwick Montgomery

Published by:
New Reformation Publications
PO Box 54032
Irvine, CA 92619-4032

Printed in the United States of America

Publisher's Cataloging-In-Publication Data
(Prepared by The Donohue Group, Inc.)

Names: Montgomery, John Warwick, author. | Preus, Jacob A. O. (Jacob Aall Ottesen), 1920–1994, writer of supplementary textual content.
Title: Crisis in Lutheran theology : the validity and relevance of historic Lutheranism vs. its contemporary rivals / [written and edited] by John Warwick Montgomery ; with a preface by Dr. J.A.O. Preus, President, The Lutheran Church-Missouri Synod.
Description: V. 1 & 2 [3rd edition]. | V. 3 [1st edition, revised]. | Irvine, California : NRP Books, an imprint of 1517 the Legacy Project, [2017] | Includes bibliographical references and index. | Contents: Volume I. Essays / by John Warwick Montgomery— volume II. An anthology / edited by John Warwick Montgomery—volume III. Reformation 2017 and the Kloah Catastrophe : essays / by John Warwick Montgomery.
Identifiers: ISBN 9781945978616 (3 volume set) | ISBN 9781945978319 (hardcover: v.I) | ISBN 9781945978333 (hardcover: v.II) | ISBN 9781945978593 (hardcover: v.III, 1st ed.) | ISBN 9781945978326 (softcover: v.I) | ISBN 9781945978340 (softcover: v.II) | ISBN 9781945978906 (softcover: v.III) | ISBN 9781945978586 (softcover: v.III, 1st ed.) | ISBN 9781945500305 (ebook: v.I) | ISBN 9781945500756 (ebook: v.II) | ISBN 9781945978913 (ebook: v.III) | ISBN 9781945978609 (ebook: v.III, 1st. ed.)
Subjects: LCSH: Lutheran Church—Doctrines—History. | Theology, Doctrinal— History—20th century. | Theology, Doctrinal—History—21st century.
Classification: LCC BX8065.2 .M6 2017 (print) | LCC BX8065.2 (ebook) | DDC 230/.41—dc23

NRP Books, an imprint of New Reformation Publications, is committed to packaging and promoting the finest content for fueling a new Lutheran Reformation. We promote the defense of the Christian faith, confessional Lutheran theology, vocation and civil courage.

To
CONCERNED LUTHERAN LAYMEN
in the
Northern Illinois District

Matthew 12:30

INTRODUCTION

The eminent church historian Winthrop S. Hudson concludes his Chicago History of American Civilization volume on *American Protestantism* (1961) with high praise for Lutheranism and bright hope for its future:

> The Lutheran churches . . . exhibited an ability to grow during the post-World War II years, with the Lutheran Church-Missouri Synod making the greatest gains. The Lutheran churches are in the fortunate position of having been, in varying degrees, insulated from American life for a long period of time. As a result they have been less subject to the theological erosion which so largely stripped other denominations of an awareness of their continuity with a historic Christian tradition. Thus the resources of the Christian past have been more readily available to them, and this fact suggests that they may have an increasingly important role in a Protestant recovery. Among the assets immediately at hand among the Lutherans are a confessional tradition, a surviving liturgical structure, and a sense of community which, however much it may be the product of cultural factors, may make it easier for them than for most Protestant denominations to recover the "integrity of church membership" without which Protestants are ill-equipped to participate effectively in the dialogue of a pluralistic society.

Professor Hudson's analysis is sound and his prediction is well grounded; yet there are disquieting indications that the future of American Lutheranism may fall far short of his expectations. Why? His argument is based squarely on the consideration that, unlike other denominations, the Lutheran Church has been "less subject to theological erosion" and has therefore been able to retain "the resources of the Christian past." But the last decade has made painfully clear to all who have not worn the colored glasses of naiveté that the Lutheran churches in America — the Missouri Synod included — are now experiencing the very "theological erosion" which, as Hudson correctly notes, produces ecclesiastical deadness and irrelevance.

The essays in the two volumes of *Crisis in Lutheran Theology* endeavor to point up the extreme peril of the current theological situation. A conscious effort has been made to include not only papers directed to professional theologians but also essays that laymen untrained in theology will readily comprehend. (In general, the essays in Part One of each volume are orientated to the theologically sophisticated, and those in Part Two are suitable for lay study.) All who contribute to these volumes look with wonder and with thanksgiving to the Lutheran heritage that has provided so clear a testimony to Christ and to His inerrant Word; and every contributor prays the Lord of the Church that these volumes, published in the 450th anniversary year of the Reformation, may rouse sleeping churches from their torpor and drive them to "cast off the works of darkness and put on the armour of light."

5

Charles Porterfield Krauth, who fought and won a not dissimilar battle a century ago, speaks directly to us today in his *Conservative Reformation and Its Theology;* may we have the ears to hear him:

> Had a war of three hundred years been necessary to sustain the Reformation, we now know the Reformation would ultimately have repaid all the sacrifices it demanded. Had our fathers surrendered the truth, even under that pressure to which ours is but a feather, how we would have cursed their memory, as we contrasted what we were with what we might have been.
>
> And shall we despond, draw back, and give our names to the reproach of generations to come, because the burden of the hour seems to us heavy? God, in His mercy, forbid! If all others are ready to yield to despondency, and abandon the struggle, we, children of the Reformation, dare not. That struggle has taught two lessons, which must never be forgotten. One is, that the true and the good must be secured at any price. They are beyond all price. We dare not compute their cost. They are the soul of our being, and the whole world is as dust in the balance against them. No matter what is to be paid for them, we must not hesitate to lay down their redemption price. The other grand lesson is, that their price is never paid in vain. What we give can never be lost, *unless we give too little.* . . . If we maintain the pure Word inflexibly at every cost . . . we shall conquer . . . through the Word; but to compromise on a single point, is to lose all, and to be lost.

JOHN WARWICK MONTGOMERY

15 January 1967:
The Transfiguration of Our Lord

° ° °

Continued high interest in the *Crisis* volumes, as evidenced by their five printings over a six-year period, has dictated a second edition, with the opportunity to correct minor errors and to include additional essays bearing on the latest aspects of the struggle for a faithful Lutheran confessionalism.

Non-Lutherans who chance upon these volumes should not find themselves in alien territory. Since the work was first published, it has been of considerable service to Christians in many communions (such as the Presbyterian, Anglican, Methodist, Baptist, and Roman Catholic) where deterioration of historic Christian doctrine has paralleled the Lutheran problem on which these volumes especially focus. In actuality, the *Crisis* volumes do not deal narrowly with a crisis in *Lutheran* theology but with the general crisis in biblical and doctrinal authority which has become so endemic in the modern church.

This new edition thus goes forth to serve all those Christian believers who can pray the magnificent words of Duke Henry's Saxon Order of 1539: "O Lord God, heavenly Father, pour out, we beseech Thee, Thy Holy Spirit upon Thy faithful people, keep them steadfast in Thy grace and truth, protect and comfort them in all temptation, defend them against all enemies of Thy Word, and bestow upon Christ's church militant Thy saving peace."

JOHN WARWICK MONTGOMERY

6 January 1973:
The Epiphany of Our Lord

. . .

Does "history repeat itself," as the ancients taught? Not in an ultimate way, for the history of a fallen race will finally end in the glory of our Lord's return. But in lesser ways, there is certainly repetition. As George Santayana wisely put it, "Those who fail to learn from history are doomed to repeat it."

In the Lutheran Church-Missouri Synod of the 1960s and 1970s, the issue for biblical inerrancy was the so-called higher criticism; this book dealt with that problem in depth, offering help to all Christian churches faced with the same problem. Now, in that same conservative church body, the inerrancy of Holy Scripture is threatened by an unfortunate philosophy of lower or textual criticism; this third edition of *Crisis in Lutheran Theology* includes new material dealing with that sophisticated, contemporaneous technique capable of undermining total biblical truth.

But in a time such as ours, plagued by terrorism and political uncertainty, how really important is such a theological concern? To paraphrase the sage Black aphorism ("All dem dat's talkin' 'bout heaven ain't necessarily a-goin' there"), "All dem dat's using the word 'inerrancy' ain't necessarily a-talkin' 'bout the same thing." If we lose the revelatory Scriptures, we shall surely lose the Christ on whom those Scriptures center.

JOHN WARWICK MONTGOMERY

31 October 2017:
The 500th anniversary year Festival of the Reformation

ACKNOWLEDGEMENTS

The articles contained in this book have appeared previously in various American and German theological journals; bibliographical data on their original publication follows:

Sasse, Hermann. "The Inspiration of Holy Scripture," *Christianity Today*, March 16, 1962. (Copyright 1962 by *Christianity Today;* used by permission.)

Preus, Robert D. "The Doctrine of Revelation in Contemporary Theology," *The Evangelical Theological Society Bulletin*, Summer, 1966. (Used by permission.)

Friberg, H. Daniel. "The Locus of God's Speaking," *The Christian Century*, April 11, 1962. (Copyright 1962 by Christian Century Foundation; used by permission.)

Preus, Robert D. "Notes on the Inerrancy of Scripture," *The Evangelical Theological Society Bulletin*, Autumn, 1965. (Used by permission.)

Surburg, Raymond. "Implications of the Historico-Critical Method in Interpreting the Old Testament," *The Springfielder*, Spring and Summer, 1962. (Used by permission.)

Preus, Robert D. "Biblical Hermeneutics and the Lutheran Church Today," *Proceedings, Twentieth Convention, Iowa District West of the Lutheran Church-Missouri Synod*, 1966. (Used by permission.)

Spitz, Lewis W., Sr. "Luther's *Sola Scriptura*," *Concordia Theological Monthly*, December, 1960. (Used by permission.)

Carter, Douglas. "Luther As Exegete," *Concordia Theological Monthly*, September, 1961. (Used by permission.)

Bohlmann, Ralph A. "Principles of Biblical Interpretation in the Lutheran Confessions," *Aspects of Biblical Hermeneutics: Concordia Theological Monthly, Occasional Papers No. 1*, 1966. (Used by permission of Concordia Publishing House.)

Friberg, H. Daniel. "The Word of God and 'Propositional Truth'," *Christianity Today*, July 5, 1963. (Copyright 1963 by *Christianity Today;* used by permission.)

Neiswender, Donald R. "Found Too Late: The Word of God," *Christianity Today*, November 25, 1966. (Copyright 1966 by *Christianity Today;* used by permission.)

Preus, Robert D. "The Lutheran Church and the Ecumenical Movement" [original title: "Die ökumenische Bewegung und der lutherische ökumenizitätsbegriff"], *Lutherischer Rundblick*, February-March, 1964. (This essay appears for the first time in English in the present volume. It is used by permission.)

No effort has been made to harmonize the bibliographical styles of the several essays. It has been assumed that each author has chosen the format most appropriate to his subject content.

CONTENTS

Part One

Revelation and Inspiration

Part Two

Biblical Interpretation and Ecumenicity in Light of Luther and the Confessions

Part One

Revelation and Inspiration

I.

THE INSPIRATION OF HOLY SCRIPTURE

Hermann Sasse

Holy Scripture is the inspired Word of God. Whether we like it or not, this affirmation is a fundamental dogma of the Church universal. Christ himself made it a doctrine binding on his Church when he accepted it from the synagogue (cf. Matt. 22:43; Mark 12:36). Inspiration of the Scriptures was proclaimed by the apostles (Acts 1:16; 3:21; 4:25; 28:25; II Cor. 3:14 ff.; II Tim. 3:16; Heb. 3:7; 9:8; 10:15; II Pet. 1:19 ff.). It was confessed by the Church in that great ecumenical creed which binds together all churches of Christendom. For the words of our "Nicene Creed," (A.D. 381) concerning the Holy Spirit, "who spoke by the prophets," not only refer to the historical fact of the oral preaching of the prophets in the past, but also to the prophetic books (which include in the Old Testament also the preexilic historical books), as the words "according to the Scriptures" in the passage on Christ's resurrection (cf. I Cor. 15:3 f.) show. This scope is confirmed by both contemporary (Epiphanius) and later (for example, the Armenian) versions of the Creed; they contain formulas like "who spoke in the Law, and in the Prophets, and in the Apostles and in the Gospels." With the Nicene Creed, all Eastern and Western Catholic churches accepted this doctrine, and all churches of the Reformation reaffirmed it. The doctrine of the divinely inspired Scriptures is so closely linked to the central doctrines of the Creed, namely the doctrines on the Trinity and the Person of Christ, that any decay in understanding the Holy Scripture as God's Word leads necessarily to decay in believing in the God-Man Jesus Christ and in the Person of the Holy Spirit. The tragic history of modern Protestantism corroborates this relationship.

It is strange indeed that the common possession of all Christians should always be the center of disunity. All churches agree that the Bible is the Word of God. But what is the Bible? Not only the Canon but even the text of the Scriptures differs in East and West, in Rome and in the Protestant churches. This difference, incidentally, already existed in the Church of the New Testament, which used side by side the Septuagint and the Hebrew Old Testament.

But even where the same books and the same text are read, deep differences exist concerning crucial questions. Does God's revelation come to us in the Scripture only, or also in the unwritten tradition of the Church and in an inner experience of the soul? Is Scripture its own interpreter or did Christ

13

institute in his Church a teaching office which has to interpret Scripture with binding authority? These fundamental differences of opinion produce so many interpretations that the Bible has been called the book wherein everybody looks for his own views and finds them. Of what value, then, is the common conviction that the Bible is the Word of God?

The Great Unifying Factor

The Bible, despite all contradictory interpretations thereof, is the great unifying factor of Christendom. Christians have the content of Scripture in common. More than this, as long as they recognize the Scriptures as the Word of God they recognize a divine authority to which all must submit, an objective truth which transcends all subjective interpretations. Even Rome, which considers the teaching office of the Church (in the magisterium exercised by the Pope) as the divinely appointed, authoritative, and infallible interpreter of the Scriptures, could never subordinate the Scriptures to the Church in the manner that some modern Anglicans and Protestants are doing who regard the New Testament as a product of the Church. While the Church has created the canon by determining which books should be "canonical," that is, recognized by the Church, she was not at liberty to select just any book. She could receive only the "sacred" books, those which "as written by the inspiration of the Holy Spirit have God as their author and have been given as such to the Church," as the Vatican Council declares (Denzinger 1787). The Church therefore is bound to the divinely inspired Scriptures. Whatever the coordination of "Scripture" and "Tradition" in the decree of Trent and the coordination of "Holy Writ" and "Holy Church" by modern Catholics may mean in practice for the authority of Holy Writ, the Vatican dogma of the inspiration of the Scriptures makes it a heresy for any Catholic to declare any authority higher than Scripture.

This dogma of Holy Scripture as the inspired Word of God, together with the Trinitarian and Christological dogmas, was the common possession of all Christendom at the time of the Reformation. What Luther said to Rome concerning these "sublime articles of the divine majesty" is true also of the doctrine of the Bible as the Word of God: it is not a matter of dispute and contention. This fact explains why the early Protestant confessions contain no article on Holy Scripture. Only after the Council of Trent's doctrine of Scripture and Tradition and its definition of the Canon were the churches of the Reformation forced to speak on these issues. But even behind the controversies over the *Sola Scriptura* lies the common belief that Holy Scripture is the Word of God. However deep and irreconcilable are the doctrinal contrasts between Rome, Wittenberg, Zürich, Geneva, and Canterbury, these types of Christianity showed considerable agreement in their common acceptance of the teaching of the Nicene Creed including its doctrine of the Scriptures. Only from this perspective can we understand the various confessions of the sixteenth and seventeenth centuries as attempts to interpret not define Holy Scripture. It is really moving to note how they all had "the aim," as the Council of Trent puts it, "that errors may be removed and the purity of the Gospel be preserved in the Church."

The Loss of the Bible

Perhaps the greatest tragedy in Western Christendom has been, not the loss of unity in the sixteenth century, but rather the loss of what for generations still remained the common possession of even the separated churches. This tragedy began when Trent decided that the Gospel is contained both "in written books and in unwritten traditions, which were received by the apostles from the lips of Christ himself, or, by the same apostles, at the dictation of the Holy Spirit, and were handed on to us." Both the Scriptures and the traditions must be received and venerated, therefore, "with equal pious affection and reverence." Never before had the Western Church dared so to equate "traditions" and the Scriptures. Even when theologians like Hugh of St. Victor called the writings of the Fathers "Holy Scriptures," they distinguished them clearly from the canonical books which alone merited absolute faith and which alone were the valid basis of a dogma. In referring to Augustine's famous statement on the difference between canonical and all other writings, Aquinas makes very clear where Christian doctrine finds its authority: ". . . our faith rests on the revelation which has been made to the apostles and prophets who have written the canonical books" (*Summa th.* I, 1, 8). It is wrong to superimpose on medieval theology such a question as "Holy Writ or Holy Church?" which stems from a certain type of modern Catholic Dogmatics which removes the doctrine of the Church from its context in the Creed and puts it side by side with the doctrine of Holy Scripture into the "Fundamental Theology" which expounds the sources of revelation (for example, the new "Summa" of the Jesuits in Spain). The bishops at Trent who opposed the equation of "Scriptures" and "Traditions" saw the danger of just such a new dogma. They could hardly have realized the full extent of the tragedy that was to come. Since the content of tradition is never fully known, the teaching office of the Church responsible for interpreting tradition was bound to become a veritable new source of revelation. This danger has been corroborated by the development of modern Mariology into a counterpart to Christology. The dogmas of the Immaculate Conception (1854) and the Assumption of Mary (1950) cannot be proved from Scripture. Nor do the first four centuries of the Church supply any foundation for such traditions. That such tradition extends back to the apostles is believed solely on the authority of the pope. When he defines these dogmas, he declares them "revealed by God, and therefore to be believed by all the faithful." Those who reject these dogmas because they are found neither in the Scriptures nor in the old traditions of the Catholic Church "have suffered shipwreck concerning the faith and have fallen away from the unity of the Church." To what extent the great Bible movement now asserting itself in Roman Catholicism can restore what has been lost of the authority of Holy Scripture remains to be seen.

Protestants have always recognized the tragic development of Roman theology since the juxtaposition of Scripture and Tradition by Trent in 1546. Have they realized, however, the corresponding tragedy that has overtaken the churches that call themselves Churches of the Reformation? Do we perhaps behold the mote in our brother's eye but do not consider the beam in our own? That the mariological doctrines, which (as many Catholics expect) may some day be followed by the definition of a dogma of Mary as the co-redeemer and mediatrix of all graces, are not only unbiblical but also interfere with Christ's honor as the only mediator is certainly true. But why, in 1950, was the protest against the dogma of the Assumption so unimpressive? Why do our modern Protestant criticisms of Rome all lack authority which characterized the doctrinal statements of our fathers in the sixteenth and seventeenth centuries? The answer is clear enough.

A Scriptural Witness

The Protestantism of those days was not a negative protest against Roman errors. Rather, it was a positive witness to the authority of Holy Scripture as the only source and rule of all doctrines of the Church. To these Protestants Holy Scripture was the Word of God. We must recognize that the *Sola Scriptura* of the Reformation depends on the firm belief that the Bible *is* the Word of God. Where this belief is shaken or even abandoned, the authority of Scripture collapses. This is the tragedy of modern Protestantism. We cannot deal here with the process of this collapse. We only note that first the theologians and then one after another of the churches severed Scripture from the Word in their official statements of faith. They were satisfied with the assumption that this Word is only contained somewhere in the Scriptures, or that the Scriptures are only a record of a past revelation in the mighty acts of God which were the true Word of God. Or we hear that under certain circumstances the Bible can become the Word of God.

Because it is no longer understood, the doctrine of the inspiration of Scripture has been abandoned by the theologians in the majority of the Protestant churches. It is regarded as untenable. But the biblical doctrine of the *fact* of inspiration must not be confused or equated with Augustine's and Gregory's theories of the *method* of inspiration. Unfortunately, the psychological speculations of the Fathers have been accepted uncritically by theologians of the older Protestant groups. Strangely enough, it is a theological tradition of the Western Church that has prevented the churches of the Reformation from understanding the inspiration of Scripture as a work of the Holy Spirit, the Paraclete, a work which defies all psychological explanations.

Authoritative Doctrine

This loss of the authority of the Scriptures deprives modern Protestantism of its power to discuss doctrine with Rome. Roman Christians ask their "separated brethren" in the Protestant churches, if you reject the doctrine of Mary's immaculate conception as unscriptural, then why do so many of you reject also Christ's virgin birth, a doctrine which your fathers confessed with the Church of all ages and which undoubtedly is based on Holy Scripture? You reject the assumption of Mary as unbiblical legend, but you reject also the ascension of Jesus as myth even though it is taught in the Bible. You deny the right of the pope to interpret Holy Scripture authoritatively. But the great miracles of the virgin birth and of Christ's bodily resurrection, which are so inseparably linked to the incarnation of the eternal Son of God, the pope would never dare to interpret as legends and myths. Such liberty seems to be the privilege of Protestant professors of exegesis!

Bishop Hanns Lilje recently noted the significance of the conversion to Rome of Professor Heinrich Schlier of Bonn. This outstanding disciple of Bultmann, one of the most learned New Testament scholars in Germany, confessed that it was Bultmann's approach to the New Testament that led him in this direction. "What tribunal is to make decisions about these various strata of tradition which have been worked out, and who is to decide about their relative value? He preferred to attach himself to a tradition historically established as that of the Church of Rome rather than to trust himself to the unsure path of conflicting human opinions" (*Lutheran World*, Sept. 1961, p. 135). We do not expect many to follow Schlier. It is far easier and more respectable for a Protestant scholar to accept the authority of Bultmann, of Tillich, or of whatever other leader may arise. But Schlier's conversion reminds us of his predecessor's at Bonn; Erick Peterson also had turned to Rome. Such facts point up the sad condition of modern Protestant theology which has lost the Bible as the Word of God. The Church of the Reformation lives and dies with the *Sola Scriptura*.

One wonders which tragedy is greater: to add another source of revelation to the inspired Scriptures, as in Roman Catholicism; or to lose the Scriptures as the inspired Word of God, as in modern Protestantism? Which is worse: to add a mediatrix of all graces to the only true Mediator between God and man; or to lose Christ as the Mediator entirely? Of Jesus' earthly existence, the Church of all ages confesses "Who was conceived by the Holy Ghost, born of the Virgin Mary . . . the third day He rose again from the dead, He ascended into heaven." If this statement is mere myth and legend, then the incarnation becomes mere "symbol." Then the man Jesus was not the eternal Son of God. Then we have no Saviour. Paul long ago recognized these implications (I Cor. 15:17). What we previously stated about the connection between the doctrines of inspiration, of the Trinity and of the Person of Christ, is true.

Which error is worse, that of Rome or that of modern Protestantism? However we answer, one thing is clear: Rome can interpret but not revoke one of its doctrines; they are "irreformable" and must abide until the Last Judgment. But what of Protestantism? A Church of the Reformation is, or ought to be, a repenting church. Can our churches still repent? Or is their day for repentance forever past? Thank God, if they will "hear what the Spirit saith unto the churches," they can yet return, by His grace, to the Word of God.

II.

THE DOCTRINE OF REVELATION IN
CONTEMPORARY THEOLOGY

Robert D. Preus

Modern theologians have spoken with renewed emphasis and vigor on the subject of divine revelation and its underlying importance for the Church. Such an emphasis has been both necessary and welcome, and this for two reasons. First, we must consider that these theologians (Barth, Brunner, and many concerned with Biblical theology) emerged — and sometimes only after intense struggle — from a period dominated by classical Liberalism, evolutionism and pantheistic Idealism. Kant's denial of any rational or factual knowledge of transcendent reality seemed to cow an entire era of theologians. Following his lead, Ritschl reduced all theology to a matter of value judgments to which there was no corresponding reality and the only basis of which was the enlightened reason of the believer. Thus, there was no need and no place for revelation. Unable to answer Kant, Schleiermacher retreated into subjectivism, making Christianity not a matter of cognitive knowledge at all, but a matter of feeling, a dependence upon God. The Bible for him was *ex hypothesi* not a revelation expressing God's thoughts toward man, but rather a book expressing man's thoughts toward God, man's religious experiences. And so it went through the century, Luthardt drawing his theology from the "Christian consciousness," Kahnis from the "consciousness of the Church," these theologians all the time turning their faces persistently in the wrong direction, away from that revelation which is the Scripture of God, either ignoring the concept of revelation altogether or, by centering it exclusively in God's past acts of which there is no reliable witness, making the revelation (whatever it is) quite inaccessible.

The strong emphasis of modern theology upon the doctrine of revelation is necessary and welcome secondly because of the climate and Zeitgeist of our own day which lies under the heavy influence of scientism, positivism, Whiteheadianism, and Pragmatism with their immanent gods. None of these movements could have any possible concern with a special revelation; in fact, special revelation is impossible on their terms. All these ideologies are committed to a rigid Humean empiricism coupled with a simple and unquestioning adherence to the uniformity of nature (with the exception of Whitehead who seems uneasy about evolution as a unifying principle, about an immanent god, and about the scientific method as the method of knowledge).

It is not strange, then, that in such a climate Barth and even Brunner will

18

appear as new prophets and even champions of conservative theology and that their systems will be dubbed a "theology of the Word."

As a matter of record, however, we must point out that this stress upon the doctrine of revelation is not new; it is merely new in certain circles. In the eighteenth and nineteenth centuries before and after the devastation wreaked upon natural religion and natural theology by Hume, Kant, and even by the proponents of natural theology like John Stuart Mill, many theologians were writing prodigious works on the subject of supernatural revelation. Bishop P. Browne and H. Prideaux had argued that revelation was the Gospel which was a series of propositions to which faith gives assent. On the other side was the practical anti-intellectualism (in the wake of Kant) of such men as S. T. Coleridge, Julius Hare, and F. D. Maurice who like many continental theologians (Kierkegaard) taught a subjective view of revelation. To them revelation was the encounter with the divine, the bestowal of faith. Coleridge broke totally with Schleiermacher who insisted that revelation was not an inbreaking of God, but merely the upsurging of human personality, pious self-consciousness. Coleridge's reaction against Schleiermacher and his position on revelation is remarkably similar to that of Barth today. To him, as for Barth, Scripture is not revelation but the possibility of revelation. Even in the seventeenth century, before the later intense interest in natural revelation and apologetics, there was in certain quarters serious study concerning the nature and mode of special revelation. One might refer merely to Abraham Calov, a Lutheran, who devoted most of the first volume of his great *Systema* to a discussion of divine revelation, offering a presentation unequaled in depth and scope even by A. Hoenecke who of modern Lutherans gives most attention to the idea.

But somehow the great interest and many writings on the subject of revelation did not catch on until modern Biblical theology and Neo-orthodoxy arrived on the scene and dealt with the theme. What, then, is the position of modern theology which has influenced the thinking of so many on this important matter? How are we to interpret and assess it?

I. Two Contemporary Views on Revelation

Modern theology wavers between two poles of opinion, between two extreme positions, in speaking of revelation. When pressed these theologians often revert from position A to position B and vice versa. It is therefore in some cases difficult to describe the precise opinion of these men.

A. Position A makes of revelation a confrontation of God with man. This encounter is always on the personal level. Brunner calls it "personal correspondence" (*Divine-Human Encounter*, pp. 94 ff.). Personal correspondence is opposed to the usual subject-object antithesis: it is rather subject-subject. God does not reveal something, but Himself. In ordinary personal relationships there is always a blurring of the "thou" and "something" about the "thou."

> But when God speaks with me the relation to a "something" stops in an unconditional sense, not simply in a conditional sense as in an ordinary human encounter (*ibid.* p. 86).

Thus revelation cannot be "communication", but is rather "communion." Bultmann calls it "personal address" (*Existence and Faith,* 64).

> God does not give us information by communication: He gives us Himself in communion (Baillie, p. 47).

That revelation is in no sense a communication of information is sometimes pushed to the point where such a communication is not even *involved* in revelation (thus Brunner, Bultmann and emphatically Nygren, *En Bok om Biblem,* "Revelation and Scripture"). To Bultmann revelation is neither an illumination in the sense of a communication of knowledge nor is it to be construed as a "cosmic process which takes place outside of us and of which the world would merely bring a report" (*op. cit.,* p. 78). The result is that

> there is nothing revealed on the basis of which one believes. It is only *in* faith that the object of faith is disclosed; therefore, faith itself belongs to revelation (*ibid.,* p. 79).

Consistent with this view that revelation is address is the opinion that revelation is always contemporary. According to Heinecken, revelation is always "contemporaneous", i.e. "it is always in the now." Always involving the recipient of the revelation, revelation is an ongoing activity of God, wherever and whenever God imparts Himself. It does not have the *ephapax* of the incarnation and the atonement ("The Meaning of Revelation," *The Voice,* p. 23).

Summing up, we might make the following observations concerning Position A:

1. It seeks to be monergistic, making God the author of every revelation. A strong stress is placed on God's sovereignty. Thus, revelation occurs only *ubi et quando* God wills. After all, if revelation is God's address to man, then it is He in His sovereign grace who chooses the time and place of this direct encounter.

2. The revelation of God is a self-disclosure. The content (*objectum*) of revelation is God Himself. And He reveals Himself always as subject.

3. The place of Scripture in revelation is rather vague. Scripture for Barth is merely the "possibility" of revelation or the "occasion" for revelation (Reid, *The Authority of Scripture,* p. 196). For Bultmann Scripture would appear to be merely the locus of the kerygma by which God addresses man. Brunner calls Scripture a "witness to the revelation" (*Revelation and Reason,* pp. 118 ff.), but this can only pertain to past revelations and therefore begs the question. Modern theology seems to be rather embarrassed to find any open niche for Scripture in its doctrine of revelation.

4. Revelation is practically identified with the call or with conversion. This is seen from the fact that there is no revelation apart from faith (Bultmann, Heinecken, Barth, Baillie).

5. Closely associated with this position is the conviction that faith is in no sense directed toward facts about Christ. The emphasis is totally on faith *in,* it is never a matter of faith *that* (Brunner, *op. cit.,* pp. 38 ff.;

Baillie, *op. cit.*, p. 47). The noetic element in faith is played down or denied. But cf. Rom. 10:9; I Th. 4:14; I John 5:5; Gal. 2:20; Rom. 6:8; Rom. 5:4; Luke 24:45; Acts 24:14; I Tim. 1:15; Acts 26:27. These passages all make Scripture or some particular doctrine the object of faith. Thus, Neo-orthodoxy comes perilously close to the old position of Schleiermacher and Ritschl who made the Person, not the work of Christ, the object of faith. Neo-orthodoxy often appears to have a faith in Christ abstracted from everything that can be said *about* Him.

6. Position A emphasizes the dynamic nature of revelation almost to the exclusion of its dianoetic (informative) nature and purpose. Again this leads either to subjectivism or mysticism. Nygren (*op. cit.*) is the most adamant on this point. According to him, the so-called "static and intellectualistic view" of revelation, that it is the "communication of formerly hidden knowledge," must be utterly rejected. "Not a fiber of its roots must remain." We reply with our hearty agreement that revelation is always dynamic, charged with the very attributes of God and conveying God Himself (cf. Isa. 45:23; Ps. 107:20; 148:8; Gal. 1:16). This is an old Lutheran emphasis which must not be neglected. But on the other hand God does reveal information (Gal. 2:2; 1:12). God has revealed to Paul the Gospel which is a verbal, informative message. Again certain factual information is revealed to Simeon before he died (Luke 2:26). On his final journey to Rome information was revealed to Paul about his shipwreck, the survival of all passengers and his eventual arrival in Rome (Acts 27:22). Peter says that information was revealed to the Old Testament prophets that their predictions were meant for our time rather than their own. (I Pet. 1:12).

7. Position A has a strong and sometimes healthy emphasis (Nygren) on the contemporaneousness of revelation; not always in the sense of *Deus loquens*, however. The emphasis is upon *Deus revelans*, not upon *Deus revelatus*. Revelation is therefore not a *datum*. To varying degrees this cuts off revelation from history, from God's great acts of redemption (which are fully historical, and necessarily so if Christianity is to be an historical religion, and not degenerate into a form of deism or transcendentalism). To Bultmann, for instance, there is no factuality behind any of the redemptive "myths" connected with Christ's activity recounted in the New Testament. The only historical and real referent he has for revelation is the so-called kerygma which is merely the theology of the early Church.

8. The means of grace are played down on this view. In the case of none of the theologians espousing position A are the Word and Sacraments *per se* powerful to confer forgiveness or work faith. This is in line with the general existentialist orientation.

B. Position B describes revelation as an act of God, sometimes as an act plus human appreciation of it. Whereas position A is held chiefly by systematic theologians (including Bultmann however), position B is more popular with those who interest themselves in Biblical theology. Position B avoids the supremely subjectivistic element in position A. Position B does not seem to be oriented so strongly in existentialism.

We offer G. Ernest Wright as a rather typical proponent of this position.

To him (*God Who Acts*) Biblical Theology is the theology of recital, the theology which recounts the formative events of Israel's history as the redemptive handiwork of God (pp. 38 ff.). This was Israel's faith, a uniquely Israelitish insight. Wright does not say, so far as I can discern that God *revealed* this unique understanding to Israel, but it appears that Israel worked this out for herself. Thus, for instance, Israel takes over an older Canaanitish myth and works it into an account of creation which fits this framework. In a later book with Reginald Fuller this position becomes a little more articulate: boiled down, it implies that the history of Israel was a series of natural events, that is, events which could be explained by natural causes and were not necessarily wonders or miracles to those outside of Israel. Revelation seems then to be the addition of an interpretation which takes God into the picture. The interpretation makes these events revelatory. Thus the same event becomes something quite different when interpreted. The believer (in retrospect) sees it one way, the outsider another (*The Book of the Acts of God*).

Some direct comment is necessary concerning this position. Operating with a naturalistic a priori the position makes miracles and all divine intervention into our cosmos something less than what they must be (if they are miracles and wonders at all) and something less than they were thought to be by those who record them. As a matter of fact, the Bible is filled with accounts of divine intervention into our realm, and that of a stupendous nature. It is true that the full meaning of all that was transpiring in the history of God's people was not open to Pharaoh, Sennacherib, the Amorites in Gibeon, the Canaanites and others. But certainly all these people must have known that something awful and supernatural was happening. To deny that these events occurred is actually to take away the basis for Israel's faith in God's Lordship and redemptive activity and to represent her faith either as naive or fraudulent, at any rate something we today could hardly respect. If these events did not take place as they were recorded, Israel's interpretation is merely pious guesswork. Thus we see modern theology operating with a closed system of a closed universe. Something happened to engender Israel's faith, but not something truly miraculous, nothing which represents God breaking through the nexus of nature. And so modern theology has become deistic.

Now the fact of the matter is that God's interpretation of His relation to Israel (e.g., His sovereignty, His Lordship, His providence, His redemptive purpose and activity) is bolstered and attested *by* His mighty acts (the Exodus, the story of Gideon, Jericho, etc.). Modern theology (Wright, Bultmann, Fuller, *et al.*) reverse this order. It is not a matter of Israel interpolating or embellishing some harrowing escape or victory which she has experienced; it is a matter of her miraculous escape or victory vindicating God's previous word of promise and comfort. In other words, the right order in speaking of revelation is often not, act plus interpretation, but interpretation plus act.

C. Similarities between position A and position B can be noted. This is particularly true when we consider certain negative aspects.

1. Both positions seem to be a tour de force against the old evangelical doctrine which made special revelation something broader than a mere con-

frontation (Bultmann, Barth) or than act plus commentary (Wright, Temple, Baillie), something both *ephapax* and dynamic. The old Lutheran view (and this view seems to be uniquely Lutheran) thus spoke of revelation as something objective, something there, something always available, but at the same time spoke of the continuity of revelation (*Deus revelans*), of God who discloses Himself and speaks to us *now*. This is tied to the uniquely Lutheran doctrine that Scripture *is vere et proprie* God's Word (in the sense that it is God's power and revelation). Only the Lutheran teaching that Scripture is efficacious can retain the Biblical doctrine of revelation in its entire breadth.

It is doubtful whether (with the exception of Barth) Neo-orthodoxy which has never really studied Luther's theology or that of the later orthodox Lutherans was ever aware of this position. At least Baillie in his discussion of the idea of revelation in the seventeenth century seems blissfully ignorant when he describes the era as "defining revelation as a communicating of a body of knowledge, some part at least of which could be independently obtained, or at least verified, by 'the light of reason and nature,' while the remainder was supplemental to what could be so obtained or verified" (*op. cit.*, p. 5). Be all that as it may, Neo-orthodoxy could not have accepted the old Lutheran position, for modern theology is committed to the presuppositions of higher criticism, that the Bible was a mere human response to God's activity among His people and is therefore errant.

2. Both positions deny the possibility of propositional revelation. Heinecken (*op. cit.*, p. 43) categorically rejects "identifying written sentences and propositions with special divine revelation and speaking of 'an inscripturated propositional revelation.'" Abba (*The Nature and Authority of the Bible*, pp. 83, 247) who holds essentially to position B, but who like Baillie, Temple and others, when in trouble, sometimes retreats to position A, has the following to say:

> Revelation was therefore the resultant, as it were, of two factors: it was given through two things — the historic event and the prophetic mind [!]. Neither was sufficient of itself, but through the interplay of both God spoke.

Such a statement might suggest a propositional revelation of some sort. But then Abba retreats behind position A when he says much later in his book, "Revelation does not consist of a series of statements about God: it is the self-disclosure of God." His reason for rejecting any idea of propositional revelation is the same as that of Baillie and Temple whom he follows: he has abandoned the belief that Scripture is inerrant, and God's revelation therefore cannot be contained within fallible, human language. That the Biblical writers think in terms of propositional revelation has already been indicated in our discussion of revelation as information. Certainly when Scripture speaks of a revelation of a mystery (Rom. 16:25; Eph. 1:9; 3:3) or of the Gospel (Rev. 1:1 ff.; Gal. 1:12; cf. also Luke 2:17), the reference is to a mystery of Gospel which is articulated.

3. Both positions deny that there can be a revelation of truth. One oft-cited quotation from Temple will serve to illustrate this point.

> What is offered to man's apprehension in any specific revelation is not truth concerning God but the living God Himself (*Nature, Man and God*, p. 322).

Note the alternative Temple leaves. This seems to be the position also of Barth, Brunner, Baillie and Abba. *Either* God reveals Himself, *or* He reveals a truth about Himself. That revelation could embrace both of these alternatives is a possibility not seriously entertained. Yet this is precisely what occurs and what the Lutheran Church has taught throughout its history. Temple goes on to say:

> There is no such thing as revealed truth. There are truths of revelation; but they are not themselves directly revealed (*ibid.*, p. 316).

This means that there can be no possibility of *revealed* doctrine (truth), or of *revealed* theology.

It has been conjectured that the Bible does not operate with a correspondence theory of truth, and therefore it would be quite meaningless to claim that Scripture reveals truth in the sense of statements. This desperate position seems to lie behind the allegation (Abba) that "there is no biblical warrant for making inerrancy a corollary of inspiration". We should not waste much time answering such a conjecture. The purpose of declarative statements is to make words correspond to fact (except in the case of deliberate lies). Without the correspondence theory of truth there can be no such thing as *informative* language or *factual* meaning. The eighth commandment entirely breaks down unless predicated upon the correspondence theory of truth. So much for the logical impossibility of the above theory. As a matter of fact Scripture is replete with evidence that it operates throughout with the correspondence idea of truth (cf. Eph. 4:25; John 8:44-46; I Ki. 8:26; Gen. 42:16, 20; Zech. 8:16; Deut. 18:22; John 5:31 ff.; Ps. 119:163; I Ki. 22:16, 22 ff.; Dan. 2:9; Prov. 14:25; I Tim. 1:15; Acts 24:8, 11). It is utterly irrelevant when Brunner counters that Scripture teaches a *Wahrheit als Begegnung* (which is the title of one of his books). This is only to confuse truth (which pertains to statements) with certitude. So too is it irrelevant to point out that *aletheia* and *emeth* often refer to something more deep than mere correspondence to fact, that they refer to God and His faithfulness. God is true (faithful) simply because future events (fulfillment) *corresponds* to His word of promise, and His word is true for the same reason.

4. The fourth point of similarity between the two positions is the playing down of the dianoetic nature and purpose of revelation, and we have mentioned this above. We might merely add at this point that it would seem incredible for anyone seriously to think that the meaning of any act of God is less revelatory than the act itself, e.g. the death of Christ. On this fourth point modern theology seems to be less secure than on the first three. If revelation is not dianoetic, if God does not reveal information, there seems to be no escape from mysticism or from the equally sterile positivistic tenet that theology (language concerning God and revelation) is emotive; that is to say, theology is the use of symbolic ("mythical") tools or instruments which are

24

employed in the *practice* of religion. In either case theology possesses no cognitive value. Again there can be no *revealed* theology (cf. point 3 above), no theology which is either true or false, and this is the nature of the case.

But, as a matter of fact, the revelation of information is a Biblical teaching. Paul (I Cor. 15:3) "receives" (by revelation) the facts concerning Christ's suffering and death and resurrection on the third day (cf. John 1:11 and Col. 2:6). The prophets in receiving a vision or word from the Lord receive usually an explanation for this word as well. Information was revealed to Paul in Acts 27:24 and I Cor. 11:23 and to Simeon in Luke 2:26 — and we could go on and on.

II. General Assumptions and Predilections Behind the Modern View of Revelation

A. Modern theology assumes that the human authors of Scripture, writing out of their cultural milieu, were fallible human beings, subject to error and other human limitations. Here we quote the well-known statement of Barth:

> To the bold postulate, that if their [the Biblical writers] word is to be the Word of God they must be inerrant in every word, we oppose the even bolder assertion, that according to the scriptural witness about man [notice how Barth appeals to anthropological evidence rather than bibliological data at this point], which applies to them too [sic], they can be at fault in every word, and have been at fault in every word, and yet according to the same scriptural witness, being justified and sanctified by grace alone, they have still spoken the Word of God in their fallible and erring human word. (*Church Dogmatics,* I 2, 529-30).

On such a postulate Scripture cannot be revelation. This is the conclusion of practically all the theologians we have considered. Bultmann makes the point very clear.

> God the mysterious and hidden must at the same time be the God who is revealed. Not, of course, in a revelation that one can know, that could be grasped in words and propositions, that would be limited to formula and book and to space and time; but rather in a revelation that continually opens up new heights and depths and thus leads through darkness, from clarity to clarity (*Existence and Faith,* p. 30).

There are obviously other presuppositions underlying this statement, but Bultmann makes it clear that God's revelation cannot be contained in anything limited to space and time such as human language.

B. The basic methods of higher criticism as well as many of its tenets are assumed by modern theology when speaking of revelation. In general the dogmatic claims of Scripture concerning its origin, power and authority are ignored, and little heed is given to Jesus' attitude and use of the Old Testament. For instance, Barth and Dodd in all their writings on Scripture and its authority never seriously consider these matters. At the same time the Bible is considered only a human response to Gòd's activity, the produce of the Church's theology, which is precisely what the positive theologians of the nineteenth century taught. Theology is the product of the Church (cf. form criticism: Bultmann, Schweitzer, Schlier *et al.*). God is not the *principium essendi* of theology as our old teachers said, but rather we have Paul's theology, John's theology, James' theology etc. Abba (*op. cit.*, p. 243) remarks, for instance, that at his conversion and his meeting with Peter three years later were the only opportunities Paul had for " 'receiving' " the Christian tradition, thus ignoring the apostle's own claim that he did not "receive" his gospel from men but from God and that he spent three years in Arabia (Gal. 1:12, 17).

Such a procedure involves also fitting isagogical data into the naturalistic or evolutionary development of doctrine. Thus, the book of John is not authentic, but a Hellenized or Gnostic Tendenzschrift (Schweitzer, Bultmann). The pastoral epistles are unauthentic because of their emphasis upon doctrine which again is a late Hellenistic development. The psalms of David are not authentic because they conflict with datings concerning the emergence of such themes as resurrection, immortality, etc. Ultimately this position leads often to distorted views concerning Christ Himself, since He committed Himself concerning certain books of the Old Testament: a kenosis doctrine is taught, or adoptionism, or Jesus is called a child of His time, and all because theologians are committed to the historical-critical method. Such conclusions as these mentioned, predicated as they are upon naturalistic presuppositions, often become in turn the predilections behind modern theology's view of revelation.

C. At times a strange, atomistic view of language may account for the attitude of modern theologians toward the orthodox doctrine of revelation. Reference will be made to the thousands of textual variants in the Bible, to the rather loose quotation in the New Testament from the LXX, to the impossibility of getting to the autographic texts of Scripture, to the fact that we do not have the *ipsissima verba* of Jesus, or to the fact that there can never be an infallible interpreter of Scripture (Temple) — and all to show that the Bible cannot be revelation. Let us take the absurd reasoning of Heinecken as an example of this procedure. Speaking against the position that the Bible is an inerrant revelation, he says:

> Admittedly, this leads, in every instance, to an assertion about the autographs for which we must continue to search and which we must try, from our present manuscripts, always to restore as accurately as possible, for it is precisely those sentences and propositions which constitute the revelation and without them we would be at sea and we would have no knowledge of God or of his will and his heart (*op. cit.*, p. 43).

These words of Heinecken's and the other arguments mentioned above are classic examples of irrelevant evidence.

D. Existentialism appears to lie behind much that modern theology says in regard to revelation, particularly in respect to position A. Karl Barth in his *Epistle to the Romans* (p. 10) says that, if he has any presupposition, or "system", it is what Kierkegaard called " 'the infinite qualitative difference' between time and eternity in both its negative and positive meaning. 'God is in heaven and you are on earth.' " Schubert Ogden in the introduction to Bultmann's essays in *Existence and Faith* is most insistent that this is precisely Bultmann's point of departure in all his theological endeavor. Such a principle might be pushed to such a transcendental extreme that even miracles and the incarnation are denied (Bultmann, but not Barth or Kierkegaard); but in regard to revelation we can see that the principle would hardly allow for a permanent given revelation such as Scripture. For then (the argument goes) the absolute freedom and sovereignty of God could not be maintained. Bultmann is more consistent with this position than even Barth. To him theological thoughts cannot represent God's thoughts (but cf. I Cor. 2:16), are thoughts of *faith*, "thoughts in which faith's understanding of God, the world, and man is unfolding itself." (*Theology of the NT*, II, 237 ff.). And theological propositions cannot be the object of faith, but only the explication of the understanding of faith. Thus, there seems to be no factual knowledge of God at all, except perhaps that He breaks in upon us (revelation) with the kerygma making possible our authentic existence; but "the theological thoughts of the New Testament are the unfolding of faith itself growing out of that new understanding of God, the world, and man which is conferred in and by faith — or, as it can also be phrased: *out of one's new self-understanding* [Bultmann's emphasis]." Hence, for Bultmann revelation, as he says elsewhere (*Existence and Faith*, pp. 85, 88), is that I am given a knowledge of my own existence, my immediate now.

It is clear at this point why Barth and others will not follow Bultmann all the way in his existentialism. He has chopped Christianity away from its roots in history, in spite of what he says about the Jesus of history and the kerygma. This tendency of position A is the reason why many who espouse it sometimes veer toward position B which sets God's revelation in history. Adherents of position B, however, since their position makes revelation neither dynamic nor contemporary, will sometimes lean toward position A.

Another example of existentialist (Kierkegaardian) presuppositions is seen in Brunner's and Heinecken's (*op. cit.*, p. 49) argument that the traditional, orthodox doctrine of revelation springs from a desire for guaranteed certainty.

III. Some of the Practical Consequences of the Modern View Concerning Revelation

A. A playing down of the importance of doctrine in the Church.

B. An uneasy monergism in position B. When we refer to a revelation of God in the past, this is God's act exclusively (e.g. the Exodus or the resurrection). When we make revelation act plus appreciation we have a divine-human datum.

C. Scepticism. Position B, operating with the historico-critical method makes it difficult or impossible to get at the revelatory acts of God. Temple is frank to say concerning Jesus "that there is no single deed or saying of which we can be perfectly sure that He said or did precisely this or that." (Baillie and Martin, eds., *Revelation*, p. 114). W. J. Phythian-Adams (*The Call of Israel*, p. 64) is less radical; he says:

27

However much they may embellish the facts, or even obscure them in the interests of their particular purpose, at heart of their narrative these facts remain as a solid, resistant core, the indestructible nucleus of historical reality.

But how does he know this? Employing the same methodology Bultmann has come to quite different conclusions.

Let us now examine what G. Ernest Wright and Reginald Fuller have to say in their book, *The Book of the Acts of God*, so that we might learn just how much one can say about the so-called revelatory acts of God when the historico-critical method is applied to the Biblical account. Let us consider the one act of the resurrection. According to the authors, the resurrection cannot be an objective act of history in the same sense as the crucifixion of Christ. The latter event was open to all men as an historical happening (cf. Tacitus and Josephus). But resurrection is "perceived only by the people of faith" (p. 14). The risen Christ was seen only by a few (but cf. I Cor. 15:5-8; and note the irrelevant thesis here). Thus, Easter is "not an arena where a historian can operate." Only facts available to all men are the data of objective history. We might ask at this point, what historical event in the ancient world is available to the historian, if we ask for more evidence than offered by reliable witnesses? There is, in fact, as much historical evidence for the resurrection of Christ as for the fact that Caesar crossed the Rhein. The reason for the authors' position can only be due to an a priori prejudice against the miraculous. The authors then proceed to call the resurrection a "faith-event," unlike other events, but "nevertheless real *to the Christian community*." But we ask, is the event real? Did it happen? This is Paul's issue in I Cor. 15; he was not speaking of what the event meant to the Christian community. Wright and Fuller then say that the resurrection means Christ is alive, not dead; and finally they make their position quite clear when they conclude that language like "raised on the third day," "ascension," "going up," "sitting at the right hand of God," are simply "products of the situation," "temporal language of the first century Christians. To us they are symbols of deep truth and nothing more." Hence, we can only conclude that the most significant event in Christ's life, that event by which He is declared to be God's Son, by which He spoiled principalities and powers, which renders our preaching and our faith something other than vain, that event upon which the truth of the entire Christian religion depends, perhaps never actually happened. We might remember that Bultmann too makes the resurrection a myth, Brunner denies the open tomb, Niebuhr makes the resurrection supra-historical. Surely this is building a theology on the sands of utter scepticism. If theology is based on revelation, and we cannot be sure of any act of God's revelation, what is there left for theology to talk about except eternal truths or my understanding of my own existence (Bultmann)?

D. A retreat into mysticism is often the result of both positions. When the acids of historical science have eaten away at the roots of God's revelation in history, there is no other direction to go. Thus, we see modern theologians appealing to Kierkegaard with his emphasis upon subjective truth, employing the Kantian phenomenal-noumenal categories· (e.g. Christ of faith — Jesus of history; history and super history) and his "ideas of reason" which are totally above all empirical verification (it is true), but are also outside the very realm of the empirical, i.e. the historical. We might recall that it was only one step from Kant to the Neo-Kantians with their rejection of the noumenal, thus resulting in a belief in a god who does not exist. Is all this really so far from A. Ritschl who spoke of Jesus as the Son of God (Werturteil) but denied His deity or said it didn't matter? Is it even so far removed from the pragmatism of John Dewey with his unbounded confidence in empiricism and his "faith" in a god who does not exist? We are not accusing all these modern theologians of Pragmatism or Kantianism, although many (even Barth) are patterning their theology according to Kant's transcendental aesthetic. We are merely attempting to show the various directions which modern theology with its doctrine of revelation is taking.

IV. Conclusion

It is not within the purview of this essay to offer refutation of the ideas of modern theology on the subject of revelation, although in my previous analysis I have at times indicated the direction our answer must take. However, a concluding remark might be made lest our study seem to end hanging in air.

In replying to Neo-orthodoxy we must go back to the basic conviction of the Lutheran Church and of historic Christianity that the Sacred Scriptures are not merely metonymically or metaphorically or hyperbolically, but, as our old theologians have said, *vere et proprie* God's word, the product of God's breath (*theopneustos*), the utterances of very God (*ta logia tou theou*).

What does this mean? It has the most profound meaning and significance for the Church, not only for her theology, but for her life and activity. Christ said we *live* by His word. His words are spirit and life (John 6:63). The Scriptures as the words of God's mouth are able (*dunamena*) to make us wise unto salvation through faith in Christ Jesus (II Tim. 3:15). All the things we say about Scripture, its power, its authority, its perfection (*ophaleia*), its inerrancy, are predicated by virtue of its divine origin, its inner nature (*forma*) as God's Word.

Now what does a word do? What is its usual function? It is to communicate, to evoke, to move, to *reveal*. My words are the revelation of my heart. Christ, the hypostatic Word, who is "with God" (John 1:1), who is "in the bosom of the Father," He reveals God (John 1:18). And the prophetic and apostolic Word which on its own testimony (Matt. 4:4; Rom. 3:2; II Tim. 3:16) proceeds from the mouth of God *reveals* God. Scripture *is* revelation. How naive for theologians to speak of Scripture as God's Word and then to deny that it is a revelation!

III.

THE LOCUS OF GOD'S SPEAKING

In what manner does it bear on the effective objectivity of his Word?

H. Daniel Friberg

Many of those who nowadays make high claims for the Word of God conceive of this Word in a transcendentalist fashion only, in that for them the Holy Scriptures of the biblical canon are not truly and actually the Word of God but merely witnesses to that Word. As such witnesses they are perhaps usually declared to be primary, and by some they are even allowed to be unique. But the idea is that by the possession of the Scriptures we do not strictly have the Word of God but only man's more or less distorted hearing of it.

Karl Barth is such a transcendentalist. He does in fact call the Bible the Word of God, as he also does the proclamation of the church, and he makes great use of the Bible. But when it comes to a strict characterization of the Word of God, he denies that it can be objectified and he denies that it can be repeated (*Church Dogmatics,* Volume I, Part I, pages 159, 160, 186). God's Word is for Barth God speaking — speaking in such a way that man's holding it up for his own reflection or man's reporting it fails to possess it in its real essence. To have God's Word as it really is you must have it, as it were, coming in over the wire. Moreover, not only is that which you hold up for a close look or that which you repeat no longer strictly the Word of God, but what you heard — even if you were a prophet or an apostle — was in the very reception in some measure garbled and mutilated by your own creaturely hearing.

This view is more sophisticated than those of the common run of the transcendentalists I am now describing, but the common characteristic is that of locating God's real Word in such a manner that man cannot say of it: "Here it is. Exactly what I am now about to read or to repeat to you is without reservation the Word of God."

The convenience of this conception is patent: ultimately you have no definite or specific Word of God to uphold at all cost in the face of attack. You can, as holders of this view continually do, fire whole volleys of *ipsissima verba* of Scripture when it suits your purpose and argue from such precise details as the gender, number, tense and mood of scriptural words. But when the fighting gets tough you can always leave it to others and, like our coastal batteries of an earlier day with their retractable mountings, disappear from both range and sight, in this case upward, by affirming that after all the real Word of God remains inviolate in heaven. (Even the Psalmist locates the Word of God in heaven: "Forever, O Lord, Thy Word is settled in heaven" [119:89]. But in so doing he is clearly asserting the *unchangeableness* of God's Word and has no mind even to suggest that he could not really know here on earth what God has said.)

I

But the cost of such convenience is formidable. Here on earth we are left with at best only approximations to the Word of God — and approximations, at that, of an indeterminable degree of correspondence to the true Word. Notoriously fallible and variable human reason is left to judge on the basis of more or less distorted witnesses just what the Word of God in fact is. Difficult passages have been surrendered as expendable, but they have been traded for the insuperable difficulty of having nothing really firm to stand on.

According to Scripture, man is begotten anew by an incorruptible seed which is identified as the living and abiding Word of God (I Peter 1:23), and the continuance and growth of spiritual life is conditioned upon abiding in God's Word and upon recognizing and rejecting error. Our Lord in fighting off Satan's suggestion that he make stones into bread quoted Scripture as saying not merely that man must live by the Word of God but also that he must live by *every* word that proceeds from the mouth of God. All of God's words to men are the proper diet of man. The need of having the whole range of this utterance in certain and authoritative form should be even more obvious when we consider the deadliness, subtlety and limitless proliferation of error in the world. A desperate need of the times is for men to be shocked into realization that there is such a thing as doctrinal error and that teaching which is contrary to the words of life destroys with everlasting death. When men wake up to this fact they will pay any price for a certain and infallible standard of evaluation, and it will be small comfort to be told that there is a perfectly accurate standard kept inviolate in heaven — or that it can be issued in extended ribbons of truth that elude application by defying objectification.

In contrast to such distance and fluidity of the Word the Bible not only speaks of God's very Word having come to men but in scores of passages denominates definite utterances of men the Word of God. Again and again it describes some event as the fulfillment of this or that particular Word of God. Furthermore it praises the safety, blessing and joy of the man who makes the very Word of God the habitation of his soul. Consider the bizarre effect of substituting in the more than 100 Word-exulting declarations and confessions of Psalm 119 "primary witnesses to the Word of God" and "approximations to the Word of God" for the simple term "Word" and its synonyms! Even where the Psalmist asserts his delight in "thy testimonies" he is referring to testimonies in the sense of God's own declarations of his being, will and faithfulness rather than in the sense of "testimonies to such testimonies."

31

The transcendentalism here considered is pragmatically resourceless and as a teaching about the Word contrary to that Word's characterization of itself. Moreover, it violates a true understanding of the nature of speech. The object of speech is to produce in the hearer such thoughts, feelings, attitudes or actions as are desired by the speaker. What is not appropriate to such an end cannot be speech. Thus English is not speech to Zulus, except that they would allow it to be such on the presupposition that there are people who by it would be brought to think and feel and behave in a certain manner. It is termination of a certain kind that is the chief point in speech. In the relation of one human being to another, this termination is brought about — since spirit is not in immediate contact with spirit — by the use of conventional signs, viz., words, vocal or written, though there are also "words" of still other forms. To what extent God has used conventional signs in speaking to men cannot be known. The Evangelist on Patmos heard behind him a loud voice like a trumpet communicating to him God's message. What the angel of the Lord appearing in a dream said to Joseph constituted God's "command" to him on the occasion of his being directed to take Mary to be his wife. There may well be other ways in which God has spoken to men.

II

My point is that the termination of God's speech to man is, so to speak, in the interior of man. What does not so come through to him is not God's speech to man, and there can therefore be no transcendental Word of God to man. The transcendence of the Speaker I grant with readiness and with worship. Nor do I dispute for a moment the transcendence of certain categories of God's speech. The Personal Word is transcendent. The intratrinitarian speech is transcendent, as is also what God says to the angels and what they say to him. Nevertheless something of both of the latter two classes of speech, the intratrinitarian and that between God and the angels, has in fact been reported by God to men and has in this way come through to a termination in man. But what God has spoken to man has all been beamed to our kind of receptivity and has in fact terminated in man, and without such termination could not have been constituted God's Word to man.

In speaking of human receptivity I am abstracting from the very real truth that in order to hear God's Word unto the experience of life the hearer must receive from the Holy Ghost the special gift of faith which is in fact mediated by that Word and is absolutely necessary to the end of being made spiritually alive. This abstraction I justify on the ground that God's Word to man is not constituted such by man's hearing with the obedience of faith. It is truly God's Word to man even if man hears and rejects it with unbelief. Jesus warned his hearers that if they would not believe they would be judged by the Word which they refused to believe. God speaks truly even to those who remain unregenerate.

Incidentally, this characterization of the Word of God which stresses its termination in the hearer accounts for the widest possible play of the subjective qualities of the hearer without any infringement of the Word's being fully the Word of God. God's Word to and through the fisherman has the flavor of the seashore; his Word to and through the tax collector has something of the tinkling of coins; his Word to and through the tax rabbi echoes certain accents of the school of Gamaliel. There is indeed much of heaven in this Word, but it is entirely in the idiom of this world. A transcendent Word, even if it were about this world, would be entirely in the code of heaven.

Now if the termination of God's speech to man is within man, all talk of "witness" and "approximation" is mischievous and false. What is there *out there* and *up there* in ineffable transcendence to which we could possibly witness except in the degree that it had first come through to us? Or of which we could possibly know that it was being approximated by anything? And why should that which men have heard in their own beings be called a witness to a Word rather than the Word itself? And if God caused men to utter certain words as his own — which they could thus utter as easily as they could hear his words — why should that utterance be called a witness to God's Word rather than the very Word of God?

IV.

NOTES ON THE INERRANCY OF SCRIPTURE[1]

Robert D. Preus

This study is offered as an approach to the problem of the inerrancy of Scripture as it concerns the Lutheran Church today. The attempt is to present a position that agrees with Scripture's testimony concerning itself and with the historic position of the Christian church. At the same time the attempt is made to be timely and to take into account contemporary issues raised by modern Biblical theology.

Here we shall try to delineate and clarify what is meant by the inerrancy of Scripture, what is the basis of this doctrine, and what are its implications. It is not our purpose to become involved in the technicalities that have often obscured the doctrine or to traverse the labyrinth of intricate discussion that has not infrequently belabored studies of this basic theological truth.

Indeed, a brief treatment such as we are about to give cannot possibly solve the many hermeneutical and isagogical problems that touch upon the inerrancy of Scripture. Yet hermeneutical and isagogical concerns cannot be avoided in a study of this nature. Therefore we have endeavored to lay down general principles concerning these matters which will comport with the inerrancy and sole authority of Scripture. Our procedure will be as follows: we shall begin with a very general definition (thesis) of inerrancy, a definition that will express the conviction of the orthodox church from her beginning to the present time. We shall next explain and justify our definition with a series of subtheses or corollaries. Finally we shall with a series of adjunct comments attempt to relate the inerrancy of Scripture to hermeneutical principles and other concerns so as to clarify just what is included in this inerrancy of Scripture and what is not.

Thesis

In calling the sacred Scriptures inerrant we recognize in them (A), as words taught by the Holy Spirit (B), that quality which makes them over-

---

1. Editor's note: This essay was originally given in oral presentation to several study groups and conferences. It is offered here as a part of the ongoing discussion on Scriptural inerrancy within The Lutheran Church — Missouri Synod. For an earlier article on this topic in this journal see Arthur Carl Piepkorn, *What Does "Inerrancy" Mean?* in Vol. 36, No. 8 (Sept. 1965), pp. 577-593. See also *A Statement on the Form and Function of the Holy Scriptures*, Vol. 31, No. 10 (Oct. 1960), pp. 626 f.

whelmingly (C) reliable witnesses (D-E) to the words and deeds of the God, who has in His inspired spokesmen and in His incarnate Son disclosed Himself to men for their salvation (F).[2]

This definition is very general, seeking as it does to fit all the Biblical data (for example, the bold language of prophecy and of adoration, the promises concerning the world to come for which human experience offers only imperfect and insufficient analogies, the expressive and indispensable anthropomorphisms and anthropopathisms used of God, the symbolic use of numbers and other referents in books like Daniel and Revelation, etc.). The definition also agrees, however, with what the church catholic has believed and confessed through her entire history. We offer a few typical examples to bring out this fact.

Augustine, *Epist. 82*, 'to Jerome: "Only to those books which are called canonical have I learned to give honor so that I believe most firmly that no author in these books made any error in writing. I read other authors not with the thought that what they have thought and written is true just because they have manifested holiness and learning!"

Thomas Aquinas, *In Ioh. 13, lect. 1*: "It is heretical to say that any falsehood whatsoever is contained either in the gospels or in any canonical Scripture."

Luther (W² 15, 1481): "The Scriptures have never erred." (W² 9, 356): "It is impossible that Scripture should contradict itself; it only appears so to senseless and obstinate hypocrites."

Preface to the Book of Concord (Tappert, p. 8): "We have in what follows purposed to commit ourselves exclusively and only, in accordance with the pure, infallible, and unalterable Word of God, to that Augsburg Confession which was submitted to Emperor Charles V at the great imperial assembly in Augsburg in the year 1530." *Large Catechism* (Baptism 57 [Tappert, p. 444]): "My neighbor and I — in short, all men — may err and deceive, but God's Word cannot err." *Formula of Concord* (Ep VII, 13 [(Tappert, p. 483]): "God's Word is not false nor does it lie."

Calov, *Systema locorum theologicorum* (Wittenberg, 1655-1657), I, 462: "Because Scripture is God's Word which is absolutely true, Scripture is itself truth (Ps. 119:43, 86, 142, 160; John 17:17, 19; II Sam. 7:28; Ps. 33:4; Gal. 3:1; Col. 1:5; II Tim. 2:18; 3:8; Titus 1:1; and James 1:8). Thus whatever the sacred Scriptures contain is fully true and to be accepted with utmost certainty. Not only must we hold that to be true which is presented in Scripture relative to faith and morals, but we must hold to everything that happens to be included therein. Inasmuch as Scripture has been written by an immediate and divine impulse and all the Scriptures recognize Him as their author who cannot err or be mistaken in any way

---

2. Majuscule letters A-F refer to the six corollaries which will shortly be given in support and clarification of the major thesis.

(Heb. 6:18), no untruth or error or lapse can be ascribed to the God-breathed Scriptures, lest God Himself be accused."

Turrettin, *Institutio Theologiae Elencticae* (Genevae, 1688), I, 79: "We deny that there are any true and real contradictions in Scripture. Our reasons are as follows: namely, that Scripture is God-breathed (II Tim. 3:16), that the Word of God cannot lie or be ignorant of what has happened (Ps. 19:8-9; Heb. 6:18) and cannot be set aside (Matt. 5:18), that it shall remain forever (I Peter 1:25), and that it is the Word of truth (John 17:17). Now how could such things be predicated of Scripture if it were not free of contradictions, or if God were to allow the holy writers to err and lose their memory or were to allow hopeless blunders to enter into the Scriptures?"

C. F. W. Walther (*Lehre und Wehre*, 21, 35): "Whoever believes with all his heart that the Bible is the Word of God cannot believe anything else than that it is inerrant."

C. F. W. Walther (*Lehre and Wehre*, 14, 4): "Whoever thinks that he can find one error in holy Scripture does not believe in holy Scripture but in himself; for if he accepted everything else as true, he would believe it not because Scripture says so but because it agrees with his reason or his senti-ments." (Translation in CTM, 10, 4, p. 255).

Brief Statement: "Since the Holy Scriptures are the Word of God, it goes without saying that they contain no errors or contradictions, but that they are in all their parts and words the infallible truth, also in those parts which treat of historical, geographical, and other secular matters. (John 10:35)."

Tromp, *De Sacrae Scripturae Inspiratione* (Rome, 1953), p. 121: "Everything which is contained in sacred Scripture, as attested by the author and in the sense intended by him, is infallibly true."

Dei Verbum of Vatican II (See *Verbum Domini*, 44, 1 [1966], p. 8; also *The Documents of Vatican II*, ed. by Walter M. Abbott, S. J. [New York, 1966], p. 119): "Therefore, since everything asserted by the inspired authors or sacred writers must be held to be asserted by the Holy Spirit, it follows that the books of Scripture must be acknowledged as teach-ing firmly, faithfully and without error (*firmiter, fideliter et sine errore*) the truth which God wanted put into the Sacred Writings for the sake of our salvation."

Such statements written under different circumstances and at different times evince the remarkable unanimity on this matter which obtained in the church throughout her history. The statements also indicate or infer the following six corollaries which will serve to delineate and further explain our definition.

Corollary A

This "recognition" of the truthfulness of the written Word of God is not primarily intellectual: it takes place in the obedience of faith. The truthful-ness and reliability of the Scriptures is an article of faith.

Corollary B

The basis of inerrancy rests on the nature of Scripture as God's Word. Inerrancy is an inextricable concomitant of inspiration. Our conviction is that since Scripture is truly and properly speaking God's Word, it will not deceive nor err.[3] Admittedly this is an inference (as in the case of the doctrine of the Trinity or the two natures of Christ), but it is a necessary inference, because God is faithful and His Word (Scripture) is truth — and no Christian theologian until the period of Rationalism ever shrank from this inference. It is to be noted that both Christ and the apostles drew the same inference. (See not only John 10:34; Mark 12:24; Matt. 5:18-19 but also Christ's and the apostles' use of the Old Testament; they simply cite it as unconditionally true and unassailable.)

Corollary C

Our recognition of the reliability of the witness of Scripture is graciously *imposed* on us by the Spirit of God and this through the power of Scripture itself.

Corollary D

The nature of inerrancy is essentially twofold: Scripture does not lie or deceive, and Scripture does not err or make mistakes in any affirmation it makes (*falsum formale and falsum materiale*). In other words, the holy writers, moved by the Spirit of God, infallibly achieve the intent of their writing (see the statement of Tromp above). This is what is meant when we say that Scripture is a *reliable witness* to the words and deeds of God. Of His people God demands in the second and eighth commandments that they tell the truth; of His prophets and apostles, that they do not lie, God will not countenance lying and prevarication (Prov. 14:5; 19:22; Ps. 63:11; Jer. 23:25 ff.; Zeph. 3:13; Acts 5:3; I John 2:21, 27). And God Himself will not lie or deceive (Prov. 30:6-7; Num. 23:19; Ps. 89:35; Heb. 6:18). In His written Word He will not break or suspend that standard of truth which He demands of His children. Thus we hear frequently from God's inspired witnesses the claim that they do not deceive, that they are not mistaken, that they tell the truth (Rom. 9:1; II Cor. 11:31; Gal. 1:20; I Tim. 2:7). The whole impact of entire books of the Bible depends on the authoritative and truthful witness of the writer. (John 21:24; I John 1:1-5a; II Peter 1:15-18)

Pertinent to what was just said is the following. The truth of the sacred Scriptures must be determined from the sense which is intended (in verse,

---

3. Cf. M. Nicolau et I. Salaverri, S. J., *Sacrae Theologiae Summa* (Madrid, 1958), I, 1095: "Inerrantiam Scripturae non derivari praecise ex fine scriptoris, ad illa tantum quae ipse docere intendit, sed derivari ex natura inspirationis, ad illa omnis quae vi huius influxus asseruntur." The alluding to many contemporary Roman Catholic sources in notes does not necessarily imply full agreement with these statements or that we should use these statements in any final study on inerrancy. The statements are, for the most part, quite sound and useful. The fact is that Roman Catholics are the majority of those who write on inerrancy today from a point of view similar to ours.

pericope, book) by the author. This sense in turn must be determined according to sound hermeneutical rules.

It is obvious that such a position on the nature of Biblical inerrancy is predicated on a correspondence idea of truth which in part means this: declarative statements (at least in those Biblical genres, or literary forms, which purport to be dealing with fact or history) of Scripture are, according to their intention, true in that they correspond to what has taken place (for example, historical statements), to what obtains (for example, theological affirmations and other affirmations concerning fact), or to what will take place (for example, predictive prophecy). It really ought to go without saying that with all its different genres and figures of speech, Scripture, like all cognitive discourse, operates under the rubrics of a correspondence idea of truth. (See John 8:46; Eph. 4:25; I Kings 8:26; 22:16, 22 ff.; Gen. 42:16, 20; Deut. 18:22; Ps. 119:163; Dan. 2:9; Prov. 14:25; Zech. 8:16; John 5:21-32 ff.; Acts 24:8, 11; I Tim. 1:15; note, too, the forensic picture which haunts all of Scripture — for example, such concepts as witness, testimony, judge, the Eighth Commandment, etc.; John 21:24.)

To speak of inerrancy of purpose (that God achieves His purpose in Scripture) or of Christological inerrancy of Scripture is indeed relevant to the general question of inerrancy, but may at the same time be misleading if such a construct is understood as constituting the nature of inerrancy — for then we might speak of the inerrancy of Luther's Small Catechism or of a hymn by Paul Gerhardt, since they successfully achieve their purpose.

The first purpose of Scripture is to bring us to faith in Christ (John 20:31; II Tim. 3:15). Involved with this prime purpose of Scripture is Luther's doctrine of the Christocentricity of Scripture (Old Testament as well as New Testament). Such Christocentricity has a soteriological purpose. Only when I understand that Scripture and Christ are *pro me* will I understand the Scriptures (or the inerrancy thereof). But to say that Scripture is inerrant only to the extent that it achieves its soteriological purpose is a misleading position if it is made to be identical with inerrancy or confused with it. How does Scripture achieve this soteriological purpose? By cognitive language, among other things. By presenting *facts,* by telling a history (Old Testament as well as New Testament). To say that there is a purpose in Scripture but no intentionality (that is, intent to give meaning) in the individual books or sections or verses, or to maintain that Scripture is inerrant in its eschatological purpose but not in the intentionality of its individual parts and pericopes would not only be nonsense, reducing all Scripture to the level of some sort of mystical utterances, but would be quite un-Scriptural (Luke 1:1-4, etc.). The eschatological purpose of Scripture does not cancel or vitiate or render trivial and unimportant the cognitive and factual content of assertions (and the truth of assertions) throughout the Scripture, but requires all this (Rom. 15:4). And on the other hand, formal and material inerrancy does not threaten or eclipse the Christological purpose of Scripture but supports it. Nor does such a position (formal and material inerrancy) become tantamount to reading Scripture atomistically. Language is a primary structure of lived experience and cannot be studied in isolation from it. Because the language of imagery in Scripture may not always be adequately analyzed or ever completely exhausted implies neither that it is meaningless (positivism) nor that it is errant ("Christian" positivism). Not orthodoxy but neo-orthodoxy has a positivistic, wooden theory of language.[4]

Corollary E

Inerrancy is plenary or absolute. 1) It pertains not only to the substance of the doctrines and narratives in Scripture, but also to those things which are nonessential, adjunct, *obiter dicta,* or things clearly assumed by the author. (Quenstedt, *Systema,* I, 77: "Doctrine, ethics, history, chronology, topography, or onomastics." *Brief Statement:* "historical, geographical, and other secular matters"). 2) It covers not only the primary intent of the various pericopes and verses but also the secondary intent (for example, a passing historical reference within the framework of narrative, such as that Christ was crucified between two thieves, that wise men visited Him at His birth, that Joshua led the Children of Israel into Canaan, that Ruth was a Moabitess, Nimrod a hunter, etc.), not only soteriological, eschatological, and religious intent and content of Scripture but also all declarative statements touching history and the realm of nature.

There are various reasons for this strict position. 1) The New Testament cites what might often be considered to be passing statements or negligible items from the Old Testament, accepting them as true and authoritative (Matt. 6:29; Matt. 12:42; John 10:35). Jesus accepts the basic framework of the Old Testament history, even those aspects of that history which seem unimportant to many today, for example, Sodom and Gomorrah (Luke 17:27), Lot's wife turning to salt, the murder of Abel (Luke 11:51), Naaman (Luke 4:27). The New Testament does not recognize *levicula* in the Old Testament (Rom. 15:4, II Tim. 3:16). 2) The primary intent of a passage or pericope is often dependent on the secondary intent(s). This is so in the nature of the case. For instance, the Exodus as a deliverance of God depends on the miraculous events connected with it. 3) The most common argument for the full inerrancy of Scripture as advanced by the older theologians was as follows: if errors of fact or contradictions are admitted in minor matters recorded in Scripture (matters that do not matter [?]), by what right may one then assume that there is no error in important or doctrinal concerns? How does one determine what matters are important? And does not, after all, everything pertain at least indirectly to doctrine (II Tim. 3:16)? In other words, to maintain that "things which do matter" in Scripture (doctrinal matters) are inerrant and "things which do not matter" (nondoctrinal matters) are errant is both arbitrary and impossible to apply. (See Calov, *Systema,* I, 606 ff.; also FC SD XI, 12)

---

4. Hoepfl insists that inerrancy is made irrelevant when it is said that historical errors do not affect the intent of Scripture. Cf. *Introductio Generalis in Sacram Scripturam* (Rome, 1958), p. 123: "Pro ipsis Protestantibus liberalibus magis 'conservatoribus,' qui inspirationis notionem saltem valde deprimunt, quaestio inerrantiae omnino non exsistit, cum errores historici fini S. Scripturae non noceant."

Corollary F

The practical importance of the doctrine must always be recognized; it consists in this, that, as God is true and faithful, the reader of Scripture can have the assurance that he will not be deceived or led astray by anything he reads in God's Word, Holy Scripture. In no discussion of inerrancy do we find merely an academic interest in maintaining purely a traditional position or in hewing to a party line. Such a practical concern must also be emphasized in our day. Any approach to Scripture or method of interpretation which would make of Scripture something less than trustworthy is sub-Christian and does not take Scripture at its own terms. It must also be borne in mind that the truthfulness of Scripture is never an end in itself, but serves the soteriological purpose of Scripture.

Adjuncts to the Doctrine of Biblical Inerrancy

1. Inerrancy does not imply verbal exactness of quotations (for example, the words of institution, the words on Jesus' cross). The New Testament ordinarily quotes the Old Testament according to its sense only, sometimes it only alludes to a pericope or verse in the Old Testament, sometimes there are conflations, and so forth. In the case of extra-Biblical citations we ought to assume that the holy writer stands behind and accepts the truth of his quotation unless the context would indicate otherwise (see II Chron. 5:9; 8:8 where there are citations from documents which say that a situation obtains "to this day," that is, when the original document was written). It is helpful to distinguish between the *veritas citationis* (lies, statements of evil men, or the quotation of the statements of Job's friends, etc.) and the *veritas rei citatae*. (Acts 17:28; Num. 21:14 and possibly II Kings 1:18)

2. Inerrancy does not imply verbal or intentional agreement in parallel accounts of the same event. For instance, the portrayal of creation in Gen. 1 and in Job 38 are radically different because of a radical difference in the aim of the author. Again, the different evangelists write about our Lord from different vantage points and out of different concerns: therefore their accounts will differ not only in details (as in the case of any two or three witnesses of the same event) but in aim. We must exercise caution here, however, lest we impose a point of view on an author which cannot be drawn inductively from the Scripture itself. For instance, there is no certain evidence that Matthew is writing for Jews, tying up Christ's life with Old Testament prophecy (John also cites the Old Testament often: 22 times); this is merely a rather safe conjecture. The same may be said concerning John writing on Christ's divinity against Cerinthus. We have no right or good reason to assume that the holy writer tampers with or distorts the facts to maintain a point of view; the evangelists claim to be faithful and careful witnesses (John 21:24; Luke 1:1 ff.). However, it must be clearly recognized that incomplete history or an incomplete presentation of doctrine in a given pericope is not false history or a false presentation.

3. Scripture is replete with figures of speech, for example, metonymy (Luke 16:29), metaphor (Ps. 18:20), personification (Matt. 6:4), synecdoche

40

(Luke 2:1), apostrophe, hyperbole (Matt. 2:3). It should go without saying that figurative language is not errant language. To assert that Scripture, by rounding numbers and employing hyperbole, metaphors, and so forth, is not concerned about precision of fact (and is therefore subject to error) is to misunderstand the intention of Biblical language. Figurative language (and not modern scientifically "precise" language) is precisely the mode of expression which the sacred writers' purposes demand. To imply that figurative language is *ex hypothesi* meaningless or that it cannot convey information — truthful and, from its own point of view, precise information — is the position of positivism, not the result of sensitive exegesis (for example, "Yanks slaughter Indians" is a meaningful and precise statement). How else does one speak of a transcendent God, of His epiphanies and revelations, than in metaphors and figures of speech? Demetaphorize, deanthropomorphize, and you are often not getting closer to the meaning of such expressions, but losing their meaning. Figurative language, then, meets all the canons necessary for inerrancy: (1) that statements perfectly represent the author's meaning; (2) that statements do not mislead the reader or lead him into error of any kind; and (3) that statements correspond to fact when they purport to deal with fact, and this in the case of poetry as well as in the case of straight narrative.

It must be added at this point that when we interpret or read Scripture we identify ourselves with the writers, not only with their *Sitz im Leben* and their use of language but with their entire spirit and their faith (which is more important, I Cor. 2:14-16). We not only understand them but feel and live and experience with them; we become totally involved. To stand back dispassionately and assess and criticize as a modern man would Shelley or Shakespeare or Homer is to fail to interpret Scripture.

4. Scripture uses popular phrases and expressions of its day, for example, bowels of mercy; four corners of the earth; Joseph is called the father of Christ. No error is involved in the use of such popular expressions. See Ps. 7:9; 22:10.

5. In describing the things of nature Scripture does not employ scientifically precise language, but describes and alludes to things phenomenally as they appear to our senses: for example, the fixity of stellar constellations and the magnitude of the stars (Is. 13:10; Judg. 5:20; Job 38:31; Amos 5:8; Job 9:9); the sun and moon as lights and the implication that the moon is larger than the stars (Gen. 1:16) [it *is* larger from our vantage point]; the earth as motionless in a fixed position (Eccl. 1:4; Ps. 93:1); the sun as going around the fixed earth (Eccl. 1:5; Matt. 13:6; Eph. 4:26; note that in the Hebrew Bible there is even a phrase for the rising of the sun: *mizrach shemesh*, which means "east," Ps. 50:1). Phenomenal language also explains why the bat is classified with birds (Lev. 11:19; see Lev. 11:6; Ps. 135:6). Such a classification offers no attempt to be scientific.

Many things in the realm of nature are spoken of in poetic language: the spreading out of the heavens (Is. 40:22; Job 9:8), the foundations of the earth (Job 38:6), the pillars of the earth (Job 9:6) and of heaven (Job 26:11), the ends of the earth (Ps. 67:7; 72:8). Note that there is much apostrophe and hyperbole (Mark 4:31) when Scripture speaks of the things of nature.

In none of the above instances is inerrancy threatened or vitiated. The intention of the passages cited above is not to establish or vouch for a particular world view or scientific explanation of things. Because the language is not scientific does not imply that it is not true descriptively.

6. The various literary forms used by Scripture.

a. Certain alleged forms are not compatible either with the purpose of Scripture or with its inerrancy. For instance, in principle, purely scientific, purely historical, or purely salacious literary forms cannot be reconciled with the serious, practical, theological purpose of Scripture. Specifically, any literary genre that would in itself be immoral or involve deceit or error is not compatible with Biblical inerrancy and is not to be found in Scripture, for example, myth, etiological tale, midrash, legend or saga according to the usual designation of these forms. None of these genres fits the serious theological purpose of Scripture. Thus we do not find Scripture presenting material as factual or historical when in truth it is only mythical. (II Peter 1:16 ff.; I Tim. 1:4; 4:7; II Tim. 4:4)[5]

b. Apart from the above strictures any form of ancient literature is hypothetically compatible with Biblical inerrancy, for example, allegory (Gal. 4) and fable (Judg. 9:8-15), provided the genre is indicated directly or indirectly. At the same time it does no violence to inerrancy if the language of folklore or mythical elements serves as a means to clothe a Biblical author's presentation of doctrine (for example, "helpers of Rahab" in Job 9:13; "Leviathan" in Job 3:8 and in Ps. 74:12-15; Idumea as inhabited by centaurs, satrys, and other strange creatures [Is. 34:14], meaning that Idumea will be devasted so that only such animals can live there). We do the same today if in a sermon a pastor refers to a "dog in a manger." As for the midrash, there is no reason to maintain that Scripture cannot employ midrashim any

---

5. Cf. A. Bea, *De Inspiratione et Inerrantia Sacrae Scripturae* (Rome, 1954), p. 44: "Myth is the expression of some religious or cultic idea through personifications which are regarded as divine entities (e.g., the fertility of the earth and of animals — Astarte). Such myths must be distinguished from mythic literary elements (metaphors, personifications) employed from selected mythology for illustrative purposes. Cf. Is. 27:1 (= Ugarit A + I, 1-2?); Ps. 74:12-17; 89:10-14; 48:3; Job 26:7; Is. 32:20. Myth, properly so-called, cannot be found in the sacred Scriptures (cf. EB n. 60-333); however, that literary elements could be used to adorn or illustrate was already granted by the holy Fathers; cf. S. Greg. Nyss, PG 44, 973. On individual passages, see *Biblica* 19 (1938), 444-448; F. Porporato, *Miti e inspirasione biblica*, 1944; id. in *Civ. Catt.* 94 (1943/I), 329-340.

"*Midrashim* technically speaking are rabbinic literary efforts — writings from that era — which are not strictly exegetical but composed for establishing rules for living (*halachah*). II Chron. 13:22 and 24:27 do not use the term in this technical sense. but signify merely 'study' or 'work' (cf. Eissfeldt, *Einl.*, p. 605). Since it arbitrarily confused true and false things, midrash *per se* is excluded by the holy Scriptures (cf. EB n. 474). It can be admitted only if the holy writer clearly indicated that he is writing only for the sake of edification and not for setting forth properly history (cf. EB n. 154)."

more than other literary forms. In many cases midrash approaches parable in form and purpose. However, the fanciful examples of midrash with the indiscriminate admixture of truth and error and the production of pure fiction to stress a certain lesson is not compatible with the historical character and the inerrancy of Scripture.[6]

7. Biblical historiography.

a. Some Biblical writers use and cite sources for their history. We must assume that the Biblical author by the way in which he cites sources believes that these sources speak the truth, that they are reliable sources; and therefore he follows them. The contrary contention is certainly possible, but it must be proved in individual cases (implicit citations, see II Sam.). In the case of explicit citations (the words of a character in a history) we assume the truth of the matter cited, but this again depends on the intention of the hagiographer. We can assume the truth of the matter cited only if the holy writer formally or implicitly asserts that he approved it and judges to be true what he asserts in the citation. (See Acts 17:29)

b. Historical events are not described phenomenally as are the data of nature.[7]

c. The historical genre employed by Scripture is apparently a unique form. As it cannot be judged according to the canons (whatever they may be) of modern scientific historiography, it cannot be judged by the mythological and legendary or even historical forms of ancient contemporary civilizations;

---

6. See J. M. Lehrmann, *The World of the Midrash* (London, 1961); see also *Sacrae Theologiae Summa*, I, 1097: "All literary genres are quite compatible with inspiration, if they are not by their very nature immoral (as in the case of certain classical poetry) or if they do not tend to lead into error. Thus myths considered as false religious fables (e.g., the personification of natural things such as the fertility of the earth as divine beings) is a literary form not consonant with inspiration. But a myth merely cited in Scripture or used as a mere literary adornment may be admitted, but as something merely cited, or as something purely metaphorical. . . . We can even allow that fictitious narratives (are present) in the Scriptures, provided that they are recognized as such and that of necessity the truth related by the words of the story is in the proper sense not historical. Thus there is the allegorical mode of speaking in Scripture, such as we find in the Song of Songs, which is an allegorical song describing the love and mystical union between Jahveh and His people. And it is true that in the different literary forms of Scripture, whether poetical or doctrinal or narrative, (fables) are interspersed."

7. Cf. Bea, p. 45: " 'History according to appearance' is based upon a false foundation, namely this, that principles which obtain relative to matters of nature can be transferred to historical concerns. Historical sources or general opinion are not 'appearances of happenings'; the telling of a certain happening *per se* does not amount to announcing that something appeared to the senses, as in the realm of nature, nor is it tantamount to say what the common people think about a happening; rather it is the announcing of the happening itself." Cf. also *Sacrae Tehologiae Summa*, I, 1097: "On the other hand, history is not concerned with phenomena which are continuously apparent and with things which men describe according to appearance, but history concerns itself with *things that have happened, just as they have happened*" (italics theirs).

43

for example, we take the ancient Babylonian and Ugaritic accounts of creation as pure myth, but quite clearly the Biblical cannot be taken as such.[8]

d. Chronology and genealogies are not presented in Scripture in the full and orderly manner in which we might present a chronicle or family tree today. Scripture often spreads out time for the sake of symmetry or harmony, *hysteron proteron* is often employed, and also prolepsis (John 17:4; 13:31). Again, genealogies often omit many generations. (See I Chron. 26:24, where Moses, Gershom, Shebuel are given, covering a period of perhaps more than

---

8. Cf. Bea, pp. 46-48: "In its own characteristics Israelite writing of history far surpasses all other Semitic historiography. . . . W. F. Albright, *The Archaeology of Pal.* (1932), 128. . . . In a certain sense Hebrew historiography can be compared with the Hittite (cf. *Annales Mursilis* II, ca. 1353-1325; *Apologia Hattusil.*, ca. 1295-1260), but the Israelitish writing of history surpasses this in liveliness, in its simple manner, and sincere way of narrating, in psychological depth and breadth; in particular it is not a 'courtly' or 'official' manner of narrating. . . .

"The manner of writing among the ancients definitely differs from the modern. Firstly, the ancients considered the writing of history to be an art (cf. Cicero). Thus it was adorned greatly, for instance, with fictitious speeches to express certain ideas. Such historiography pays more attention to giving the sense of a speech than to bringing out the exact words; it employs numerical schemata (30, 40, 70); it uses mnemonic techniques (such as etymologies); it is careless concerning exact chronology; it uses genealogies as shortcuts to history; it narrates in 'concentric circles' rather than in straight continuous exposition, etc. Now all of these devices, provided that they are properly considered, in no way conflict with the integrity of the narratives. . . .

"Ancient history is not a genre of its own peculiar type which is less interested in telling the truth than modern history. Rather it has different aims, different ways of exposition from modern history. Therefore it is necessary in the case of all the individual authors to investigate accurately what sources they use, how they make judgments from these sources, what style they employ, what purpose they intend. Only then are we able to assess rightly and judiciously concerning their historical merit. . . .

"The intention of the inspired historiographers is to write *true* history. When they made use of the narrative genre, this presupposes per se that they desire to tell of things that *have happened*. . . .

"That these stories have a religious aim does not imply that the *facts* which they refer to are any less true. 'Religious history' is not necessarily fictional narrative. Thus, for instance, the evangelists, although they write with a religious aim in mind, are very careful about the truth of the facts (cf. Lk. 1:1; Jn. 19:35; I Jn. 1:1 . . .)

"That the facts connected with revelation are sometimes (e.g., in the first eleven chapters of Genesis) presented in a simple manner, a manner accommodated to the comprehension of less cultured men, that they are presented figuratively and anthropomorphically, does not imply that we can call these narratives any less truly historical although they are not history in our modern technical meaning of the term; cf. EB 581, and *Verb. Dom.* 25 (1946), 354-56.

"The Judaic as well as the Christian tradition understood the Biblical narratives in the strictly historical sense; cf. the sayings of Christ (Lk. 4:25; 6:3 ff.; 17:32; Matt. 12:40) and the sayings of the apostles (Heb. 11:17-40; II Pet. 2:5-8), in which facts of minor or secondary importance are set forth as history. . . . That Christ and the apostles simply 'accommodated' themselves to their own contemporaries cannot be asserted a priori, but must be proved in each individual case where there might seem to be some special reason for granting this."

400 years; or Heb. 7:9-10, where Levi is said to be in the loins of Abraham, his father, when Melchisedec met him; thus any ancestor is the father of all his descendants.)

8. We must grant that there is often a *sensus plenior* in Scripture pericopes in the sense of I Peter 1:10-12. That is to say, the writer of Scripture is not in every respect a child of his time, conditioned by his own cultural milieu, but he often writes for a later age. However, we cannot countenance a *sensus diversus et disperatus relate ad sensus litteralem obvium hagiographi*, which would conflict with Biblical inerrancy and turn Scripture into a waxen nose. We hold only to a profounder and sometimes more distinct sense than the writer may have perceived as he expressed himself. This has serious implications relative to the New Testament use and interpretation of the Old Testament; the New Testament does not misinterpret or do violence to the Old Testament when it interprets. *Sensus litteralis Scripturae unicus est* does not imply that the sacred writer understands the full divine implication of all his words.

9. Pseudepigrapha. Pseudonymity in the sense of one writer pretending to be another in order to secure acceptance of his own work is illicit and not compatible with inerrancy. That the motives for such action may be construed as good does not alter the fact that fraud or forgery has been perpetrated. The fact that such a practice was carried on in ancient times does not justify it nor indicate that the practice was considered moral. When in ancient times a pious fraud was found out and the authenticity of a work disproved, the work itself was suspect. (See *Fragmentum Muratorianum*, 5, where the *finctae* letters of Paul to the Laodiceans and the Alexandrians were not accepted by the church for that very reason.)

Pseudonymity must be carefully delimited. Pseudonymity is deliberate fraud (for any reason whatsoever). It has nothing to do with anonymity. Nor would it be pseudonymity if a later writer culled under inspiration all the wisdom sayings of Solomon, gathering them into a volume and presenting them for what they are, Solomon's wisdom. His contemporaries know that Solomon has not written the book, but understand the sayings and the wisdom to be Solomon's (similar to this, that we have the words of Christ in the Gospels). In such a case no deception is involved. In the case of the pastoral epistles such a conclusion could not be assumed by any stretch of the imagination. The letters are written to give the impression that they come directly from Paul, claiming his authority. If they were not in fact Pauline, a deception has taken place, a successful deception until lately.[9]

---

9. Cf. J. I. Packer, *"Fundamentalism" and the Word of God* (Grand Rapids, Mich., 1958), pp. 182 ff.; D. Guthrie, *The Pauline Epistles, New Testament Introduction* (London, 1961), pp. 282-294. Cf. also the chapter by Guthrie, "The Development of the Idea of Canonical Pseudepigrapha in New Testament Criticism," in *The Authorship and Integrity of the New Testament* (Theological Collections, No. 4), London, 1965. In another chapter of the same book entitled "The Problem of Anonymity and Pseudonymity in Christian Literature of the First Two Centuries" Kurt Aland takes the contrary position, that there are pseudepigrapha in the New Testament. Aland insists that psychological

10. Etymologies in Scripture are often according to sound and not (obviously) according to modern linguistic analysis. This fact does not affect inerrancy. The ancients are not thinking of etymologies in the modern sense.[10]

11. The inerrancy and the authority of Scripture are inseparably related. This fact has been consistently recognized by Lutheran theologians, who have often included inerrancy and authority under the rubric of infallibility. What is meant is that without inerrancy the *sola scriptura* principle cannot be maintained or practiced. An erring authority for all Christian doctrine (like an erring Word of God) is an impossible and impracticable *contradictio in adjecto*.

12. In approaching the Scripture as children of God who are under the Scriptures, we shall do well to recall and observe two basic principles of our Lutheran Fathers: (1) Scripture is *autopistos*, that is to say, we are to believe its utterances simply because Scripture, the Word of God, makes these utterances (inerrancy is always to be accepted on faith!), and we are to believe without the need of any corroborating evidence. This would apply to statements about God but also to statements about events in history. (2) Scripture is *anapodeiktos*, that is, self-authenticating. It brings its own demonstration, the demonstration of the Spirit and of power. Again no corroborating evidence is necessary or sought for. Now *sola scriptura* means all this; and it means as well that there are no outside criteria for judging the truthfulness or factual content of Scriptural assertions (for example, neither a modern scientific world view nor modern "scientific historiography"). We accept the assertions of the Scripture on faith. For instance, the fact that the creation story or the flood or the story of Babel has some parallels in other Semitic and ancient lore gives no right to conclude that these accounts in Scripture are mythical (any

---

considerations and ethical viewpoints cannot be considered in any discussion of the problem of pseudepigrapha; but such a move is, among other things, clearly a proposal to turn the idea of inerrancy out of court and permit no inquiry into its applicability at this point.

10. Cf. J. Levie, *The Bible, Word of God in Words of Men* (New York, 1962), pp. 220 to 221: "We know that in all countries the common people very often invent as an afterthought etymological explanations for the name of a given place or given tribe on the basis of quite arbitrary associations of ideas or words. Is it legitimate to admit that here too the sacred writer is content to hand down to us the popular derivations customary in his environment, or should we be obliged to believe that, by virtue of inspiration, these derivations are the true linguistic explanations of the words in question, and should therefore be accepted by present-day scholars?

"It is now generally recognized that the inspired writer is only reporting these attempted etymologies as he found them in the folklore of his country. The literary form he adopts, which is that of popular history, clearly shows that he has no intention of offering us scientific derivations of the modern kind, but popular derivations in the style of his own times.

"Here are a few examples taken from ten chapters of Genesis, 16 to 26: — 16:13 (Atta el Roi); 16:14 (Lackai Roi); 17:17; 18:12-15; 21:6 which give three derivations of the name Isaac (these clearly show by their differences that the writer intended to give a simple report and to make no attempt at criticism); 19:22 (Segor); 21:31 (Bersabee); 22:14 (Yahweh Yireh); 25:25 (Jacob); 25:30-1 (Edom); 26:20 (Eseq); 26:21 (Sitna); 26:22 (Rechoboth; 26:33 (Schibea)."

more than we have the right to conclude that Christ's resurrection is not historical because there are mythical resurrections recorded in history). Such an interpretation would involve a violation of the *sola scriptura* principle. At the same time it is possible that a changed world view (for example, our modern view as opposed to the Newtonian view of absolute space and time) will open for consideration a new interpretation of a Biblical pericope, although it can never determine our interpretation of Scripture.

It is particularly important to maintain the above principles in our day in view of the tendency to allow extra-Biblical data (particularly historical and archaeological data) to encroach on the absolute authority of Scripture.

V.

IMPLICATIONS OF THE HISTORICO-CRITICAL METHOD IN INTERPRETING THE OLD TESTAMENT

Raymond Surburg

In dealing with the interpretation of a Biblical book, students are required to employ Biblical criticism which is often divided into lower and higher criticism. The former endeavors to recover the text that was produced by the original author. This type of criticism is also called textual, the foundation upon which higher criticism builds.[1] By "lower" criticism is not meant inferiority to so-called "higher" criticism.

I.

Since the original autographs are no longer available, the first step in interpretation of a Biblical book is to ascertain the true text. The original Scriptures of the Old and New Testament were inspired in their actual wording by the Holy Spirit. Our present printed texts are based upon manuscripts copied by amanuenses during the course of about 3,500 years. Throughout the centuries much effort has been expended by many competent scholars to produce a reliable text. Especially during the last four hundred years, textual criticism has been developed to a point where today it is a science that employs reliable norms for ascertaining the true text of the Bible. Such men as Tischendorf, Weiss, Westcott, Hort, Nestle, Kittel, Kahle and a host of scholars have devoted years of painstaking research to make available to Biblical students correct texts of the Old and New Testaments. The American Textual Criticism Seminar has been working for a number of years to give the world a new critical text of the New Testament, while discovery of the Dead Sea Biblical Manuscripts and portions of Biblical manuscripts have opened up new vistas for textual criticism of the Old Testament. The Christian Church is greatly in debt to the men who have specialized in this area for their earnest endeavors to ascertain what were the *ipsissima verba* of Holy Writ in Hebrew, Aramaic, and Greek. Every Christian should be interested in the efforts of present day scholars to restore the Biblical text in all its original purity.

---

1. Jean Steinmann, *Biblical Criticism* (New York: Hawthorn Books, Publishers, 1958), p. 12.; Erwin L. Lueker, *Lutheran Cyclopedia* (St. Louis: Concordia Publishing House, 1954), 1044.

Task of Higher Criticism

After the textual critics have completed their task of preparing a text which they believe to be a facsimile of the original, the higher critic begins his task of delving into questions of authorship, literary form, and historical background. Some scholars divide higher criticism into literary and historical criticism.

In describing the importance of literary criticism, Father Steinman wrote: "Literary criticism is no less necessary. Its function will be to determine exactly what the inspired writer had in mind and what the import of his statements was. We must know what literary form a book of the Bible belongs to before we can understand it properly and suggest how it should be interpreted.[2] Literary criticism tries to localize a given writing, determine its author, if possible, and ascertain all that is known about him; the place where the book was composed; the time of writing; the person or groups of people to whom it was addressed, and the occasion, cause, or circumstances for penning the document. These steps in the localization of a book have been summarized under six questions: Who? Where? When? To whom? Why? and What? The genuineness of a writing, whether it is pseud-epigraphic or whether in the course of tradition the book has been given a false ascription, is a problem closely related to the localization of a literary document.

Under "Who?" the problem of authorship is discussed. Literary criticism employs the same techniques as the student of English literature does in his evaluation of the claim that Bacon wrote Shakespeare. Two types of evidence are considered in the determination of the authorship of a document: external and internal. External evidence embraces two considerations: the tradition as to authorship, and the light cast on the problem by its original recipients. Internal evidence is based on the vocabulary and style of a book together with reference to other literary productions of the writer, which are compared for ideas and content. Liberal scholars claim that the objective application of these literary canons to Biblical literature has resulted in the repudiation of some erroneous ideas held about the origin and purpose of many Biblical books.

Under "What?" the literary features of a book are considered. A knowledge of literary form is necessary. The Bible contains such literary types as history, narration, parable, dialogue, proverb, drama, and essay. Matthew Arnold was convinced that the "first step toward a right understanding of the Bible was to appreciate that its language was not rigid, fixed and scientific, but fluid and literary."

A problem closely related both to the authorship and nature of the contents of a writing is the necessity of determining the sources that were employed by its writer. In a literary work, oral or written, or even both, sources may have been used which should be identified and, if possible, localized. The Book of Joshua and the Books of Chronicles refer to written sources besides those indicated in the writings themselves which latter sources

---

2. Steinmann, *op. cit.*, p. 17.

have become a passion with most liberal and neo-orthodox scholars, especially in the Old Testament field. A perusal of R. H. Pfeiffer's *Introduction to the Old Testament* will reveal how practically every book of the Old Testament has been torn apart so that many Biblical writings resemble a patch quilt.[3] Colwell claimed that in the writing of Hebrew literature, "the scissors and paste" method was employed, thus enabling the modern student to discern the sources used in writing, re-writing, and editing the Old Testament books.[4]

In the study of the Gospels, scholars are convinced that it is possible to detect the literary sources. Mark, Luke, Matthew, and John are supposed to have written their Gospels in the same manner as the pre-Christians wrote their histories. Confidently, Colwell has announced: "The identification of these sources made a sane interpretation of Gospel parallelisms possible and dealt a death-blow to superficial harmonizing of the Gospels."[5]

Since many books of the Old Testament, according to the understanding of liberal scholars, give a great deal of evidence of editorial activity, called redaction, the work of this redactor (a hypothetical personality) must be taken into account. Most of the redactional activity is supposed to have taken place in post-Exilic times.

The dating of a document, the "When?" is another problem the Biblical student encounters. There are two categories into which the evidence is grouped: external and internal. External evidence comprises the testimony derived from literature other than the document under consideration. Thus a number of New Testament books give information about other books in the canon which were written earlier. Peter refers to the Epistle of St. Paul as in existence as he writes II Peter 3:16. The non-canonical literature of the second century contains valuable information about the writing and formation of the New Testament canon. Internal evidence, on the other hand, consists of data furnished by the books themselves. An example of internal evidence as an aid to the dating of the Book of Luke is the statement of 3:1, giving the 15th year of Caesar Tiberius as the beginning of Christ's public ministry, which means that the Gospel must have been written after this year. The opening verse of the sixth chapter of Isaiah gives the year in which Isaiah began his ministry and consequently must have been written subsequently to this date. Evidence as to the date of a book is often found in a quotation or quotations from other books that are datable. Again, when the sources are dated or datable, it is possible to date the document of which they are a part. Often the place of origin of a literary document is sometimes datable. A book purporting to originate at a certain time and place, written, however, in a language never used at the time in question or in the locality, cannot be genuine in its claim.

---

3. Robert H. Pfeiffer, *Introduction to the Old Testament* (New York: Harper & Brothers, 1948), 909 pp.; cf. also Robert H. Pfeiffer, *The Books of the Old Testament* (New York: Harper & Brothers Publishers, 1957), 335 pp.; Walter R. Roehrs, "Higher Criticism," *Lutheran Cyclopedia, op. cit.,* pp. 466-469.
4. E. C. Colwell, *The Study of the Bible* (Chicago: The University of Chicago Press, 1947).
5. *Ibid.,* p. 139.

After these considerations have been determined, the next step for the user of the historical method is to consider comparatively the book being interpreted, especially with reference to its historical, cultural, social, economic, intellectual, and religious background, which may be determined by a study of the geography, epigraphy, numismatics, and archaeology of the period from which the book claims to have come.

Historico-Critical Method

The use of both lower and higher criticism is often referred to as the employment of the "historico-critical method." It is not easy to define what is meant by this method since it is more than simply resorting to the critical use of all helps available today, whether historical, linguistic or archaeological in the study of Scripture. Such well known scholars as Luther, Calvin, Flacius, and Calov were proponents of this methodology. However, the birth of the modern use of the historico-critical method is usually traced by historians of Biblical exegesis to Richard Simon, Jean Astruc, Pascal, and Spinoza. The "historico-critical method" was born during the period of rationalism which generally rejected miracles and the inspiration of Scripture. The latter half of the eighteenth century produced a type of theology that was "destructive" of the theological position of the reformation and post-reformation periods. With the historico-critical method also arose a school of biblical criticism which was based on rationalistic presuppositions. Early studies by Astruc (1753), Eichhorn (1783), DeWette (1805) and Ewald (1823) resulted in "the documentary hypothesis" of the Pentateuch, claiming that the first five books of the Hebrew Bible had their origin in a combination of a series of documents which were not committed to writing until four or five centuries subsequent to Moses' death. After this hypothesis had gone through various stages, and Old Testament scholars had made many additions and changes, there emerged the final documentary hypothesis, sponsored by two Hebrew scholars, Graf and Wellhausen. Wellhausen's *Prolegomena to the History of Ancient Israel* resulted in the stabilization of a theory which before had been subject to much flux.[6]

One of the contributors to the *New Bible Handbook* wrote regarding the philosophy behind the Wellhausen theory: "Not believing in the possibility of miracles, they elaborated a theory which pictures the religion of Israel as a gradual evolution from primitive animism, through a stage when Jehovah was taken as a tribal god, like the gods of the heathen, until, under the influence of the later prophets, a lofty level of monotheism was reached. The whole Old Testament was radically affected by this theory; the sources of the various books were dated in accordance with it, using as a criterion the stage of development which they were thought to reflect. The late dating of the documents opened the way for attributing their supernatural elements

---

6. For the rise and development of biblical criticism cf. Samuel Terrien, "History of the Interpretation of the Bible. III. Modern Period," George A. Buttrick, *The Interpreter's Bible* (New York and Nashville: Abingdon-Cokesbury Press, 1952), I, pp. 127-135.

to the growth of myth or legend, and the history was completely reconstructed from this point of view."[7]

The early proponents of the historico-critical approach to the Old Testament were strongly influenced by the philosophy of Wolff and Kant, and such advocates as Spinoza, Lessing, Kuenen, Strauss, F. Baur, Eichhorn, and De-Wette were guided in their study and interpretation of the Bible by two positions: 1) all were certain that the new criticism must be applied indiscriminately to the Bible, and 2) all had adopted a new and freer view of what the Bible was and what was involved in Biblical revelation. Robert Preus writes: "Without these two developments there would never have been a 'historical-historical' method in the modern sense."[8]

The development of the views that resulted from the use of the historico-critical method had its origin in the rejection of the orthodox view of Scripture. One of the first theologians of the age of enlightenment to reject the traditional view was Sigmund Baumgarten (1706-1757). He failed to grasp the truth that Holy Scripture was but one mode of divine revelation, claiming the traditional view identified revelation and inspiration. He looked upon the Old and New Testaments merely as the original source of revelation (*Urkunde*). Baumgarten was followed by Johann Semler (1725-1791) often called the father of modern Biblical criticism. The latter distinguished between the Word of God and revelation and claimed that the Bible was only then relevant when and to the degree that it had a message for the internal life of man. When this was evident then it was proper to speak of Holy Writ's inspiration. In his approach to the Bible, Semler was thoroughly rationalistic, which meant a rejection of the supernatural under the form of miracles and predictive prophecy. For him these were necessary presuppositions that must be utilized by any interpreter that would adequately comprehend the message of the Biblical books. It was uncritical to ascribe a priori God's authority to Scripture and proceed with its interpretation on this assumption.

Semler's position was adopted and perpetuated by Vatke, a member of the Hegelian school, by Kuenen and F. Baur and many others in the first part of the nineteenth century. They all rejected the divine origin and unique character of Israel's religion. The consequent result for all these men was the adoption of skepticism. In the same manner as all those who had rejected the inspiration of Scripture and its teaching that the Bible was the inerrant Word of God, Semler, like Lessing, Fichte, and Kant, resorted to moralism as the essence and core of religion.[9]

Upon the foundation of his predecessors Wellhausen built and rejected the accounts of the miraculous in the Old Testament as either legend or myth and proceeded to explain the religious development according to an evolution-

---

7. "Modern Criticism," in G. T. Manley, *The New Bible Handbook* (Chicago and Toronto: The Inter-Varsity Christian Fellowship, 1949), pp. 40-41.
8. Robert D. Preus, "Current Theological Problems Which Confront the Church," *A Conference of the College of Presidents and the Seminary Faculties*, November 27-29, 1961, Concordia Seminary, St. Louis. p. 32.
9. Cf. Otto Pfleiderer, *The Development of Theology in Germany Since Kant and Its Progress in Great Britain Since* 1825 (London: George Allen & Unwin Ltd., 1923), pp. 253-276.

ary scheme. "This involved the abandonment of the story of revelation as told in the Bible, and the reconstruction of what was conceived to be the true history which lies behind its fables and traditions. The documentary analysis rendered this possible by affixing to each document, or fragment, a date corresponding with the critic's view of the history and religious progress. Thereby a book which purports to be a true narrative derived from contemporary sources was turned into a late compilation derived from varying traditions, myths and legends."[10]

Two of the main pillars of the Wellhausen position were to the effect that writing was unknown before the days of the monarchy, and that Israel's religion could be traced back to totemistic animism, from which it progressed through the stages of polytheism, henotheism, and finally monotheism. These assumptions resulted in the necessity of holding the narrative of the Old Testament to have been handed down for long ages by oral tradition.

J, E, D, P, etc.

"The New Document Theory" (associated with Hupfeld, Reuss, Graf, Kuenen, Wellhausen) postulated four sources for the Pentateuch, which came to follow the general order of J, E, D, and P.[11] In essence, the theory holds that J (ca. 850 B.C.) and E (ca. 750 B.C.) were combined by a redactor (Rj^e) ca. 650 B.C.; D (621 B.C.) was added by R^d ca. 550 B.C.; P (ca. 500-450) by R^p ca. 400 B.C., bringing the Pentateuch in general to its present form. By the beginning of this century this theory was accepted in many Protestant circles. In 1891 Professor Driver issued his *Literature of the Old Testament*, a book which closely followed the position set forth by Julius Wellhausen. Later Oesterley and Robinson in a number of volumes propounded the same theory with the result that modern criticism (called by conservatives "negative criticism") eventually permeated the textbooks of colleges and theological seminaries in England and America.

Higher criticism, however, in the twentieth century did not remain static. Many changes were introduced into the scholarly understanding of the origin and development of the Old Testament. Flack asserted: "Critics have posited not only divisions and alterations in the four principal sources, J, E, D, and P, but also numerous additional documents. Smend, for example, found two parallel strands in J (J^1 and J^2. Hempel named three phases in J (J^1, J^2 and J^3) corresponding to the three divisions of Genesis 1-11, 12-36, 37-50."[12] Most critics assign J to Judah, the southern kingdom, and E to Israel, the northern kingdom. Mowinckel, outstanding Scandinavian scholar, assigns E to Judah and denies the independence of J. Eissfeldt, a German scholar of

---

10. Manley, *op. cit.*, pp. 44-45.
11. Cf. the history of Pentateuchal Criticism by Elmer E. Flack. "Pentateuch" in Lefferts A. Loetscher, *Twentieth Century Encyclopedia of Religious Knowledge* (Grand Rapids: Baker Book House, 1955), II 862-864; Edward J. Young, *An Introduction to the Old Testament* (Grand Rapids: Wm. B. Eerdmans Publishing Company, 1960), pp. 130-164; Solomon Goldman, *The Book of Books: An Introduction* (New York: Harper & Brothers, 1948), pp. 39-67.
12. Flack. *op. cit.*, p. 863b.

repute, finds a document called L in the Pentateuch, which is in contrast to P, a priestly source. Morgenstern posits a Kenite document called K, which is supposed to be the source for the life of Moses. R. Pfeiffer, on the other hand, postulates a document S, whose origin was in the south or around Seir.

One of the four documents of the Pentateuch is D (Deuteronomy) placed by Wellhausen around 621 B.C. Hoelscher has challenged the Josianic date and claims it originated after the Exile about 500 B.C. Other scholars, A. C. Welch and Th. Oestreicher, have assigned it to a period earlier than the reign of Josiah. Edward Robinson assigns it even to the time of Samuel.

P, the latest document of the Pentateuch, was originally assigned to the Exilic period, ca. 550 B.C. Many believe that Ezekiel wrote it. Found in Genesis, Exodus, Leviticus, and Numbers, it is supposed to be recognized by a formal style, its systematic arrangement, a unique vocabulary and its predilection for genealogies, numbers, cultural laws, and the rights of priests. Yet, outstanding authorities like Max Loehr and Paul Volz have rejected its existence, while Gerhard von Rad has divided it into two parallel writings, designated by him as P[a] and P[b].

In addition to the alleged existence of J, E, D, P, S, L, K, scholars have also advanced the idea that in the Old Testament writings there are separate units of laws, as the Decalogue, the Covenant Code, and other legal sections, which as Flack asserts had the result "that the documents in question have become less distinct than formerly, particularly as their origin as the work of a single author or school."[13]

In the twentieth century many of the positions espoused by Wellhausen have been rejected. That aspect of his views which may be called the Development hypothesis has been surrendered, although most scholars insist on employing some form of the Documentary Hypothesis.[14] According to Bright[15] and Mendenhall,[16] Wellhausenism in its classic form has almost ceased to exist. Mendenhall asserted: "Perhaps the most important gap in the field of Old Testament history is the lack of an adequate hypothesis to replace that of Wellhausen."[17] In place of the regnant Wellhausian theory, new views have been proposed, such as those of the Form Critical School, the Myth and Religion School, the Traditio-historical or Uppsala School. Although these new schools differ in some respects, they have one feature in common: They all repudiate the Mosaic dating and the full trustworthiness of the Pentateuch.

Form-Criticism Evaluated

Herman Gunkel introduced the study of oral tradition into Old Testament field. By the use of "Form-Criticism" Gunkel was able to raise the question of the pre-literary course of the Old Testament religion and his-

---

13. *Ibid.*, p. 863.
14. John Bright, "Modern Study of Old Testament Literature," in G. Ernest Wright. editor, *The Bible and the Ancient Near East* (New York: Doubleday & Company, Inc., 1961). p. 18.
15. *Ibid.*, p. 18.
16. *Ibid.*, p. 34.
17. *Ibid.*, p. 38.

tory. Robinson says "that the net result has been to overthrow the construction of Wellhausen, by tracing the roots of the post-exilic law and of the interpretation of Israel's historical origin in terms of *Heilsgeschichte* (history of salvation) back into the period of the Israelite origins itself."[18] The materials which are found written down in J, E, D, P, were first handed down in oral traditions, and with few exceptions, were not written till the time of David, or somewhat later. Hebrew historiography began only in the time of David and Solomon, with the account of David's rise to power (I Samuel 16:14 through II Samuel 5:25) and the narrative as to his successor (II Samuel 7:9-20; I Kings 1-2). These narratives are considered by the critics as factual and sober. However, before this time, history was handed down only as a mass of legends clustering about cultic formulas which gave them their meaning, and this meaning was *Heilsgeschichte*. The traditions which were transmitted orally for generations are not to be considered reliable because they have been molded and modified in the course of being handed down, so that it becomes the task of the scholar to remove the accretions and get back to the core or the kernel. This means that it is up to the critic to establish the amount of material in the Pentateuch that is reliable.

Does the new approach support the traditional understanding of the five books of Moses? To this Robinson replies: "The historical implications of this study of oral tradition are thus not a confirmation of the sequence of the story as we have it in the Pentateuch. Abraham, Isaac, and Jacob were not the kin, did not worship the same God. The band which escaped from Egypt, the people who received the law at Sinai, and the nomads who over a period of centuries settled in Palestine are not one and the same group."[19]

Alt by his emphasis upon the existence of legal units and Albright by the employment of comparative Near Eastern archaeology, have tended to emphasize the complexities of oral tradition, which must be grasped, it is contended, before the history and theology of Israel can be understood.

According to Flack, there has occurred in recent decades as a result of the work of the Swedish School (Mowinckel, Nyberg, Volz, Engnell, etc.) and that of Von Rad and others, a weakening of the case for the documentary hypothesis. Thus Flack asserts: "It is now clear that the present Pentateuch cannot be fully accounted for by a mechanical process of piecing together diverse documents. Nevertheless, the theory of the four major literary sources, J, E, D, and P, still holds the field in recent criticism in general."[20] In 1951, Prof. North asserted concerning the status of Pentateuchal criticism: "Thirty years ago it looked as if the problem of the Pentateuch was reaching a definite solution. . . . The Graf-Wellhausen theory had triumphed and it seemed that little or nothing remained to be done."[21] However, the attacks by scholars like Dahse, Lohr, Möller, Cassuto, Eerdmann, Rethpath, Wiener, Dornseiff, James Orr, and others have led to a serious questioning

---

18. James M. Robinson, "The Historical Question," in Martin E. Marty, editor, *New Directions of Biblical Thought* (New York: Association Press, 1960), p. 75.
19. *Ibid.*, p. 82.
20. Flack, *op. cit.*, p. 863b.
21. C. R. North, "Pentateuchal Criticism," in H. H. Rowley, (ed.), *The Old Testament in Modern Study* (New York: Oxford University Press, 1951), p. 48.

of the validity of the classical literary analysis of the Graf-Wellhausian theory. Already in 1945, Ivan Engnell of Uppsala maintained in *Gamla Testamentet* that the Wellhausian theory "represents a modern, anachronistic *book-view* (*boksyn*), and is therefore an interpretation in modern categories, an *interpretation europeica moderna*. For a right judgment of the problem, a 'modified' or 'moderate view' of literary-critical type is, therefore, not enough; what is demanded is a radical break with this whole method. There never were any parallel continuous documents in the Mosaic books of the kind that are assumed. That large parts of the material in the Mosaic books were from the beginning or at a very early stage fixed in writing is quite another matter."[22] The present status of Pentateuchal criticism has, therefore, resulted in considerable confusion and uncertainty as to the sources. John Bright recently contributed an article to Essays in honor of William Fox Albright in which he asserted: "One should begin by warning the reader that it is impossible to make general statements regarding any phase of Biblical criticism today without running the risk of oversimplification. The whole field is in a state of flux. It is moving, certainly, but it is not always easy to say in what direction. Sometimes it gives the impression that it is moving in several mutually canceling directions at once. Even upon major points there is often little unanimity to be observed. As a result, scarcely a single statement can be made about the state of the field that would not be subject to qualification. Indeed, perhaps the only safe generalization possible is that the critical orthodoxy of a generation ago, with its apparent certainties and assured results, has gone, but that no new consensus has taken its place. Nevertheless, in spite of confusion and disagreement, certain significant trends can perhaps be chartered."[23]

Cyrus Gordon of Brandeis University, world famous as an archaeologist and an authority on Ugaritic, wrote an article for *Christianity Today* in which he rejected the JEDP theory, claiming it is "the badge of interconfessional academic respectability."[24] At one time a devotee of the JEDP source-structure of the Pentateuch, he became convinced of its untenability as a result of archaeological evidence. On the basis of his study of the description of the ark in the Gilgamesh Epic, he rejects the arguments of the critics that the P source for the Flood story is from the time of the Second Temple. Thus Gordon writes: "The pre-Abrahamic Genesis traditions (such as the Deluge) are not late P products; they are essentially pre-Mosaic and it is not easy to single out even details that are late."[25]

Different styles found in a document do not mean different authorships as modern criticism asserts. Just as a lawyer employs different styles in preparing a brief than in writing a letter to his mother, or as a clergyman

---

22. *Gamla Testamentet. En traditionshistorik inledning* (Stockholm, 1945), I, 189 f. as quoted by Merrill F. Unger, "H. H. Rowley and the New Trend in Biblical Studies," John F. Walvoord, (ed.), *Inspiration and Revelation* (Grand Rapids: Wm. B. Eerdmans Publishing Company, 1957), p. 196.
23. Wright, *op. cit.*, pp. 13-14.
24. Cyrus H. Gordon, "Higher Critics and Forbidden Fruit," *Christianity Today*, 4:4, November 23, 1959.
25. *Ibid.*, p. 3.

uses one style when conducting a religious service and still another when speaking to his children at breakfast, so the description of the Ark in Genesis in technical language is no more proof for different authorship from that of the narrative which surrounds it.

One of the reasons why higher criticism posits different authorships in the Old Testament is the existence of accounts that are repetitious, with variants. Judges 4 gives a prose version of Deborah's victory, while Judges 5 is a poetic account of the same historical event. Between the two versions there are variants. According to higher criticism the poetic version is much older; the prose account written centuries later. However, Gordon points out that in Egyptian literature historic events were recorded "simultaneously in prose and poetic versions, with the major differences appropriate to the two literary media."[26]

One of the cornerstones of the JEDP hypothesis is the supposition that the occurrence of "Jahwe" indicates a J document and "Elohim" an E document. When Jahwe-Elohim is found, it is supposed to represent a conflation of J and E into JE. However, Gordon calls attention to the Rash Shamra or Ugaritic texts where the gods often have compound names, such as: Qadish-Amrar, Ibb-Nikkal. Sometimes an "and" is placed between the two names, as in Qadish-and-Amar, Nikkab-and-Ibb, Koshar-and-Hasis and many others. One of the best known deities of Egypt was Amon-Re, a name representative of a widespread practice of fusing two names into one for designating a god. To claim that "Yahweh-Elohim" is the result of combining names from two divergent sources would just as logically demand postulating Amon-Re from two documents, an "A" and an "R" source, which no Egyptologist has thought of doing.

The Old Testament indicates in a number of books that the inspired writers used literary sources. But Gordon contends that JEDP are artificial ones, for whose existence there is no evidence. The uncertainty of these ever having existed is shown also by the fact that Old Testament authorities disagree where J, E, D or P begin or end.

Excavations at RasShamra have revealed a highly developed civilization in Canaan before the emergence of the Hebrew people as a nation. The simultaneous existence of prose and poetry in a developed form is clearly shown by the Ugaritic literature. Eight different languages have been found at RasShamra, with dictionaries compiled in four different languages for the scribes' use. In the days of the Patriarchs, Canaan was the center of a great international culture. Thus the beginnings of the Chosen People "are rooted in a highly cultural Canaan where the contributions of several talented peoples (including the Mesopotamians, Egyptians, and branches of the Indo-Europeans) had converged and blended."[27]

Higher Criticism and Conservative Churches

In the first three decades of the twentieth century there were generally two camps in regard to the use of higher criticism as developed by Protestant

26. *Ibid.*, p. 4.
27. *Ibid.*, pp. 5-6.

theologians of the last two hundred years. Liberal Protestantism espoused the conclusion of higher criticism and used its findings in the study and teaching of the Old Testament. Conservative Protestantism rejected modern literary and historical criticism because of its denial of the doctrine of plenary inspiration, the supernatural element in the Bible, the miracles, and prophecies of the Old Testament. The Roman Catholic church with few exceptions before 1942 also rejected the views of higher criticism of liberal Protestantism.

However, with the advent to America of the views of neo-orthodoxy, many liberals as well as many neo-evangelicals have joined this theological camp. A perusal of the writings of neo-orthodox writers on Old Testament subjects reveals the fact that they accept "the assured results of Biblical criticism." William Hordern, in his book *The Case for a New Reformation Teology,* has clearly indicated that neo-orthodoxy or new reformation theology is not opposed to Biblical higher criticism, but espouses and uses it.[28] He berates fundamentalism for its refusal to bow before the findings and dictates of Biblical criticism.[29]

In the last two decades there has been a trend among Southern Baptists[30] and Roman Catholics[30a] and conservative Lutherans[31] to accept the neo-orthodox position on revelation and the Scriptures. They have also been adopting higher critical views on isagogics which were foreign to their denominations and were not previously promulgated in their divinity schools. Seminaries of American Lutheranism which once rejected higher criticism as it pertained to the Old Testament have turned to the neo-orthodox concept of revelation and inspiration and with it have accepted the view of higher criticism on the Old Testament.[32]

In the following treatment of this matter an attempt will be made to set forth and evaluate the implications which flow from the use of the historico-critical method for the interpretation of the Old Testament. It will be the purpose of the writer to show that in the light of the position of

28. William Hordern, *The Case for A New Reformation Theology* (Philadelphia: The Westminster Press, 1959). pp. 53-54; 107-108.
29. *Ibid.,* pp. 107-108.
30. Compare the position of Ralph H. Elliott, *The Message of Genesis* (Nashville: Broadman Press, 1961), pp. 1-16, or Eric C. Rust, *Judges, Ruth, I and II Samuel* (Richmond: John Knox Press. 1961), pp. 11-12. 77-79, with John R. Sampey, *Syllabus for Old Testament Study* (New York: George H. Doran Company, 1924), pp. 52-64; or Josiah Blake Tidwell. *The Bible Period by Period* (Nashville: Broadman Press, 1923), pp. 1-128. Cf. also "The Message of Genesis," *Christianity Today,* 6:39, March 2, 1962.
30a. C. Unhau Wolf. "Recent Roman Catholic Bible Study and Translation," *The Journal of Bible and Religion,* 29:280-289, October, 1961. Cf. also Frederick J. Moriarity, *Foreward to Old Testament Books* (Weston, Mass.; Weston College Press, 1954). p. 115; John L. McKenzie, *The Two-Edged Sword* (Milwaukee: The Brace Publishing Company, 1956), p. 317.
31. A. A. Jagnow. "Revelation Today," E. C. Fendt (ed.), *What Lutherans Are Thinking* (Columbus: The Wartburg Press, 1947). pp. 72-84.
32. Cf. articles in *The Ambassador,* February, 1961. published by the students of Wartburg Theological Seminary, Dubuque, Iowa; *Book News Letters of Augsburg Publishing House,* September, 1961, p. 6; cf. also *Lutheran Synod Quarterly,* 2:31, September, 1961.

Scripture subscribed to by The Lutheran Church-Missouri Synod in its official pronouncements, the conclusions of higher criticisms are in conflict with Synod's position on the inerrancy of Scriptures and with its doctrine of the attributes of Holy Scripture.

II.

The views of the historico-critical method cannot be harmonized with the traditional view on the inspiration of the Bible as held by conservative Christians in the past nor by The Lutheran Church-Missouri Synod. Paragraph 1 of *The Brief Statement* sets forth the doctrine of the verbal inspiration of the Bible. In the same paragraph we read: "Since the Holy Scriptures are the Word of God it goes without saying that they contain no errors or contradictions, but that they are in all their parts and words the infallible truth, also in those parts which treat of historical, geographical, and other secular matters, John 10:35."[33] The "Statement on Scripture" adopted at the 1959 Synodical Convention asserts: "We believe and teach that all Scripture (that is, all the canonical books of the Old Testament) is given by inspiration of God and is in its entirety, in its parts, and in its very words inspired by the Holy Spirit." Again: "We condemn and reject any and all teachings and statements that would limit the inerrancy and sufficiency of Scripture or that deny that divine authorship of certain portions of Scripture." Inspiration applies not only to such statements as speak directly of Christ but also to such as may seem remote (e.g. in the field of history, geography, and nature).[33a]

Both liberal and neo-orthodox writers repudiate the doctrine of verbal inspiration and the inerrancy of Scripture. C. H. Dodd in *The Authority of the Bible* devoted the first chapter to repudiating the historic view of the Church concerning the authority of the Bible. Thus he wrote: "The old dogmatic view of the Bible therefore is not only open to attack from the standpoint of science and historical criticism, but if taken seriously it becomes a danger to religion and public morals. A revision of this view is therefore an imperative necessity."[34] Again he said: "God is the Author not of the Bible, but of the life in which the authors of the Bible partake, and of which they tell in such imperfect human words as they could command."[35]

Professor W. F. Albright, one of the leading archaeologists and Semitic scholars of America, claims that modern Biblical scholarship has made untenable this "once reputable doctrine of verbal inspiration."[36] Professor H. H. Rowley, leading Semitic scholar of Great Britain, claims that relinquishing the doctrine of verbal inspiration might mean for many the "abandonment

---

33. *Brief Statement of the Doctrinal Position of the Missouri Synod* (St. Louis: Concordia Publishing House, no date), p. 3.

33a. *Reports and Memorials, Forty-Fourth Regular Convention, The Lutheran Church Missouri Synod* (St. Louis: Concordia Publishing House, 1959). pp. 483-484; and *Proceedings*, p. 189.

34. C. H. Dodd. *The Authority of the Bible* (New York: Harper & Brothers, 1958), p. 14.

35. *Ibid.*, pp. 16, 17.

36. W. F. Albright, *The Archaeology of Palestine* (Baltimore: Penguin Books, 1960), p. 255.

of any real belief in the inspiration of the Bible" and asserting on the other hand, "that while modern scholarship has made impossible the old view of inspiration, it does not threaten a truer view of inspiration."[37] Eric Kuhl asserts that the critical evaluation of the Old Testament which was initiated by the Enlightenment was only possible when churchmen broke away from the prevailing doctrine of inspiration. Rejection of verbal inspiration made it possible to obtain "a better and more correct understanding of the Scriptures."[38] In the same book in which Rowley claims that modern scholarship has produced a truer view, he also tells his readers that "for the New Testament no more than the Old . . . can inspiration be supposed to yield verbal infallibility. Because human beings wrote the Scriptures, they may be said to have been the result of a divine-human process, which in the end means that as far as the human side was concerned it was subject to error."[39] Rowley says regarding those through whom revelation was vouchsafed: "Not only did their failings mar the word which God spoke through them, and pervert the perfect revelation reaching men by their means, but those same failings marred their own vision of Him. They also had false ideas of God and cherished false hopes, and their false hopes dimmed their eyes. They could neither communicate the perfect Word of God."[40] In discussing his view of the inspiration of the Bible, Rowley claims that "All that we learn of God in the Old Testament that is in harmony with the revelation given in Christ is truly of God. . . . And all that we learn of God in the Old Testament that is not in harmony with the revelation given in Christ is not of God. It represents the misunderstanding of God by sincere men, whose view was distorted by the eyes through which they looked upon Him."[41] Elmer Homrighausen states: "Few intelligent Christians can still hold to the idea that the Bible is an infallible book, that it contains no linguistic errors, no historical discrepancies, no antiquated scientific assumptions, not even bad ethical standards. Historical investigation and literary criticism have taken the magic out of the Bible and have made it a composite human book, written by many hands in different ages. The existence of thousands of variations of *texts* makes it impossible to hold the doctrine of a book verbally infallible. Some might still claim for the 'original copies' of the Bible an infallible character, but this view only begs the question and makes such Christian apologetics more ridiculous in the eyes of sincere men."[42]

Contradictory Accounts?

In harmony with the belief of the fallibility and errancy of the Bible is the documentary hypothesis which assumes that there are contradictory accounts of the same events in Scripture; in fact, it was because of existing

37. H. H. Rowley, *The Relevance of the Bible* (Philadelphia: The Westminster Press, 1944), p. 21.
38. Eric Kuhl, *The Old Testament. Its Origins and Composition* (Richmond: John Knox Press, 1961), p. 10.
39. Rowley, *op. cit.,* p. 48.
40. *Ibid.*, p. 28.
41. *Ibid.*, p. 33.
42. Elmer Homrighausen, *Christianity in America* (Nashville: Abingdon Press, 1936), p. 121.

doublets in the earlier books of the Old Testament that scholars were supposed to have been helped to discover different sources used by the redactors or compilers of the Pentateuch.[43] Genesis 1:1-2:4a is said to come from "P" and Gen. 2:4b-25 is ascribed to "J". These two accounts are presumed contradictory because they differ in the order of creation, in the names used for the deity (God and Lord God), and in vocabulary. Furthermore, they are imputed to have a different point of view. In the "P" account, God creates by divine fiat and stands in contrast to the God of the "J" account which has God strolling through the garden in the cool of the evening. There are also two different genealogies in Genesis 4 and 5. Genesis 4:7-26 and Genesis 5 are said to differ in vocabulary, style and outlook. Genesis 4:7-26, it is claimed, corresponds to Gen. 2:4b-25 (J), while Genesis 5 corresponds to Gen. 1:1—2:4a. In Genesis 6-9 the critics contend there are two stories of the flood interwoven. In "P" one pair of every species is to be brought into the ark (Gen. 6:19) while in "J" seven of each clean species are to enter the ark (7:2). In the Joseph cycle of stories in the "J" account, Joseph is sold to the Ishmaelites; in verse 38 (E) the Midianites buy Joseph. In the Abraham narratives, according to the critics, there are two different accounts of Abraham's deception. In Gen. 12:10-20 Abraham is portrayed as telling Pharaoh that Sarah was his sister (J); in chapter 20 Abraham tells the same half truth to Abimelech. Old Testament higher critics also assert that there are many duplicate narratives of the same event in other historical books of the Old Testament; these contradictory accounts clearly indicating the use of different sources. An examination of the lists of duplicate accounts as given by Driver and other Old Testament Introductions at first appears to be formidable. Conservative Old Testament commentaries and conservative Biblical Introductions have examined these individually. Those scholars and Bible students who accept the trustworthiness, inerrancy and infallibility of Scripture will endeavor to explain difficult passages insofar as this is possible. William Arndt has done this in two writings of his: *Does the Bible Contradict Itself?* and *Bible Difficulties.*[44] Examination of the so-called duplicates, however, shows that the majority of them can be explained as either (1) expansions, where the second part supplements the former, or (2) where the accounts are referring to *different* events which have certain features in common, or (3) they are entirely fictitious, because they are produced by an artificial division of a single story. A comprehensive examination of all alleged doublets in the Pentateuch is made by Oswald T. Allis, *The Five Books of Moses,* chapters IV and V.[45]

---

43. G. W. Anderson, *A Critical Introduction to the Old Testament* (London: Gerald Duckworth, 1959), pp. 23-24.
44. W. Arndt, *Does the Bible Contradict Itself* (St. Louis: Concordia Publishing House, 1926), p. 142; W. Arndt, *Bible Difficulties* (St. Louis: Concordia Publishing House, 1932), p. 117.
45. Oswald T. Allis, *The Five Books of Moses* (Philadelphia: The Presbyterian and Reformed Publishing Company, 1943), pp. 79-110; Wilhelm Möller, *Die Einheit und Echtheit der 5. Bücher Mosis* (Badsalzuflen: Selbstverlag des Bibelbundes, 1931), pp. 202-248; G. Ch. Aalders, *A Short Introduction to the Pentateuch* (Chicago and Toronto: Inter-Varsity Christian Fellowship, no date), pp. 43-53.

In accepting the documentary hypothesis and the methodology by which many Old Testament scholars treat other Biblical books, the rejection of the belief in the inerrancy of the Bible logically results. This is a fact which all liberal and neo-orthodox scholars have asserted and reiterated in their writings. The adherence to higher critical views on the Old Testament necessitates the adoption of a view regarding the Scriptures' inerrancy which is foreign to that formerly held by Lutheran theologians and exegetes in the twentieth century. Professor Hove in *Christian Doctrine* wrote of the Bible: "All parts are *equally* inspired, are equally true. Even those parts which do not directly speak of the sublime matters that constitute our Christian faith are given by inspiration of God." According to Hove matters which belong to the range of that which is naturally known to man, references to historical events, or physical occurrences, or geographical facts, were written under the inspiration and guidance of the Holy Spirit, Who preserved the writers from penning anything that was untrue (p. 10). Professor Reu in the revised 1951 edition of his *Lutheran Dogmatics* asserted that the Scriptures are to be viewed from the standpoint of saving faith. "All other items of knowledge are subordinate to saving knowledge. This does not imply, however, that errors are found in these subordinate elements, i.e. matters of history, genealogy, natural science, etc." (p. 54). The Pittsburgh Agreement, adopted by the A.L.C. and the U.L.C.A., stated that the Scriptures "taken together, constitute a complete, errorless and unbreakable whole."

III.

The acceptance of viewpoints of higher criticism, whether set forth by liberal or neo-orthodox authors, also eventuates in a rejection of the reliability of the historical narratives of the Bible. G. W. Wade in *A New Commentary On Holy Scripture* said: "In connection with the religious pronouncements of the Old Testament historian upon the events related by them, it is desirable to distinguish between the reasonableness of the view taken of the general fortunes of their race, and that of some of the explanations furnished by particular occurences."[46] According to Wade, the writer of II Sam. 6:6-7 ascribes the death of Uzzah to God's anger because Uzzah touched the sacred ark. However, Wade believes that if this account had been written later, when the Jews had a more highly developed concept of God, they would have attributed this catastrophe to some physical cause, such as heart disease or apoplexy.[47]

Robert Pfeiffer claims that "the tribal memory of Israel does not go beyond Moses (except for Simeon and Levi's attack on Schechem) but even the most historical stories from Moses to David are not accurate in all details."[48] The same authority contends that the biographies of Moses, Joshua, Gideon,

---

46. G. W. Wade, "Introduction to the Historical Books," Charles Gore, Henry Leighton Goudge, and Alfred Guillaume (eds.), *A New Commentary on Holy Scripture Including the Apocrypha* (New York: The Macmillan Company, 1958), p. 170b.
47. *Ibid.*, p. 170b.
48. Pfeiffer, *The Books of the Old Testament, op. cit.*, p. 8.

Samuel, David, Solomon, Elijah, Elisha, as well as other outstanding personalities, tend to become legendary even before the time that Jewish piety portrayed them as saints or reprobates.[49] The episodes of Moses' birth, the meeting of Saul with Samuel, or the slaying of Goliath by David are, in Pfeiffer's opinion, classical examples of legends, and that many Old Testament stories have no factual basis at all but are popular explanations of certain natural (myths) or historic (sagas) phenomena.

Is Genesis a Factual Account?

Liberal and neo-orthodox Old Testament writers will not accept the historicity of many of the historical narratives of the book of Genesis. Thus the accounts recorded in Genesis 1-11 are not considered reliable history. John Bright begins his *A History of Israel* with the patriarchal narratives, completely omitting Gen. 1-11.[50] A. M. Barnett claims that with the story of the patriarchs, we begin to cross the threshold of history.[51] According to the critics, the early chapters of Genesis contains myths and sagas which were stripped of their polytheism, brought originally by the Patriarchs from Babylonia, where they had grown up in centers influenced by Summerian and Babylonian religious ideas. In not accepting Old Testament history as factual, modern critical scholars justify their rejection by claiming that the Old Testament writers were not much concerned about mere events in their chronological sequence but more with their theological significance. It it is the contention of liberal and neo-orthodox higher critics that Genesis 1-3 does not contain a factual record of the manner in which God created the world, made Adam and Eve, established marriage or how sin entered the world.[52]

While many scholars as a result of archaeological evidence are willing to admit that in Genesis 12:50 we have a record of historical events and that Abraham, Isaac, Jacob and Joseph were historical personages, yet there are those who claim that these narratives cannot be used without critical scrutiny. Cornfeld in *From Adam to Daniel* states: "We must be on our guard against deducing actual 'historical' information from such narratives as the parallel Abraham and Sarah stories . . . As in all ancient folk literature, the story-cycles of Abraham, Jacob, or Joseph consisted of kernels of historical facts in enveloping layers of legend."[53] The inconsistencies in the narratives, he states, are due to the fact that the stories of the patriarchs were compressed from different oral traditions by different chroniclers who failed to make adjustment in the details. According to Cornfeld there are inconsistencies that

49. *Ibid.*, p. 8. Cf. also Robert H. Pfeiffer, *Religion in the Old Testament* (New York: Harper & Brothers, Publishers, 1961), p. 12.
50. John Bright, *A History of Israel* (Philadelphia: The Westminster Press, 1959), p. 60. Cf. also the position of M.-J. Steve. *The Living World of the Bible* (Cleveland and New York: The World Publishing Company, 1961), p. 11.
51. A. M. Barnett, "Genesis," *The Encyclopedia Americana* (1959 edition), XII, 389.
52. S. H. Hooke, "In the Beginning," *The Clarendon Bible* (Oxford: Clarendon Press, 1947), pp. 1-13.
53. Gaalyahu Cornfeld, *Adam to Daniel* (New York: The Macmillan Company, 1961), p. 71.

the compilers failed to eliminate and this is a phenomenon found throughout the Pentateuch.

The editors of the *New Commentary on Holy Scripture* in "Advice to the Ordinary Reader of the Historical Books" believe that the history in the Old Testament is idealized for the purpose of edification.[54] They contend that the historians of the Old Testament were not critically precise about the facts they recorded but were more concerned with the meaning of history. "They are true interpreters, but not true recorders."[55]

Rowley maintains that while it is possible to accept the Biblical account which brings Abraham from Ur of the Chaldees to Haran and later into Canaan, and afterwards describes his descendants as going into Egypt, it must nevertheless be remembered that these accounts were transmitted orally and took the form of saga rather than history.[56] "The recognition of a historical kernel does not mean that every detail of the tradition can be accepted without hesitation."[57]

The account of the exodus from Egypt to the Sinai peninsula, from Sinai to Kadesh Barnea, and from Kadesh Barnea to the plains of Moab is not considered accurate by many liberal and neo-orthodox scholars.[58] Some Israelites are alleged to have entered Canaan in the fourteenth century, and should likely be identified with Habiru referred to in the Amarna Letters. Those who were lead out of Egypt by Moses were principally the Joseph tribes, although Levites were also linked with this tradition. The Biblical reader knows that this interpretation is not in agreement with the facts recorded in Exodus, but critical scholars contend that the Bible version represents a fusion of two separate traditions. Some of the facts reported in the Pentateuch are not from the Mosaic period, according to the critical school, but are ascriptions from a much later period which redactors depicted as coming from the past. Many words and deeds are credited to Moses which were never spoken by him or performed by him. It is believed that the Book of Numbers, where the census of the tribes is recorded, may have exaggerated the numbers of those who left Egypt. The figure of 600,000 men reported by Moses to have left Goshen may mean a multitude of over two million who entered the Sinai Peninsula. Liberal and neo-orthodox scholars believe that it was impossible for such a multitude to have found sustenance in the wilderness.[59]

The trustworthiness of historical records of the Book of Joshua has been questioned by the users of the historico-critical method. There is considerable disagreement among them regarding the story of the conquest. Those who

54. Gore, Goudge, and Guillaume, *op. cit.*, p. 188a.
55. *Ibid.*, p. 188a.
56. H. H. Rowley, "The History of Israel," G. Henton Davies, Alan Richardson and Charles L. Wallis, *Twentieth Century Bible Commentary* (New York: Harper & Brothers, Publishers, 1955), pp. 53-54.
57. *Ibid.*, p. 54.
58. Bernhard W. Anderson, *Understanding the Old Testament* (Englewood Cliffs: Prentice-Hall, 1957), pp. 60-70.; Norman K. Gottwald, *A Light to the Nations* (New York: Harper & Brothers, Publishers, 1959), p. 129.
59. G. E. Wright, *Biblical Archaeology* (Philadelphia: The Westminster Press, 1960), p. 42.; Gabriel Hebert, *When Israel Came Out of Egypt* (London: SCM Press, 1961), p. 82.

reject the skepticism which many scholars manifest over against the Book of Joshua, claim however that the Book of Joshua presents a simplified and schematized account of events, since as Bright asserts "there is much evidence from the Bible (e.g.) Judges and elsewhere that the Israelite occupation of Palestine did not take place in a single onslaught but was a process that went on for a matter of centuries."[60] Joshua and Judges contain contradictory accounts of the conquest of Canaan by the children of Israel.[61]

Bicknell thinks that the Book of Chronicles is bad evidence for the truth of what happened in the days of David. However, he contends that Chronicles is good evidence for the beliefs and opinions that were current among the priestly class in the third century B.C.,[62] the time when these books were allegedly composed.

Who Wrote the Books of Samuel?

According to higher criticism, in the Books of Samuel and Kings, the Biblical student has to distinguish between the Biblical account as recorded and what really transpired, especially where there are doublets for the same happening. The editor in the 7th century B.C., who wrote the Books of Samuel combined two sources that allegedly displayed contradictions, duplications, fusions, and differences in points of view, style and diction. Critics who divide the book into two main documents drawn from J and E contend that there are two divergent views about Samuel, the judge; one document makes him an unknown figure, the other describes him as a great national personality. Other critics divide the books of Samuel still further. They also maintain that there are two different accounts of the introduction of David to Saul (I Sam. 16:17; 17:55); two diverse reports in which Saul met his death (II Sam. 1 and I Sam. 31); two varied accounts of the origin of the proverb: "Is Saul among the prophets?" (I Sam. 10:11; 19:24), as well as other incidents. Definite evidence for divergent sources for the Samuel books is said to be found in the existence of two attitudes toward the monarchy; one, rejecting the request of the people for a king, and the other, favoring it.

Conservative scholars, on the other hand, believe that "the careers of Samuel, David and Saul are so interwoven that they present an orderly progressive narrative. Although events are not always recorded chronologically, a consistent plan is discernible throughout. The plan is most naturally explained as the result of one and the same writer (who, however, most certainly used documents) rather than as the result of later editors who simply combined conflicting sources."[63]

The critical view of the origin of the books of Samuel depict the compiler or editor as an incompetent blunderer. Unger says that "it is more inconceivable

---

60. John Bright, "Joshua, Book of," *The Encyclopedia Americana* (1960 edition), XVI, 216a.
61. Stephen Szikszai, *The Story of Israel* (Philadelphia: The Westminster Press, 1960), p. 42.
62. E. J. Bicknell, "The Function of Literary and Historical Criticism," Gore, Gouge, and Guillaume, *op. cit.*, p. 19.
63. Merrill F. Unger, *Introductory Guide to the Old Testament* (Grand Rapids: Zondervan Publishing House, 1951), p. 295.

that the editor should have left the alleged contradictions and fusions stand in the text, when his precise task as editor was to eliminate such discrepancies."[64] Those who are not biased by the presupposition of the higher critical theory would be able to make an honest attempt to harmonize the accounts. "As in the Pentateuch many of the alleged parallels are accounts of different events with merely similar features, others are records of the same event from a different point of view. Still others are not parallel at all but brief allusions to events already related which are referred to again because they have a special connection in the progress of the narrative. Alleged contradictions are only apparent, and may in every case be satisfactorily explained."[65]

Neil admits that there is in the Bible a story emphasis on history, but it is history with a difference. The Bible contains a record of certain events which happened in the Middle East between about 2,000 B.C. and A.D. 100. Yet Neil affirms that "the writers do not consider it to be their prime function to give us a painstaking factual narrative, complete with maps and dates, of the political, economic and military fortunes and misfortunes of the group. . . . As in the case of its scientific data, the Bible does not stand or fall by the accuracy or inaccuracy of its historical information. Its writers did not aim to provide either science or history. They were writing theology. The Bible is primarily a book about God and ourselves."[66]

IV.

The acceptance of the historico-critical method has further resulted in the rejection or rationalization of the miracles of the Old Testament. Miracles are interwoven with the entire fabric of the history of Israel; especially is this true of certain periods of Old Testament history. The early course of Israel's history is dominated by miracles, such as her liberation from the Egyptian yoke (e.g. the plagues), the passing through the Red Sea, Israel's sojourn in the wilderness (e.g. the manna, water from the rock, sending of quails, and blooming of the staff of Aaron), the conquest of Canaan (e.g. the crossing of Jordan and conquest of Jericho). During the period of the Judges there is the miraculous account of the fleece on the threshing floor (Judges 6:36-40). Within the time of the divided monarchy, Elijah and Elisha are outstanding as the greatest thaumaturgists of the Old Testament. Through Elijah the supply of meal and oil for the widow of Zarephath did not fail during the famine, later her dead son was restored to life, fire was brought from heaven and caused to consume the sacrifice on Mt. Carmel. Finally, Elijah was taken into heaven by means of a fiery chariot.

Elisha divided the water of the Jordan, purified with salt the waters of the spring at Jericho, fed a hundred men with twenty barley loaves and a few ears of grain and cured Naaman from leprosy; after the death of Elisha, a man placed in the same sepulcher, on touching the bones of the prophet,

---

64. *Ibid.*, p. 295.
65. *Ibid.*, p. 295.
66. William Neil, *The Plain Man Looks at the Bible* (London and Glasgow: Collins, Fontana Books, 1959), pp. 49-50.

was restored to life. There are eight and sixteen miracles recorded as performed by Elijah and Elisha respectively in I and II Kings. In the writings of the literary prophets, only one miracle is recorded, namely, the retrogression of the shadow on the sun dial in Hezekiah's palace. Prophecies, frequently predicting events many years before their occurrence, take the place of miracles in the literary prophets. During the Babylonian exile there are the miracles of the rescue of three men in the fiery furnace and the preservation of Daniel in the lions' den.

Old Testament Miracles: History or Myth

Theological liberals have always rejected the miracles of the Old Testament as impossible and therefore as unhistorical. Neo-orthodox scholars interpret the miracles somewhat differently, but in the last analysis arrive at the same conclusion. Aage Bentzen claimed that in dealing with Biblical narratives, it is necessary to distinguish between the problems of historical research and the Christian faith.[67] When working with the history of Israel the question of credibility must be raised. This is especially needed when operating with miraculous events. Although Bentzen says that historical science cannot deny the possibility of miracles or the existence of God, neither can it assert their existence.[68] Miracles, he claims, lie outside the field of experience, which is determined by nature as known to all men. It is the aim of historical research to show how everything happened quite naturally. "Therefore historical research must dismiss miraculous stories as of no use to describe events of history. It cannot deny that they are true. But it cannot use them. It may assume in many cases an 'historical nucleus' behind the miraculous 'embellishment' worked into the story by tradition and poetry. But it cannot accept the whole story as it stands as credible. It must leave it unused."[69] Although the Old Testament historian cannot employ the miracles in the sense that they record objective history, they are still valuable, according to Bentzen, because they aid the modern reader to understand the Israelite religion at a given period in its historical development.

Neo-orthodox theologians reject the historicity of the Old Testament miracles by protraying the Biblical writers as employing "the myth" in their writings. To interpret "mythological" accounts literally is to be guilty of wooden-hearted literalism, the great error of orthodoxy. Reinhold Niebuhr warns against the error of regarding "the early form in which the myth is stated as authoritative."[70] "Religion" says Niebuhr "is involved in myth as a necessary symbol of the faith."[71] Charles Kean, an adherent of the "mythological" school, demands as a first requisite for dealing with Biblical history "a rejection of Biblical fundamentalism, because no appreciation of mythology is possible if the myths themselves are literalized."[72]

67. Aage Bentzen, "Biblical Criticism, History and Old Testament Criticism," *The Evangelical Quarterly*, 23:85, January, 1951.
68. *Ibid.*, p. 85.
69. *Ibid.*, p. 85.
70. Reinhold Niebuhr, *Beyond Tragedy* (London: Nisbet, 1944), p. 28.
71. *Ibid.*, p. 34.
72. Charles Duell Kean, *The Meaning of Existence* (London: Latimer House, 1947), p. 150.

Leading interpreters at the present time look upon the discussion of miracles in the Old Testament as out of place in the presentation of objective history. Stories that record the miraculous are to be regarded "mythologically." It is their contention that the miraculous element in the Biblical narratives is of no ultimate consequence for the historical character of those parts of Scripture in which the miracles are imbedded.

Although Alan Richardson recognizes the fact that the concept of the miraculous is essential to the proper understanding of God and the Bible narratives, yet he still maintains it is important for readers to examine critically the miraculous incidents of the Old Testament and to scrutinize them in the light of modern knowledge.[73] There are two main groups of miracles that require examination: 1. those associated with the Exodus (The Ten plagues, Ex. 8-12; the crossing of the Red Sea, Ex. 14; the miracles of Moses in the wilderness); and 2. those found in the biographies of Elijah and Elisha.

The Elijah-Elisha complex of miracles are, according to Richardson, best understood as "legendary tales of wonders which accumulate around famous men" and testify to the impression their personalities made upon their contemporaries.[74]

The Exodus Miracles

Regarding the miracles associated with the exodus of Israel from Egypt, neo-orthodox historians will not admit them as true historical happenings. Thus William Neil calls the exodus story "a saga" concerning which the student does not know what is behind it. To quote him: "Taken separately, most of the details — the plagues, the crossing of the water, the pillar of fire — can be rationally explained."[75] Neil attributes these miraculous stories now found in the Bible to embellishments by story tellers.

Muilenberg, in *The Way of Israel*, in discussing the passing of the Children of Israel through the Sea of Reeds, states that if the historian is asked what really happened there, he would be forced to answer that he does not know.[76] Faith, however, responds to the same question: "Our God delivered us from bondage." Coert Rylaarsdam explains the account of the passing of the Israelites through the waters of the Red Sea as a story which in the course of time went through the process of communal embellishment. "The crossing was an event which lay wholly within the nexus of nature and history as these are scientifically understood."[77] The event of the deliverance of the Israelites was simply caused by an east wind which drove back the water, enabling the Israelites to cross over safely. A different account makes the parting of the water due to Moses' use of a magic wand. A third account (Exodus 14:17-18, 22b) has the waters separated by the rod as to stand like walls.[78]

---

73. Alan Richardson, "Miracles," Davies, Richardson and Wallis, *op. cit.*, p. 14.
74. *Ibid.*, p. 15.
75. Neil, *op. cit.*, p. 60.
76. James Muilenberg, *The Way of Israel* (New York: Harper and Brothers, Publishers, 1961), p. 49.
77. J. Coert Rylaarsdam, "The Book of Exodus," *The Interpreter's Bible*, I, p. 935.
78. *Ibid.*, p. 936.

Bernhard Anderson informs the readers of the Book of Exodus that it is essential when interpreting the Egyptian plagues to realize: "The Israelites did not have our kind of historical curiosity. These narratives do not purport to be an objective photographic report of exactly what took place, devoid of all bias and interpretation. Rather, they testify to events as Israel experienced them, as they were interpreted within the community of faith."[79] Anderson in discussing the various miracles in the Exodus story advises the readers to be aware of the existence of "irregularities, inconsistencies, and folk elements in the narratives as they are now in the Bible. The material in Exodus has been colored by Israelite faith. Since the whole account is interpretative, it is very difficult to separate sharply the central elements of the tradition from the late accretions."[80]

Richardson denies the reliability of the narratives of the exodus miracles because their portrayal comes from a late period which makes it impossible to reconstruct any of them in terms of reliable accounts of what transpired.[81]

Like liberal theologians of the last hundred years, so also neo-orthodox writers reinterpret the miraculous accounts of the Old Testament. In contradistinction to the traditional understanding of miracles, the position of neo-orthodoxy rejects the possibility and reality of miracles. The traditional understanding, accepted by all branches of Christendom before the age of rationalism, interprets miracles as "events due to an incursion of God into human life and history beyond what could occur by any merely natural means."[82] This position has been stated by Pieters: "We believe that these things so recorded, are true, and actually happened as related, in spite of the fact that they are impossible and incredible to the man who does not believe in an almighty God."[83] The New Testament also bears out the interpretation of the miracles of the Old Testament. Christ and the Apostles regarded the Old Testament miracles as actual interventions of the power of God in the course of human history. This was also the view of the Ancient Church Fathers and of the Protestant Reformers.

The position of neo-orthodox writers who deny the historicity and reliability of miracles of the Old Testament is in essence repeating the objections of Strauss (1808-1874) who regarded miracles as mythical accretions to the original narrative, and entirely unhistorical. The rejection and rationalization of miracles rests upon a rationalistic attitude toward Scriptures. For the most part this interpretation of miracles is based upon *a priori* philosophical principles that are false. In other instances, it involves the rejection of human testimony, or the manipulation of evidence in the interest of preconceived theories. The writer finds himself in strong disagreement with the "mythological" interpretation because of the latter's view of God and Scripture. The rejection of miracles of the Old Testament goes hand in hand with the

---

79. B. W. Anderson, *op. cit.*, p. 40.
80. *Ibid.*, p. 44.
81. Alan Richardson, *A Theological Word Book of the Bible* (New York: The Macmillan Company, 1951), p. 152.
82. Albertus Pieters, *Can We Trust Bible History?* (Grand Rapids: Wm. B. Eerdmans Publishing Company, 1954), p. 35.
83. *Ibid.*, p. 35.

concept that Scripture is not a direct revelation from God to man but merely the record of what certain Israelites imagined they had experienced or of the interpretation they placed on certain acts of God.

The Books of Daniel and Jonah are denied their historical character by assigning them to the area of fiction; at the same time thus disposing of three miracles in these two books, which have always been a stumbling block to rationalistic interpreters.

V.

Higher criticism, as espoused by liberal and neo-orthodox theologians, has resulted in the rejection of many Old Testament prophecies formerly conceived of as Messianic, as well as the proposing of a new concept of the nature of Messianic prophecy. An unprejudiced reading of the Old Testament shows that it has a two-fold purpose: 1. to preserve the knowledge of the true God among the Israelites; and 2. to prepare the Israelites for the coming of Christ and the New Testament era. Immediately after the fall, God announced the coming of a Redeemer. At first the references to Him were revealed in a general manner, but later the promises bcame specific and assume in the prophetic literature a definite form and pattern. Bible-believing Christians of different denominations have considered the following passages as Messianic: Gen. 3:14-15; 9:24-27; 12:1-3; 49:8-12; Numbers 24:15-19; Deuteronomy 18:15-18; II Sam. 7:12-17; 23:1-7; Job 19:25-27; Proverbs 8:22-31; Psalms 2, 8, 16, 22, 45, 72, 110, 118; Amos 9:11-15; Hosea 1:10-11; 2:18-23; 3:4-5; Isaiah 2:2-4; 4:2-4; 7:13-14; 9:1-7; 11:1-5; 40:1-6; 42:1-7; 49:1-9a; 50:4-11; 52:13—53:12; 60:1-6; 61:1-3; Micah 5:1-4; Jer. 23:5-6; 31:31-34; 33:16-17; Ezekiel 17:22-24; 21:30-32; 34:23-24; 37:22-25; Daniel 7:12; 9:24-27; Haggai 2:6-9; Zechariah 3:8-10; 6:9-15; 9:9-10; 11:12; 12:10; 13:7; Malachi 3:1-5; 4:2-4. These passages are taken from works on Messianic prophecy by L. Fuerbringer, Hengstenberg, F. Delitzsch, Reich, Stöckhardt, Mack, Riehm, Heinisch, Cooper, Sampey and Knox.[84]

The designation of the above listed passages as Messianic rests upon certain assertions by the New Testament concerning the Christo-centric character of the Old Testament. Alan Richardson admits that from the apostolic days, the view developed that "the importance of Old Testament prophecy con-

---

84. L. Fuerbringer, *Exegesis of Messianic Prophecies* (St. Louis: Concordia Mimeo Co., no date), 95 pp; E. W. Hengstenberg, *The Christology of the Old Testament* (Grand Rapids: Kregel Publications, 1956), 4 volumes; Franz Delitzsch, *Messianic Prophecies* (New York: Charles Scribner's Sons, 1891), 232 pp.; Max Reich, *The Messianic Hope of Israel* (Chicago: Moody Press, 1945), 120 pp.; George Stöckhardt, *Adventspredigten. Auslegungen der vornehmsten Weissagungen des Alten Testaments* (St. Louis: Concordia Verlag, 1887), 246 pp.; Edward Mack, *The Christ of the Old Testament* (Richmond: Presbyterian Committee of Publications, 1926), 195 pp.; Aaron Judah Kligerman, *Messianic Prophesy in the Old Testament* (Grand Rapids: Zondervan Publishing House, 1957), 155 pp.; David L. Cooper, *Messiah: His Nature and Person* (Los Angeles: Published by David L. Cooper, 1933), 224 pp.; Sampey, *op. cit.*, pp. 260-291; Ronald Knox, *Waiting for Christ* (New York: Sheed and Ward, 1960), 288 pp.

sisted chiefly in the element of prediction which it contained."[85] Again he says: "But whatever we may think of the details of their application of it, there can be no doubt about the principle which the evangelists and indeed all the New Testament writers affirm: that in Christ all the prophecies are fulfilled."[86] Jesus Christ said to the Scribes and Pharisees of His day: "Ye search the Scriptures for in them ye think ye have eternal life and they are they which testify of me." (John 5:39) To the unbelieving Jews, Christ spoke the condemning words: "Had ye believed Moses, ye would have believed me, for he wrote of me." Luke in describing the missionary activity of Apollos writes: "Thus Apollos showed by the Scriptures (namely, the Old Testament) that Jesus was the Christ" (Acts 18:28). Peter writes concerning the New Testament understanding of the Old Testament: "Of which salvation the prophets have inquired and searched diligently, who prophesied of the grace that should come unto you: Searching what, or what manner of time the Spirit of Christ which was in them did signify, when it testified beforehand the sufferings of Christ and the glory which should follow" (I Peter 1:10-11). Paul assures his co-worker and associate, Timothy, that the Old Testament Scriptures which he had learned from childhood were able to make the user of them wise unto salvation through faith in Christ Jesus. The basic attitude of the Evangelists and Apostles can be summarized in the words of Paul, that in Jesus Christ all the promises of God are Yea and Amen (II Cor. 1:20).

Christians were not the only religionists who used the Old Testament and found many predictive passages about the coming Messiah's person and rule. According to Edersheim, the number of passages in the Old Testament regarded by Jews in pre-Christian times as prophetic of the Messiah is greater in number than those cited by Christians. Edersheim lists upward of 456 references in the Old Testament considered as Messianic by the Jews, of which 75 are from the Pentateuch, 243 from the prophets, and 138 from the Hagiographa.[87] "But comparatively few of these," he adds, "are what would be termed verbal predictions." However, this interpretation corroborates the fact that the whole Old Testament is to be regarded as bearing a prophetic character. It is as Unger wrote: "The idea underlying the whole development of these Scriptures and the life dealt with therein is that of God's gracious manifestation of himself to men, and the establishment of his kingdom on the earth. This idea becomes more and more distinct and centralizes itself more and more fully in the person of the coming King, Messiah."[88] Both Jews and Christians have attached special importance to the following passages: Gen. 3:15; 9:27; 12:3; 22:18; 49:8, 10; Deut. 18:18; II Sam. 7:11-16; 23:5; Psalms 2, 16, 22, 40, 110; Isaiah chapters 2, 7, 9, 11, 40, 42, 49, 53; Jer. 23:5-6; Dan. 7:27; Zech. 12:10-14; Haggai 2:9; Mal. 3: 1; 4:5, 6.

---

85. Alan Richardson, A Theological Wordbook of the Bible, op. cit., p. 44.
86. Ibid., p. 44.
87. Alfred Edersheim, The Life and Times of Jesus the Messiah (New York: Longmans, Green, and Co., 1899), II, 710.
88. Merrill F. Unger, "Messiah," Unger's Bible Dictionary (Chicago: Moody Press, 1957), p. 718.

Messiah: Divine Prediction or Jewish Dream?

An examination of the writings of liberal and neo-orthodox theologians discloses their departure from the Scriptural position that the Old Testament spoke in a predictive manner about Jesus Christ. Burrows in *An Outline of Biblical Theology* discusses the matter of the Messiahship of Jesus. He admits that Christian theology from the beginning identified Jesus with the Messiah and that this was the burden of apostolic preaching. However, Burrows depicts the Messianic hope not as a matter of God's self-revelation, but rather as a hope which was developed and fostered by the Jewish people in the course of their history as a result of the political disappointment they experienced.[89] It is the contention of modern higher criticism that many passages traditionally interpreted as Messianic will not upon closer scrutiny of scientific exegesis bear nor allow the Messianic interpretation assigned to them. Thus the Swedish scholar Ringgren asserts that a number of Old Testament passages which from the earliest days of the Christian Church had been interpreted as fulfilled in Christ, have now been explained differently. Consequently, a gulf has been established between the interpretation arrived at by the historico-critical method and the understanding of the same passages by the Christian traditional faith.[90]

An outstanding contemporary neo-orthodox theologian says about predictive Messianic prophecy: "We can indeed no longer imagine that the Old Testament writers were given a miraculous 'preview' of the events of the life and death of Jesus, or that detailed predictions of his ministry and passion were divinely dictated to them; nor shall we look for precise fulfillments of particular Old Testament texts, as writers in the pre-critical period have done ever since the days of the author of St. Matthew's Gospel (e.g. 1:22 f, 2, 5 ff, 15, 17 f, 23, etc.)."[91] This view negates direct divine communications to the saints of old about the coming of the Christ. The discussion on "the Messiah" in *The Oxford Dictionary of the Christian Church* does not mention any prophecies regarding the Messiah prior to the passages in the Samuel books where David is told that an eternal king would rule on the throne of David.[92] According to Dentan, the Messianic teaching of the Old Testament is not a matter of divine revelation, but the product of development of Israel's experience. The conception of a divinely chosen deliverer is to be traced to the Near Eastern idea of kingship which took root in Israel during the Davidic reign. In the Near Eastern world the king was regarded as a semi-divine figure from whom there radiated power able to give prosperity, peace, and victory in battle. When the hopes of the people of Israel were disappointed by the actual kings of David's line, it was only natural that the people should transfer their hopes to some future ideal king. By the end of the kingdom of Judah

---

89. Millar Burrows, *An Outline of Biblical Theology* (Philadelphia: The Westminster Press, 1946), p. 91. Cf. also Pfeiffer, *Religion in the Old Testament, op. cit.,* pp. 156-157.
90. Helmer Ringgren, *The Messiah in the Old Testament* (Chicago: Alec R. Allenson, 1956). p. 7.
91. Richardson, *A Theological Wordbook, op. cit.,* p. 179.
92. F. M. Cross, *The Oxford Dictionary of the Bible* (New York: Oxford University Press, 1957), p. 890.

in 587 B.C. this concept of an ideal ruler had become fixed in Hebrew eschatological expectation.[93]

Psalms 2, 8, 45, 72, 89, 110 usually interpreted traditionally as Messianic and containing predictions about Jesus Christ, are said to have had their origin, according to modern critical scholars, as "royal psalms." The latter were composed and used in connection with the yearly enthronement of Yahweh or New Year's Festival of Yahweh. Before David died his admirers idealized him.[94] As the process of glorification progressed, David became a Messianic figure and was considered a prototype of the future Messianic king. In regard to the whole idea of divine kingship in Israel and the festival of the ascension of the throne (Thronbesteigungsfest), which is made the basis for the interpretation of the so-called "Royal Psalms," and also of the new concept of Messianic prophecy, it should be noted that there is no reference to such a festival in the Bible. Yahweh has always been King; he never is represented as becoming King. The alleged renewal of Yahweh's Kingship was not celebrated among the Hebrews as far as it can be determined from the Old Testament. It was especially in the exilic and post-exilic periods that the Messianic hope was supposed to have been developed. This, it is said, was due to the disappointment of the Jewish people to have a kingdom of their own, and instead of focusing their hopes in political action, they began to center their hopes exclusively in the idea of God's intervention in human affairs by setting up His eternal rule on earth. The title of "Anointed One" or "Messiah" given at first to the kings of Israel was used just before the Christian era to designate the ideal King who was to establish God's reign among men on earth.

VI.

The tenets of modern biblical criticism, which rearranges the contents of the Old Testament, are also in conflict with the authoritative teaching of the New Testament on isagogical matters. That there is likewise a conflict between modern biblical criticism and the assertions of the New Testament is recognized by various Old Testament scholars. Thus Kuhl wrote: "If the Holy Scripture was the word of God in the sense that God Himself had given it to man in this form, then indeed it was elevated above all criticism. Up till now any criticism that has been made within the confines of the Church has always been restricted to textual criticism, such as Origen's fundamental and valuable attempt with his *Hexapla;* and the intention has always been not to criticize the word of God, but rather to get closer to the true Word."[95]

The whole period from the days of Christ and the Apostles to the time of the Reformation may be labelled according to Kuhl, the uncritical period in the interpretation of the Old Testament.

---

93. Robert Dentan, "Bible — Religion and Theology" (7), *The Encyclopedia Americana* (1959 edition), III, 646.
94. Sigmund Mowinckel, *He That Cometh* (Nashville: Abingdon Press, 1954), pp. 64ff.
95. Kuhl, *op. cit.,* p. 9.

Observant readers will perceive that the New Testament writers use the Old Testament extensively. New Testament authors portray their teachings as the fulfillment of all the pious yearnings of the Old Covenant saints, and evangelists claim that many events in the life of Jesus were fulfilled as foretold in the Old Testament Scriptures. It is, therefore, no coincidence that the books of the New Testament contain over 250 quotations, some of them fairly extensive, and in individual expressions and turns of speech more than 900 Old Testament allusions are found.[96] The New Testament writers quote from 34 of the 39 books of the Old Testament.

A Question of Isagogics

According to L. M. Sweet, to understand properly the use of the Old Testament in the New Testament by Christ and the apostles, there are three constructive principles which must be grasped and adopted. These are: the unity of the Old Testament and the New Testament; the prevision of the New Testament in the Old Testament; and the authority of the Old Testament as the Word of God intended for all time.[97]

Liberal and Neo-orthodox theologians and exegetes hold that the Old and New Testament authors, because they wrote out of their cultural and religious milieu, were fallible human beings, subject to error and other human limitations.[98] Jesus Himself is faulted because He was bound by human limitations and therefore could not always give correct information for all matters on which He spoke. The basic methods of higher criticism are applied to the subject of biblical revelation, whether found in either of the two testaments. The dogmatic claims which the Bible makes about its origin and authority are not taken seriously. The Neo-orthodox theologians merely look upon the Old and New Testaments as containing a human response to God's activity, which ultimately is synonymous with making the Scriptures the product of the Church's experience. This does not, therefore, recognize God as the *principium essendi* of theology, as held by Lutheran theologians in the past.[99]

Such reasoning and procedure eventuate in the fitting of isagogical material relative to the Old Testament into the naturalistic or evolutionary development of doctrine. Thus the psalms of David are not authentic because they are considered to conflict with the dating of the religious ideas found in them. New Testament assertions attributing books to Moses or Isaiah are not accepted as true because they also conflict with the findings of higher criticism, which are placed over the assertions of Jesus, Paul or the other New Testament writers. Likewise New Testament declarations about the Old Testament, which are not consonant with the findings of modern critical scholarship, are rejected as incorrect.

---

96. *Ibid.*, p. 3.
97. Louis Matthews Sweet, "Quotations, N. T.," *The International Standard Bible Encyclopedia* (Grand Rapids: Wm. B. Eerdmans Publishing Company, 1939), IV, 2517a.
98. James D. Smart. *The Interpretation of Scripture* (Philadelphia: The Westminster Press, 1961), p. 164.
99. Robert Preus, *op. cit.*, p. 27.

Jesus and the Old Testament

What was the position of Jesus Christ on the Old Testament? How did He interpret the writings of the Old Covenant? Jesus Christ as the Personal Word is the visible expression of the invisible God (Hebrews 1:3). Christians believe that Christ is the true "expression" of God, and as the revelatory Word He makes God known and conveys God's will to mankind in such a way that what Christ says and does is inerrant and infallible. He tells us that, among other things, He came to bear witness to the truth (John 18:37). Therefore, Thomas Griffith asserted of Christ: "He came to reveal God's will, and this implies and requires special knowledge. It demands that every assertion of His be true. The Divine Knowledge did not, because it could not, undergo any change by the Incarnation. He continued to subsist in the form of God even while He existed in the form of man."[100]

In the light of this position, Christians consider the pronouncements of Christ on matters pertaining to the isagogics of the Old Testament as true. It follows that any statement by Christ as a fact about the Old Testament is, or ought to be, accepted because of His infallibility. Positions of Biblical criticism that contravene the statements of our Lord should not be accepted, but often are.

There is no doubt that the Old Testament Jesus quoted from was practically the same as that which we have today. An unbiased reading will also show that He regarded it with utmost authority, as the final court of appeal for all questions pertaining to it. There is scarcely a historical book, from Genesis to II Chronicles to which Jesus does not refer. It is interesting to note that Jesus' testimony includes references to every book of the Pentateuch, to Isaiah, Jonah, Daniel, and to the very miracles that are doubted and explained away by present-day Biblical criticism. Jesus nowhere calls into question the genuineness of any Old Testament book. The Law is ascribed to Moses, David's name is connected with the 110th Psalm, the prophecies of Isaiah are assigned to the prophet Isaiah, and the prophecies of Daniel to Daniel.

Thus we read how in Matthew 8:4 Jesus says to the leper: "Go thy way, show thyself to the priest, and offer the gift that Moses commandeth." To the Pharisees the Lord said: "Moses because of your hardness of heart suffered you to put away your wives" (Matt. 19:8). "For Moses said, Honor thy father and thy mother; and whoso curseth father or mother, let him die the death" (Mark 7:10). "And beginning at Moses and all the prophets he expounded unto them in all the Scriptures the things concerning himself" (Luke 24:27). "All things must be fulfilled which were written in the law of Moses, and in the prophets, and in the psalms concerning me" (Luke 24:40). "There is one that accuseth you, even Moses, in whom you trust. For had ye believed Moses, ye would have believed me: for he wrote of Me. But if ye believe not his writings, how shall ye believe my words" (John 5:

---

100. W. H. Griffith, "Old Testament Criticism and New Testament Christianity," *The Fundamentals* (Chicago: Testimony Publishing Company, no date), VIII, p. 22.

45-47). In the same Gospel Jesus says: "Moses therefore gave unto you circumcision; (not because it is of Moses, but of the fathers) and ye on the sabbath day receive circumcision, that the law of Moses should not be broken . . ." (John 7:22-23). The parenthetical words — "not because it is of Moses, but of the fathers" — would seem to indicate that Jesus was aware that circumcision had been given to the Patriarchs before the time of Moses, which means that Jesus was concerned about historical exactness.

Jesus frequently quoted from the Book of Psalms but only once does He mention an author. Psalm 110 is ascribed to David; in fact, the validity of Christ's argument depends on the psalm being a Davidic psalm. This reference, as far as it goes, seems to confirm the ascription of the Psalms in relationship to authorship.

Isaiah is quoted a number of times by Christ. In Isaiah 6:9 Jesus finds a prophecy of the refusal of the Jews to listen to Him. "In them is fulfilled the prophecy of Esaias, which saith, By hearing ye shall hear, and shall not understand" (Matt. 13:14, 15). Again Chapter 29:13 of Isaiah's prophecy is cited: "Well hath Esaias prophesied of you hypocrites . . . This people honoreth me with their lips, but their heart is far from me" (Matt. 15:7-8). When Jesus returned to Nazareth during the Galilean ministry, they delivered to Him in the synagogue "the book of the prophet Esaias. And when he had opened the book, he found the place where it was written. The Spirit of the Lord is upon me, because he hath anointed me to preach the Gospel to the poor . . . (Luke 4:17, 18). This passage is from Isaiah Ch. 61, which belongs to the Deutero-Isaiah or the Trito-Isaiah of the critics. In John 12: 38-41, verse 38, Jesus quoted from Isaiah 53:1 and in verse 40 Jesus again quoted chapter 6:10. Here both parts of Isaiah are ascribed to the prophet Isaiah, who is said to have seen Christ's glory.

It is argued by critical scholars that Christ and the New Testament writers were not concerned with technical introduction.[101] This may be true, but it is difficult to see how Matt. 3:3; Luke 3:4; John 1:23; and Matt. 12:18-21 can be interpreted as not referring to the actual prophet Isaiah. This interpretation also agrees with the voice of tradition for the Isaiah Manuscript of the Dead Sea Scrolls, the Septuagint evidence, Jewish tradition, Josephus, the Apocrypha, the Church Fathers and the general witness of Christian scholars to the middle of the eighteenth century.

In the Mt. Olivet discourse, Jesus predicted the downfall of the Jewish state and refers to the Roman armies as "the abomination of desolation spoken of by Daniel the prophet." In Daniel 9:27 we read: "For the overspreading of abominations he shall make it desolate" and in Chapter 12:11 that "the abomination that maketh desolate (shall) set up."

An analysis of the references to the Old Testament narratives and records reveals that Christ accepts them as authentic and historically true. Thus Caven asserts: "He (Christ) does not give or suggest in any case a mythical or allegorical interpretation. The accounts of the creation, the flood, or the overthrow of Sodom and Gomorrah, as well as many incidents and events of

---

101. Young, *op. cit.*, p. 219.

later occurrence, are taken as authentic.[102] It is said by the opponents of the historical interpretation of Gen. 1-11 that the references of Jesus to these early chapters would serve the purpose for which He refers to these episodes, even if they were not true events. However, this is not the case, for the words of Jesus would lose much of their force and appropriateness if the events referred to are not historical.

When the Pharisees ask Christ about the lawfulness of putting away a wife for any cause, Jesus responds: "Have you not read that He which made them in the beginning made them male and female, and said, For this cause shall a man leave father and mother, and shall cleave to his wife: and they twain shall be one flesh?" (Matt. 19:4-5). Again: "As the days of Noe were, so shall also the coming of the Son of Man be. For in the days that were before the flood, they were eating and drinking, marrying and giving in marriage, until the day that Noe entered into the ark, and knew not, until the flood came, and took them all away; so shall also the coming of the Son of Man be" (Matt. 24:37, 39). Again: "And thou, Capernaum, which are exalted into heaven, shall be brought down to hell; for if the mighty works which have been done in thee, had been done in Sodom, it would have remained until this day. But I say unto you, that it shall be more tolerable for the land of Sodom in the day of judgment, than for thee" (Matt. 11:23, 24). These assertions of Jesus lose their weight and solemnity if the flood as described in Genesis and the destruction of Sodom and Gomorrah were mere myths. The argument of Christ that a holy and just God will again pronounce judgment is then stripped of all validity.

Today it is customary to distinguish between the type of history recorded in Genesis chapters 1-11 and chapters 12-50.[103] In weighing Jesus' references to the early episodes of Genesis, one does not find that He distinguishes between earlier and later Old Testament records on the matter of their trustworthiness.

Jesus accepted the inspiration of the Old Testament Scriptures, its declarations about Himself and the fulfillment of many prophecies concerning Him. Here Jesus comes into conflict with modern higher criticism which denies that Old Testament writers centuries in advance made direct predictions about Christ. In the opinion, therefore, of C. H. Dodd, the interpretation of Old Testament prophetical writings has suffered because of the traditional concept that the Old Testament prophets had "foretold the Messiah."[104] In the same book, Dodd further states: "The whole Messianic belief must be understood as an imaginative expression of the conviction that the great God has purposes yet unfulfilled which He must accomplish in and through His people. According to the level of religious belief and experience the idea might become

---

102. William Caven, "The Testimony of Christ to the Old Testament," *The Fundamentals* (Chicago: Testimony Publishing Company, no date), IV, p. 50.
103. G. Ernest Wright and Reginald Fuller, *The Books of the Acts of God* (New York: Doubleday and Company, 1957), pp. 53-66; Bruce Balscheit, *L'Alliance de Grace*. Traduction de F. Ryser (Paris and Neuchatel:Delachaux et Niestle, 1947), p. 17. H. Wheeler Robinson, *The History of Israel* (London: Duckworth, 1949), p. 20.
104. Dodd, *op. cit.*, p. 11.

subservient to the most vulgar kind of chauvinism, or to a high ethical monotheism."[105]

In the Sermon on the Mount, Jesus says: "I am not come to destroy the law or the prophets, but to fulfill." Here is then a general statement to the effect that Christ came to fulfill the Old Testament prophecies about Him. When the Jewish leaders persisted in rejecting Christ as the Messiah, Jesus quoted from Psalm 118 and applied it to Himself: "The stone which the builders rejected is become the head of the corner." On Maundy Thursday evening when Jesus was deserted by His disciples, He said that the prophecy of Zechariah was fulfilled: "I will smite the shepherd and the sheep shall all be scattered" (Matt. 26:31). According to Jesus, His betrayal, seizure and death occurred that "the Scripture of the prophets might be fulfilled" (Matt. 26:56). Further, according to Jesus, Psalm 41 pronounces the treachery of Judas in these words: "He that eateth bread with me hath lifted up his heel against me" and the defection of Judas Iscariot takes place "that the Scriptures may be fulfilled" (John 17:12). The persistent opposition of His enemies is a fulfillment of what was foretold: "They hated me without a cause" (John 15:25). While in the state of exaltation, Jesus appeared to two disciples on their way to Emmaus. He removes their doubt about a suffering and dying Messiah by beginning at Moses and all the prophets, "expounded unto them in all the Scriptures the things concerning Himself." "And He said unto them: These are the words which I spoke unto you while I was yet with you, that all things must be fulfilled, which were written in the law of Moses, and in the prophets, and in the psalms, concerning me. Then opened He their understanding, that they might understand the Scriptures, and said unto them: Thus it is written, and thus it behooved Christ to suffer, and to rise from the dead on the third day" (Luke 24:44-46).

"Ignorance" and "Accommodation"

Many users of the historico-critical method are well aware of the evidence which has just been cited. An attempt is, therefore, made to explain away the significance of Christ's assertions. It is contended by those who place the conclusions of modern biblical criticism above the authority of Jesus, that He had no knowledge beyond that which his contemporaries possessed. Since the Jews believed that Moses wrote the Pentateuch, that the narratives of the Old Testament are all authentic history, and that the words of Scripture are inspired, therefore Christ held the same views on these matters, even though modern criticism has shown these views to be erroneous. To espouse such a position, it is asserted, in no way detracts from the Lord's qualifications for His proper work, which was not literary, but religious and spiritual. Modern scholars tell us that Jesus Christ was qualified to give instruction on doctrinal subjects but His infallibility did not extend to questions of scholarship and criticism. Regarding Old Testament authorship of various books, He spoke as any other man of His times. Caven claims that "This view is advanced, not only by critics who reject the divinity of Christ, but by many who profess to

---

105. *Ibid.*, p. 114.

believe that doctrine."[106] Thus Dr. S. Davidson wrote: "It should also be observed that historical and critical questions could only belong to His human culture, a culture stamped with the characteristics of His age and country."[107]

The doctrine of the Kenosis is invoked to explain Jesus' lack of correct knowledge on critical issues, such as the authorship of the Pentateuch, and the ascription of second Isaiah to the prophet Isaiah. Justification for the claims of imperfection and limitations of the Lord on Old Testament problems is found in the statement of Christ recorded in Mark that He did not know the day nor hour when heaven and earth shall pass away (Mark 13:22). Philippians 2:7 is also interpreted as supporting the allegation of modern critical scholarship to the paucity of true information on the part of Jesus about Old Testament isagogical matters. While it is true that Jesus voluntarily limited Himself in areas of human and divine knowledge (Luke 5:22; John 1:48; Matt. 20:17-19) it should also be recognized that He never spoke on subjects concerning which He was voluntarily ignorant. It is as Unger wrote: "If His kenosis is extended beyond the precise delimitation of Scripture, Christ becomes a mere man, and He is no longer infallible in matters either of history or faith."[108]

Another way in which scholars have endeavored to justify the inaccurate information allegedly given by Jesus is to say that He accommodated Himself to current opinion or belief. It is felt by modern scholars that no good end would have been served if Christ in regard to the interpretation of the Old Testament had upset and contradicted prevailing opinion. He would simply have created more suspicion about Himself and His teaching than was already in evidence against Him.

The accommodation theory, supposedly practiced by Jesus, means that He possessed more accurate knowledge but He refused to divulge it. An analysis of cases where alleged accommodation took place would reveal some which would make it difficult to vindicate Jesus' perfect integrity.

Davidson has said: "Agreeing as we do in the sentiment that our Savior and His apostles accommodated their mode of reasoning to habitual notions of the Jews, no authority can be attributed to that reasoning *except when it takes the form of an independent declaration or statement*, and so rests on the speaker's credit."[109] A study of the statements of Jesus respecting the Old Testament scripture gives the impression of being "independent declarations." How shall one regard statements such as the following: "One jot or one tittle shall not pass away, . . ." or "The Scripture cannot be broken," "David in spirit calls him Lord," "All things must be fulfilled which are written in the Law of Moses, and in the prophets, and in the Psalms concerning me."

If, on the other hand, the contention of the Biblical critics is correct that Jesus revealed a measure of ignorance about the authorship of parts of the Scripture, must it not be inferred that His statements which were misleading

106. Caven, *op. cit.*, p. 65.
107. As quoted by Caven, *op. cit.*, p. 66.
108. Unger, *op. cit.*, p. 226.
109. As quoted by Caven, *op. cit.*, p. 68.

and which stood in the way of the promotion of true scholarship raise a doubt in the minds of men about His qualifications to be the permanent Teacher of the Church? Caven says: "Here is the dilemma for the radical critic — either he is agitating the Church about trifles, or, if his views have the apologetical importance which he usually attributes to them, he is censuring the Lord's discharge of His prophetic office; for the allegation is that Christ's words prove perplexing and misleading in regard to weighty issues which the progress of knowledge has obliged us to face. Surely we should be apprehensive of danger if we discover that views which claim our adhesion, on any grounds whatever, tend to depreciate the wisdom of Him whom we call 'Lord and Master', upon whom the Spirit was bestowed 'without measure' and who 'spake as never man spake'. It is a great thing in this controversy to have the Lord on our side."[110]

An examination of the references of Christ to Moses and the law do not give the impression that He was accommodating Himself to mistaken ideas. How are we to understand the obvious accuracy of references such as the following?: "Moses, therefore, gave you circumcision (not because it is of Moses, but of the fathers)." Again: "There is one that accuseth you, even Moses in whom ye trust; for had ye believed Moses ye would have believed me, for he wrote of me; but if ye believe not his writings, how shall ye believe my words?" This is not the style of one who does not wish his words to be taken verbatim.

The Question

While it is not necessary to suppose that during His state of humiliation Christ was conscious of all truth at every moment of time, it is essential to hold to the conviction that every given pronouncement of our Lord is free from the contamination of error, unless we are to undermine completely the confidence in Christ as a reliable teacher of doctrine.[111] If Christ is not to be trusted completely in all his assertions, how is the reader of His sayings going to know where to draw the line between matters of eternal import and those of purely parochial interest? Appropriately this presentation may be concluded with a searching question from the lips of Jesus Himself: "If I have told you earthly things and ye believe not how shall ye believe if I tell you heavenly things?"

---

110. *Ibid.*, p. 69.
111. Lionel E. H. Stephens-Hodge, "Christ and the Old Testament," *The Evangelical Quarterly*, 10:373, 1938.

VI.

BIBLICAL HERMENEUTICS AND THE LUTHERAN CHURCH TODAY

ROBERT D. PREUS

Introduction

Eighty years ago Lutheranism in America was shaken and split by a violent controversy over the doctrines of conversion and election. Synods were split and at odds with each other, families were divided, and life-long friendships shattered. Historians have deplored the fact that the results of doctrinal controversy could be so severe and pervasive. But momentous issues were involved. There were synergists in the Church in those days who denied the Lutheran principle of *sola gratia*, who insisted that man must have some responsibility for his conversion and salvation. And it is to the everlasting credit of men like Dr. Walther that the doctrine of salvation by grace alone, was maintained in the Lutheran Church.

Today another of the great Reformation principles is at stake, the *sola Scriptura*. A different crisis faces the Church of the Reformation. Then there were those who would shake men's confidence in salvation by grace alone. Now there are those who would shake our confidence in the Scriptures of God. And let there be no mistake about it. The Christian Church, the Lutheran Church, our Missouri Synod, faces a crisis today on this very point. For if we let go of God's infallible Word we stand to lose more than we bargain for: not merely our claim to orthodoxy, not merely the Bible itself, but our Savior.

In a sense the present crisis is more serious than that which faced the Church in the 1880's. First the debate today over the inspiration, authority and inerrancy of Scripture and the related subject of Biblical interpretation is not confined to the Lutheran Church in America. It is world wide. No theologian or informed Christian can avoid it. Second the present controversy over the nature of Scripture and its interpretation strikes at once at every single doctrine of our faith, for every article of faith is based upon Scripture and drawn from it. Third, the debate concerning the Bible has become frightfully complicated making it exceedingly difficult for layman or pastor or professor to cope with all the problems connected with Biblical authority, inerrancy, hermeneutics, etc. Philology, archaeology, philosophy, history, all have a bearing on the problems; and it is almost impossible for anyone to qualify himself in all these fields of learning. Yet we must cope with the problems. We must face with judgment and knowledge all attacks against Scripture and its proper interpretation and refute them. Our life as a Lutheran Church depends upon this. Hermann Sasse has repeatedly said that the one question facing Lutheranism today is: Do we want to remain Lutheran? And we can only remain Lutheran by holding fast the *sola Scriptura* principle, by approaching Scripture with complete confidence, by reading and applying Scripture properly to God's children.

The purpose of the present essay is not to accomplish everything that I have suggested above, that is, to cope with all the problems. Such a task is far too great for me or any person. Neither is it my purpose to offer a review of our historic Lutheran position concerning the divine origin, authority and inerrancy of Scripture. It shall rather be my aim to discuss Biblical hermeneutics, the principles whereby one reads Scripture correctly and devoutly as God would have one do. Suffice it to say at the outset, hermeneutics, our way of reading Scripture, is not unrelated to our views of Biblical inspiration and authority, but intimately associated with our attitude toward Scripture, its power, authority and veracity. The procedure, shall be as follows. First, we shall discuss the principles of hermeneutics employed by our Lutheran Confessions and by all Lutheran theologians until the rise of Rationalism in the eighteenth century. This was also the hermeneutic of Walther, Stoeckhardt and all the fathers of our Missouri Synod. And we shall examine how these principles were actually applied. Second, we shall examine some of the modern approaches to Scripture and see if these are compatible with principles employed by our Symbols, our fathers and the claims of Scripture concerning itself. And we shall point out in passing how some Lutherans in our country are following these new principles of interpretation. Third, we shall in a brief conclusion attempt to show how seriously a disregard of the old Lutheran principles of interpretation which we in our Synod have observed these many years undermines the authority of Scripture and its veracity.

I. The Hermeneutics of the Lutheran Symbols and of Historic Lutheranism

It has been generally held that there is a uniquely Lutheran hermeneutics. And this is true. The Lutheran emphasis upon the doctrinal unity of Scripture, the divine origin and authority of Scripture, the Christ-centeredness and saving aim of all Scripture, — all such emphases constitute a series of hermeneutical presuppositions of gigantic proportions, presuppositions which will and should totally determine the interpreter's attitude and approach to the sacred Scriptures. The Lutheran doctrine of man and of the way of salvation are also part of the baggage which the Lutheran theologian brings with him as he reads and interprets Scripture. That the exegete is a poor sinner with an habitual inclination toward evil, that he is in constant need of the Spirit's enlightenment to believe what he reads and studies, that all his labors to be fruitful must be preceded by earnest prayer, that every thought even of the regenerate reason must be totally subjected to the words and revelation of God, these too are assumptions of sweeping consequence for the exegete as he goes about his task.

It is important that we as Lutherans understand fully these hermeneutical presuppositions which were not only Luther's but were the possession of the entire Lutheran Church for fully two centuries and were fundamental to the Lutheran Symbols in their approach to Scripture. A doctrinal position may well seem like nonsense until we grasp the exegetical method and canons of hermeneutics which yield this position. It is particularly important for us as Lutherans to know how the writers of our Lutheran Symbols read the Scriptures, inasmuch as we have subscribed to and are committed to the doctrine of these Symbols. And certainly subscribing to the doctrine of the Confessions involves our agreement with the basic approach and hermeneutics which were employed by the Confessions in reading Scripture and drawing doctrine from it.

May I therefore offer a series of brief observations relative to the more basic hermeneutical principles and the general exegetical procedure of our Lutheran Confessions.

A. The Scriptures as the Very Word of God Himself

The divine origin of Scripture is assumed throughout all of our Confessional writings and is a fundamental presupposition to all Lutheran exegesis. It has been said that the Lutheran Confessions have no doctrine of inspiration because there is no article in the Confessions specifically devoted to the Scriptures. But such an argument from silence is surely specious.[1] There is no special article in our Confessions on many doctrines: the existence of God, angels, even the vicarious atonement. But all these are certainly doctrines of the Lutheran Church which can be elicited from our Confessions. And so it is with divine origin of Scripture, and with Scripture's authority, sufficiency, and truthfulness which are necessary corollaries of Scripture's inspiration. This is clearly brought out first of all by those statements in our Confessions which insist that all other writings, even the Confessions themselves, are to be accepted only because they are drawn from the Word of God, i.e. the sacred Scriptures (FC SD Rule and Norm, 10). Again the Word of God is called "eternal truth," and other writings only a witness to the truth (FC SD Rule and Norm, 13). Again the Scriptures are called the pure and clear fountain of Israel, which is the only true norm according to which all teachers and teachings are to be judged and evaluated (FC SD Rule and Norm, 1; Epitome Rule and Norm, 2). Secondly, we find the divine origin and authority of Scripture alluded to by many an appeal and *obiter dictum* in the Confessions. When certain Romanists do not face up to the many testimonies in Scripture concerning justification by faith, the question is asked, "Do they suppose that these words fell from the Holy Spirit unawares?" (Ap. IV, 108). Speaking of those passages which warn against human traditions and regulations, the question is again asked, "Is it possible that the Holy Spirit warned against them for nothing?" On one occasion the adversaries are faulted for condemning "several articles in opposition to the clear Scripture of the Holy Ghost." (Ap. Preface 9). Such statements indicate with clarity that the Holy Spirit is considered to be the primary author of Scripture. The fact that they are passing statements show us that the divine origin and authority of Scripture are simply taken for

---

1. Ralph Bohlmann deals with this point most adequately in his "Principles of Biblical Interpretation in the Lutheran Confessions," in *Aspects of Biblical Hermeneutics*, Concordia Theological Monthly Occasional Papers No. 1, 1966. p. 22.

granted in our Confessions. But more than this, such passing statements reveal that the divine inspiration of Scripture was quite consciously considered as a presupposition for all exegesis by the writers of our Confessions. Thirdly, the practice in our Confessions of citing Scripture faithfully to prove their doctrine, of carrying on detailed exegesis where this is necessary, of condemning all adversaries again and again specifically for being unscriptural brings out the importance of the *sola Scriptura* principle for all faithful and serious exegesis.

That God is the author of Scripture means the Scripture is inerrant. This fact is also assumed, as we see in several passing statements within our Confessions. The Scriptures are called eternal truth (FC SD Rule and Norm, 13). They will not err or lie to us (LC IV, 57; V, 76). And God who is eternal truth does not contradict Himself in Scripture (FC SD XI, 35), for it is His "pure, infallible and unalterable" Word (Preface to the Book of Concord, p. 8).

B. The Holy Spirit as the True Interpreter of Scripture

The author of any piece of literature is the best interpreter of it. This is especially true of the sacred Scripture whose primary author is the Spirit of God. It is not merely because Scripture is an ancient book, written over a long period of time and emanating from a relatively obscure culture, that we need the guidance of the Spirit to read it with edification. Such problems of history and philology can be solved fairly well by human initiative and scholarship. No, it is because we Christians are sinful and prone to disbelief that each of us needs the grace and enlightenment of the Holy Spirit to understand and believe what Scripture says to us. This was an emphasis very strong among Luther and the early Reformers. And it is echoed in our Confessions. The Formula of Concord (SD II, 26) says very explicitly "But to be born anew, and to receive inwardly a new heart, mind, and spirit, is solely the work of the Holy Spirit. He opens the intellect and the heart to understand the Scriptures and to heed the Word." This is a very important statement, one which modern exegetes could well give heed to. In its context this statement shows that the activity of the Spirit in opening up the Scriptures to us is a part of his entire work of converting and enlightening and sanctifying man. Scripture must be read according to its soteriological purpose, and only the Spirit of God can open our hearts to do this. It is through the Word of God that the Spirit comes to us, and it is through the Word — not merely the Scriptures, of course, but the Gospel — that He brings us to faith. That the Spirit interprets the Scriptures to us today means, then, that He brings us to faith in Christ and causes us to believe the Scriptures. This means that only a Christian can read Scripture with the complete understanding in the sense of acceptance, although even a Jew or Turk can often understand the literal sense of the words, as Luther had adamantly insisted.[2]

---

2. *Martin Luther,* "That These Words of Christ, 'This is My Body,' etc., Still Stand Firm Against the Fanatics," in *Word and Sacrament III,* ed. Robert H. Fischer, Vol. XXXVII in *Luther's Works,* American Edition, ed. Jaroslav Pelikan and Helmut T. Lehmann (Philadelphia: Fortress Press, 1961), pp. 13-14.

C. The Christocentricity of Scripture and the Law Gospel Motif

Like a red thread the promises concerning Christ run through the entire Old Testament Scriptures, giving them a Christological unity with the New Testament, and proclaiming one way of salvation from the Fall of our first parents to the end of time (Ap XXIV, 55, 57; IV, 57; XII 71 cf. German text). In like manner all of Scripture is said to be distributed into two parts or to teach two works of God in men, viz. Law and Gospel and the work of terrifying and comforting men (Ap IV, 5; XII, 53; FC SD V, 1, 23). Now all Scripture must be read in the light of Law and Gospel and to confuse these two teachings is to misread Scripture (Ap IV, 218ff.). Furthermore, the article of justification by faith as the epitome of the Gospel is the chief theme of all Scripture which must inform the exegete as he goes about his task (Ap IV, 2 German text); otherwise again all is darkness, even though the grammatical sense of Scripture may well be understood by the exegete. Needless to say, a doctrinal unity is maintained by the Lutheran Confessions along with the Christological unity of Scripture, for all Christian doctrine has its center in the doctrine of the Gospel. Confidence in the doctrinal unity of Scripture is again evidenced in our Confessions as they prove doctrine (e.g. the spiritual bondage of the human will, FC II) by random citations from all over Scripture. Like Luther our Confessions see the doctrine of Scripture as one perfect golden ring (the later Luther dogmaticians called all Christian doctrine *"una copulativa"*). This means that there can be no difference in doctrine between the writers of Scripture or the Testaments. The theology of Scripture (which all points to Christ) is one, even as Christ is one. Our Confessions could well have endorsed Augustine's well-known statement, *Tempora variata sunt, non fides.*[3]

D. The Clarity of Scripture

The clarity of Scripture is maintained by the Lutheran Confessions, although no definition of the nature or extent of Scripture's clarity is offered. This is seen by the fact that, for the most part, passages of Scripture are cited in our Confessions to support Christian doctrine with little or no comment. This does not imply that there are no obscure passages in Scripture, or that extensive exegesis is not required in the case of even the clearest passages, as we see in the case of the words of institution of the Lord's Supper (FC SD VII). But again and again the Lutheran Confessions insist that the doctrine taught is based on clear passages of Scripture (Ap IV, 314; LC V, 45; FC SD II, 87; Ap XXIV 94; FC SD VII 50; AC XXII, 2, XXIII, 3; XXVIII, 43). It is obvious that clear passages of Scripture (*clarissimae scripturae*) are not necessarily those which pertain to some particular doctrine, e.g. justification (it is the very purpose of Apology IV to clarify the doctrine of justification from clear Scripture passages), but are quite simply those passages, verses, pericopes which present no problems in a) their historical setting, or b) their grammatical construction. That which would render any passage or pericope unclear would be simply the presence of

---

3. *In Johannis Evangelium Tractatus*, 45, 9 (*MPL* 35, 1722).

some obscure or unknown historical referent or some obscure syntax or vocabulary. Often unclear passages can be explained by clear passages dealing with the same subject matter.

E. The Necessity of Grammatical Exegesis: Finding the Literal Sense of Scripture Which Is One

The exegesis of historic Lutheranism consistently attempts to discern the literal sense, that is, the native and plain meaning of Scripture passages and pericopes (FC SD VII, 38, 42, 45-8, 50). This is consistent with the humanistic heritage of the day. The principle was put simply in a question: what exactly did the Biblical author wish to say, assert or affirm? And to the Lutheran Confessions whatever the sacred author asserts or affirms must be considered as asserted and affirmed by the Holy Spirit Himself, and therefore as infallibly true and authoritative. And so we find in our Confessions the constant question: What does Scripture say? (Ap IV, 231; 264; 267; XII, 84, 138). What is the intended sense and meaning of the author of any given pericope? To discern this plain, native meaning of the text all the grammatical, lexicographical and historical tools of the day were employed. Etymologies, Biblical usage, even extra-Biblical data are brought to bear in the attempt to find the meaning of terms and passages (Ap XXIV, 23; 81 ff.; FC SD V, 7 ff.; Ap IV, 246 ff.). The search for the simple and native sense of the passages of Scripture rules out allegorical and fanciful interpretations and hidden meanings (Ap XI, 106; XXIV, 35; FC SD VII, 113); and this because *sensus literalis Scripturae unus est.* Any undermining of this basic fact destroys all serious exegesis.

F. Scripture Interprets Scripture

The principle that Scripture interprets Scripture (*analogia Scripturae*) derives from the clarity of Scripture and from the fact that the Holy Spirit is the principle author of all Scripture. Therefore, since sacred Scripture is one book with one author, any passage can shed light on another passage which deals with the same subject matter. This is merely interpreting Scripture passages in the light of their widest context. This particular principle is followed by the Confessions time and again when they draw from all over Scripture to maintain a certain point (Ap XII, 44 ff.; IV, 272 ff.; 256 ff.; FC SD II, 9 ff.; 26 ff.; VIII, 70 ff.). In all such cases various Scriptures serve to compliment each other in offering a complete view of an article of faith. This principle is of especial importance as the exegete interprets unclear passages by clear parallel passages (Ap IV, 87; XXVIII, 21; Tr. 23; LC I, 65) and as one exegetes and understands Old Testament passages in the light of New Testament interpretation of the Old (Ap II, 18, 20; XXIII, 64; XXIV, 36). One can easily perceive how fundamental the principle, Scripture interprets Scripture, is to all exegesis. How better can one find the meaning of an obscure passage than by consulting a clear passage dealing with the same subject matter? To deny this principle would tend to thwart any solution to many exegetical difficulties in the only way which is often possible and would be tantamount to a denial of the unity and coherency of Scripture. Any piece of literature, if it has any coherence to it at all, is read in analogy with itself.[4]

II. Lutheran Hermeneutics Applied: A Case Study

Now, having established what are the basic presuppositions and principles for Biblical interpretation according to Confessional Lutheranism, let us see how our Confessions apply these principles in a given case. Let us choose an important pericope, a pericope concerning which there is much controversy today, also in our own circles: Gen. 1-3. And then let us compare the historic Lutheran approach to this pericope with that of several modern exegetes.

A. The Lutheran Confession and Gen. 1-3

There can be little doubt that the Lutheran Confessions, like Luther and the exegetes of the day, regard Gen. 1-3 as introducing a history, not presenting a cosmogony. Furthermore, Gen. 2 with its account of Adam and Eve in the Garden cannot be divorced from Gen. 3 which speaks of the Fall of these two people into sin. Therefore the entire three chapters are taken together as a unity (not a composite of different and differing documents), although Gen. 3 does not deal specifically with creation. One's interpretation of Gen. 3 will notably affect one's understanding and interpretation of the preceding chapter. This is very clear in the case of our Lutheran Confessions which see Gen. 2 in the light of the Fall and the promise of Gen. 3.

What then do our Confessions say about the great theological themes of Gen. 1-3? How do they read this grand pericope in the light of these themes?

1. Creation

Surprisingly little is said about creation in the Lutheran Confessions. No cosmogony on the basis of Gen. 1 and 2 is offered; although Luther, Chytraeus and others in their commentaries understand the Genesis account as a plain historical descriptive account or history of what actually took place. There is very little said in the Lutheran Symbols about the creation of the world or the universe. It is rather the theological significance of creation that is em-

---

4. It is therefore extremely odd that Curtis E. Huber, commenting on the principle, *Scriptura per scripturam explicanda,* should say: "There is no suggestion implied by that principle to the effect that one passage of a particular Biblical book will automatically [sic] throw the light of meaning on another passage which is in question." ("Meaning and the Word in Lutheran Orthodoxy," *C.T.M.*, XXXVI, 8 [September, 1965], p. 566). This is precisely what the principle meant in classical Lutheranism and this is how it was applied. Huber also says that according to orthodox Lutheranism "Biblical signs do not explain themselves" and "Verbal entities do not produce meaning. God gives meaning to men's words which makes them vehicles of God's own truth." Such a bizarre summary of the orthodox Lutheran position is quite impossible to account for. The old Lutherans never say that God gives meaning to the Scriptures. Rather, they say that He gives understanding (and this means saving understanding) to those who read Scripture. The meaning of Scripture is already there in the Scriptures, there for Christian, Jew or Turk or anyone.

phasized, and this because of various antitheses of the day. For instance, in contrast to the alleged Manicheism of Flacius the goodness of God's creation is stressed (FC, I). And to defend Luther's doctrine of original sin and total depravity against the charges of Eck and others the Augsburg Confession, Art. XIX, insists that God is not the cause of sin.

As the Lutheran Confessions treat the many texts in Scripture dealing with creation their discussions seem almost invariably to lead to man as the principal creature of God, just as Gen. 1 must lead to Gen. 2 and is incomplete without it. Man is a creature of a good and beneficent Creator God, and all of God's creation serves man. This is the practical theological significance of creation and the conclusion to be drawn from the creation accounts. Listen to Luther on this point (LC. 1st Art. 11-16):

> If you were to ask a young child, "My boy, what kind of God have you? What do you know about Him?" he would say, "First, my God is the Father, who made heaven and earth. Apart from him alone I have no other God, for there is no one else who could create heaven and earth."
> For the somewhat more advanced and the educated, however, all three articles can be treated more fully and divided into as many parts as there are words. But for young pupils it is enough to indicate the most necessary points, namely as we have said, that this article deals with creation. We should emphasize the words, "maker of heaven and earth." What is meant by these words, "I believe in God, the Father almighty, maker," etc.? Answer: I believe and hold that I am a creature of God; that is, that he has given and constantly sustains my body, soul, and life, my members great and small, all the faculties of my mind, my reason and understanding and so forth; my food and drink, clothing, means of support, wife and child, servants, house and home, etc. Besides, he makes all creation help provide the comforts and necessities of life — sun, moon, and stars in the heavens, day and night, air, fire, water, the earth and all that it brings forth, birds and fish, beasts, grain and all kinds of produce. Moreover, he gives all physical and temporal blessings — good government, peace, security. Thus we learn from this article that none of us has his life of himself, or anything else that has been mentioned here or can be mentioned, nor can he by himself preserve any of them, however small or unimportant. All this is comprehended in the word "Creator".

This statement which is typical of so many in our Confessions (AC, XVI, 4 ff.; FC Ep I, 2, 4; FC SD, 1, 34-37) stresses not the original creation of heaven but the *creatio continua* and divine providence of God (FC SD, XI, 4.6). The doctrine of creation is *used* to serve man: to humble and terrify us, for we sin daily; but also to lift us up and warm our hearts with gratitude toward God for all His blessings (LC, Creed, I, 22.23).

2. Adam and Eve

Thus far the exegesis of the Lutheran Confessions pertaining to the doctrine of creation as set forth in the first chapters of Genesis has been application more than interpretation. And this practice is in conformity with that of Scripture itself (Ps. 104; Isa. 40; Job 38; Col. 1:16 ff.) which uses the doctrine of creation homiletically, doxologically and polemically. But just as the Scriptures are not using and applying a mere myth, the Confessions too, when they apply the doctrine of creation as they do to the needs of their day, in no way minimize the importance of Gen. 1 and 2 as a factual account of a real creation and a *scdes doctrinae*. When we observe what our Symbols say about Adam and Eve we notice that more interpretation is offered than application.

There is not the slightest doubt that the Confessions receive as actual history and fact the story of Adam and Eve in Gen. 2 (FC Ep I, SD, I, 9-27). Adam and Eve were the first two people of this world placed by God in the Garden of Eden. Adam and Eve were created with body and soul (FC Ep I, 4) according to Gen. 2:7; they were created in the image of God (according to Gen. 1:27) which consisted of a wisdom and righteousness being "implanted in man that would grasp God and reflect Him, that is, that man received gifts like the knowledge of God, fear of God, and trust in God" (Ap 22, 17-18). Here Gen. 2:7 is definitely interpreted according to Col. 3:10 and Eph. 4:24 according to the analogy of Scripture, and there is no attempt to interpret Gen. 1:27 independently of the New Testament. These two people, Adam and Eve, were originally created pure, good and holy, as the Genesis account says (FC SD, I, 27). Furthermore, marriage was established between Adam and Eve, and this cannot be nullified as a pleasing institution (AC XXXII, 8. Cf. Matt. 19:4 ff.).

3. The Fall and Original Sin

We notice here at once that the historical fact of the Fall is never questioned (FC SD, I, 23:9): "The dough out of which God forms and makes man has been corrupted and perverted in Adam . . ." (FC SD, I, 38). We notice also that Satan is the instigator of sin, the one who "corrupted God's handiwork in Adam" (FC SD, I, 42. 7. 24). In this connection even details connected with the Fall narrative are considered to be factual and historical such as the devil's manner in tempting Adam and Adam's subsequent contrition (SA III. VIII, 5:Ap XII, 55). For instance, Luther says (SA III, VIII, 5): "All this is the old devil and the old serpent who made enthusiasts of Adam and Eve. He led them from the external Word of God to spiritualizing and to their own imaginations, and he did this through other external words." Third, we notice the connection, alluded to so often (FC SD, I, 28.9.11.13; Ap II, 5.2; AC II, 1), between Adam's sin (Fall) and our own sinful condition, "that since the fall of Adam all men who are propagated according to nature are born in sin" (AC II, 1), that our sin is a hereditary condition (*Erbsuende*) which we have "by conception and birth" (par. 6.11. 8.23). This connection which is not drawn from Gen. 3 but from Rom. 5; Matt. 15:19; Gen. 8:21 and other passages, although never explained; is nevertheless real and is an article of faith. Again we notice how the New Testament is simply brought in to interpret the Old Testament. Such a position on original sin, based on the Genesis account and the analogy of Scripture, is quite incompatible with such views as Karl Barth's modern doctrine of total

89

depravity (*Ursuende*), that every man is his own Adam. In other words, the actuality of the Fall as recounted in Gen. 3 is the basis of the actuality of original sin today, according to the historic Lutheran understanding of Scripture. And this is a matter of confession (SA III, I, 1): "Here we must confess what St. Paul says in Rom. 5:12, namely, that sin had its origin in one man, Adam, through whose disobedience all men were made sinners and became subject to death and the devil."

Other facts pertinent to the description of original sin, its guilt, its punishment are brought out in our Confessions, but not on the basis of Gen. 3. It is interesting that in the Confessions (FC, I) Gen. 3 (this historical narrative) is the *sedes doctrinae* for the doctrine of the Fall and original sin, and Rom. 5 and I Cor. 15 are scarcely mentioned. This indicates the importance of the historicity of the narrative for classical Lutheran theology.

4. Conclusions and Comments on the Symbols' Reading and Understanding of Great Themes of Gen. 1-3

a. The interpretation in our Confessions of Gen. 1-3 is an ingenious one which accepts the *prima facie* meaning of the story. No hidden, mystical or allegorical meanings or genres are sought. And, of course, no interpretation of the account in the light of Moses' readership or *Sitz im Leben* is attempted. The matter of the six days and their length and other problems which may disturb us today are, of course, not even broached. It is rather the *theological* significance which is emphasized (i.e., 1. a created universe with a transcendant God existing apart from the universe [against pantheism and atheism], 2. a created man and woman as the culmination of God's creation [against polygenesis which was taught also in those days, e.g. Las Cases, Augustine, Avicenna, and later Isaac Peyrerius], 3. a man created good in the image of God and being immediately at his creation the full realization of what a human is to be [against Manicheism, modern evolutionism, etc.], and 4. an historical fall of Adam and Eve involving an actual act of disobedience against a specific command of God [against any and all minimizing of the universality and seriousness and reality of original sin]). We may notice that in all four of these points other Scriptures can be brought to bear, particularly Rom. 5. We note also that the *theological significance* of Gen. 1-3 is for the Lutheran Symbols *dependent wholly* upon the factuality of the account. This means that there is in Gen. 1-3 a description of something actually happening. A non-descriptive account as suggested by modern interpreters (e.g. a demythologized poem sung to God's glory; an aetiological saga; a mere cosmogony purified of theogony, theomachy and other unworthy elements; a reworking of various older Hebrew and other myths) would be totally uncongenial to the Lutheran Confessions as being opposed to the serious theological purpose of the section and to the analogy of Scripture.

b. It is surprising how little direct attention is given in the Confessions (as they deal with the themes above) to Rom. 5. Much more attention is directed to Gen. 1-3 which tells the history. We might say that FC, I deals with original sin on the basis of Gen. 3 and uses other passages only to shed light; the entire article is a sort of commentary (polemical, of course) on Gen. 3, or better, a sort of *Gutachten* based upon Gen. 3. Articles II and III of the FC which deal with the bondage of the will and with justification are quite different, having no single *sedes*, but roving all over Scripture in presenting the Lutheran position.

c. We notice finally how clearly operative the various hermeneutical assumptions and principles (annunciated above) are as our Confessions address themselves to the Genesis pericope. We see clearly the Confessions seeking the *sensus literalis* of the pericope, the plain and native meaning of Gen. 1-3. That Scripture is its own interpreter is constantly assumed and applied as other Scriptures add light and understanding to the Gen. text. Belief in the unity of Scripture, both doctrinal and Christological, is apparent as our Confessions deal with Gen. 1-3; for everything in Scripture dealing with Creation and the Fall is related without reservation to the discussion, and both Creation and the Fall are treated in such a way as to lead us to Christ and the Gospel. Again we observe the text being interpreted in the light of Law and Gospel as the Confessions seek to understand and apply what is said about creation and the Fall.[5] And we observe that the New Testament interpretation of the Old Testament is taken for granted and accepted without any reservation; the New Testament data are never ignored or lost sight of as Gen. 1-3 is read and applied. To sum up: the Lutheran Symbols interpret the themes of Gen. 1-3 both theologically in accord with the evangelical presuppositions for all exegesis and grammatico-historically as the rules of sound hermeneutics dictate; but in no case do they allow theological assumptions to undermine sound grammatical exegesis. In other words, we would conclude that in their interpretation of Gen. 1-3 our Lutheran Confessions are faithfully following the concerns voiced in the concluding paragraphs of the Formula of Concord, XI, 92-93:

"Whatever was written in former days was written for our instruction, that by steadfastness and by encouragement of the Scriptures we might have hope" (Rom. 15:4). But it is certain that any interpretation of the Scriptures which weakens or even removes this comfort and hope is contrary to the

---

5. It cannot be conjectured that Gen. 1-3 is only remotely related to Law and Gospel and that therefore on Lutheran principles (cf. Ap IV, 2 German text) we need not insist upon a particular interpretation of this pericope, viz. that it presents historical facts. This seems to be the position of Prof. Walter Bouman in an essay on creation delivered at Valparaiso University a year or two ago. (See the unpublished, but taped essay, p. 80 *passim*). The premise of such an allegation is false. Prof. Bouman says that the Law "as a description of the predicament in which I find myself is not in the first instance that back there something happened to an individual called Adam. But the Law says to me that God Himself is my enemy and that all of the circumstances of my existence contribute and conspire to that enmity which God visits upon me." True, but the origin of my sin and God's anger are rooted in a real, historic Fall, according to our Confessions, and all true Law preaching takes account of this. The way one interprets Gen. 3 will have a profound effect upon the way he preaches the Law (and the Gospel) according to our Confessions. It is not by accident that the central doctrine of justification is preceded in the AC by the articles on God, Creation, the Fall and Original Sin, Christ and His work of propitiation. All these must be real if there is any reality in the justification of a sinner before God.

Holy Spirit's will and intent. We shall abide by this simple, direct, and useful exposition which is permanently and well grounded in God's revealed will, we shall avoid and flee all abstruse and specious questions and disputations, and we reject and condemn all those things which are contrary to these true, simple, and useful expositions.

B. Modern Approaches to Genesis 1-3

Having seen how our Confessions read Genesis 1-3 and apply these chapters (and remembering that our Missouri Synod subscribes wholeheartedly to these Confessions), let us now examine how these chapters are read by modern scholars. But let us for the sake of brevity confine our examination to just the first two chapters of Genesis which deal with Creation.

As one attempts to apprise oneself of the various theological approaches to the Genesis creation story and the different methods of interpreting this account, one is at once bewildered. First, one finds almost no two commentators in even essential agreement. Second, one finds in many instances an extreme caution on the part of exegetes to commit themselves on the large theological implications of the various sections of the pericope (although in details concerning borrowings and origins of phrases and concepts the commentators are often most dogmatic, e.g. Gunkel, Cassuto, von Rad).

Roughly speaking, however, all interpretations will fall into two general classifications:

1. Approach A

This approach interprets the account in a highly figurative manner, as non-historical or supra-historical and ultimately *non-descriptive* of anything. The literary form (*genre*) of the story may be called myth, poem, parable, epic, saga, depending upon the predilection of the exegete.

Thus the account may be understood in any number of ways, e.g. as:

1. a demythologized poem, sung to the glory of God, or
2. an aetiological saga, offering an explanation of questions which must have puzzled the Israelites in the 10th century and later, a saga purified of heathen dross, or
3. a cosmogony, like so many other epic and legendary cosmogonies of the day, but purified of theogony, theomachy and other unworthy elements, or
4. an "inspired" Hebrew borrowing from the sacred writings and legends of neighbor cultures (Babylonian, Ugaritic) on basic themes of interest, or
5. a similar reworking of ancient Hebrew myths into one organic account, didactic in nature.

The following are some representative examples of Approach A. And please bear with me now if the discussion becomes somewhat prolix.

a. Vriezen in *An Outline of Old Testament Theology*[6] contends that the doctrine of Creation did not assume great proportions for Israel. He assumes that Israel did not even worship God as Creator at an early date (this works in well with the late date of the Jahwist account of Genesis 2). Israel had no more concern with Creation than other contemporary religions. The Genesis account dates to the late kings when the idea of Creation became more prominent, and this probably because of conflict with the Assyro-Babylonian philosophy of life (8 and 7 century B.C.). We have here according to Vriezen, a reaction of Jahwism to a world-power, similar to the Christian confrontation with Gnosticism or Neo-Platonism, Israel's unique contribution was in teaching that the Creator is a good and holy God. This is the prime significance and purpose of the account. It is not meant to be descriptive. Vriezen says, "Genesis 1 shows marks of profound reflection in the field of religion as well as in that of natural science and cannot simply be regarded as naive, adopted, ancient mythological conception: it represents a deeply considered philosophy indeed. It certainly is the most 'modern' of all cosmologies known from the ancient East. But its real meaning is to be found in the attempt to place the cosmogony wholly in the light of belief in God."

b. Jacob in his *Theology of the Old Testament*[7] contends that creation in the book of Genesis serves the dominant covenant idea of the Old Testament. As an idea creation developed after the covenant idea. God creates man in His image, autonomous; and this makes the covenant possible. Jacob says: "In order that man might suitably fulfill his function of partner, God subjects the framework of nature to certain fixed laws or to certain unforeseen movements and the normal aspect of the cosmos. . . ." Elsewhere the Old Testament takes over several creation myths (Job 7:12 ff.; 26:10-13; 38:8-11; Ps. 74; 89:11 ff.; Isa. 51:9 ff.). However, Genesis 1 contains definite theological "reflections" and this takes creation out of the realm of *pure* myth (in contrast to the Babylonian account). According to Jacob the *Jahwist* account (Gen. 2) affirms the unity of the world and man as the beneficiary (garden, river, etc.). The *Priestly* writer (Gen. 1) emphasizes even more the unity of the universe. In the Priestly account God is freed from figures suggesting a demiurge and is not so directly creator (orderliness, completeness is emphasized: 10 works of creation, six days) as in the Jahwist account. To Jacob, then Genesis 1 and 2 offer a highly anthropomorphic genre employed by the writers to emphasize some basic theological themes, no more. Again the account is not meant to be descriptive.

c. Eichrodt in his *Theology of the Old Testament*[8] has rather little to say on our pericope, and it is best merely to cite his comments:

> Certainly it is possible to point to the fact that the Babylonian Creation myths and the Egyptian contemplation of Nature supplied Israelite thought with varied material — possibly through the meditation of Ca-

6. Vriezen, T. C., *An Outline of Old Testament Theology*. Oxford: B. Blackwell, 1958.
7. Jacob, E., *Theology of the Old Testament*. London: Hodder, 1958.
8. Eichrodt, W., *Theology of the Old Testament*. London: SCM Press, 1961.

naanite festivals and cultic hymns — and stimulated it in many ways. But it should not be forgotten, that the most influential assumptions supporting the subjection of the whole natural order to the mighty authority of a divine Lord were attached in the religion of ancient Israel to the covenant God, who was naturally worshipped as the giver of all blessings of nature and everything that went with the fuller life of civilization. To show how decisive these basic assumptions were for the Israelite attitude to nature we need cite no more than the independent form taken by their concept of Creation. In the work of the Jahwist narrator this concept is already marked by a firm exclusion of polytheistic mythological elements, and by a deliberate linking up of Creation with history. The result was that those heathen speculations concerning the mystery of life and death, which must have been known to Israel (cf. the Osiris and Adonis cults, and the resurrection myth of Mel-Marduk) were nevertheless rejected. Instead there was a determination to hold fast to the Idea of an immediate dependence of mankind and of the whole Creation on the preemptory, controlling will of Jahweh the only eternal God; and this leaves hardly any doubt what was really the decisive factor shaping Israel's characteristic belief in the subordination of nature to the divine *Imperium*. It was their *experience* of Jahweh's control of history working purposefully toward a goal, and brooking no contradiction of its authority.

To Eichrodt, then, the creation theology of Gen. 2 is a splendid example of Hebrew insight, based on two sources: 1) their experience of God's control of all things, 2) Babylonian and other creation myths reworked and purified to serve their purposes. Again there is no indication that to Eichrodt Gen. 1 and 2 were written to tell us what might actually have happened. In fact the intention of the two chapters is not very seriously considered.

d. Cassuto in *A Commentary on the Book of Genesis*[9] grants that many references and allusions to creation in Genesis 1 and 8 may be traced back to *Israelitish* sagas and legends (this is discernible in e.g. Ps. 104:3; Job 9:8; 38:4-7 — lay foundations, lines, bases, cornerstone, morning stars singing for joy; Isa. 40:12, 21-22; Isa. 51:9-10 — Rahab, Lord of the sea, who opposed the will of God and would not confine his waters within limits). However, the Torah was written prose, employing simple, non-figurative language for the most part. Yet, it could not employ abstract language, and thus assumes an elevated poetic form. But to Cassuto the story has actually only the "practical purpose of providing moral instruction and of assuaging the feeling of perplexity in the heart of man, who finds a contradiction between the Creator's paternal love and the multitudinous troubles that throng the world." And so it is not the actuality of the events recorded, but the theological and moral implications of the story which seem important to Cassuto. Just whether the record is descriptive or not he does not state, although it is doubtful if he believes it.

e. We shall spend a little more time with von Rad, since in his com-

---

9. Cassuto, U., *A Commentary on the Book of Genesis.* Jerusalem: Hebrew University, 1961.

mentary on Genesis [10] he gives extreme exegesis of Gen. 1 and 2 and since his works are often texts in Lutheran seminaries today.

von Rad sees Gen. 2 as a beautiful testimony by the Jahwist of the activity of God in the profane as well as in the religious. He sees the Jahwist more as an artist than as a historian or narrator or witness of things which really happened, Jahweh is still with Israel, is the message. The genre of Gen. 2 is saga, religious tale; and so we cannot know what really happened. von Rad says, "The circumstances in every single saga are different. Thus one may reckon correctly with subsequent expansion of old traditions by means of fictional material, even by means of fairy tale motifs. This does not endanger the 'historicity' of the saga in any way, in so far as with the help of such means it elucidates real events and experiences." The power of forming sagas was faith.

Now all this is interesting, although speculative; for we do not know that the genre is saga. But von Rad has not yet come to the question of the *sensus literalis*. What do the words of the pericope really say? von Rad, like the other exegetes we have studied, is dealing more with motives, reasons for writing, tendenz; not with the "what" of the text. He would have us sift the theological meat from the pericope.

Turning to Gen. 1, the genre is not saga or myth, according to von Rad, but priestly doctrine, "preserved and handed on by many generations of priests, repeatedly pondered, taught and reformed and expanded most carefully and compactly by new reflections and experiences of faith. . . ." The possibility of the account telling what actually took place is out of the question. But what about the intent of Moses, we would ask? von Rad would admit that the author of the section intended to tell what really happened. He says, "Certainly in this respect too they [the statements of the chapter] present what was thought at that time about the primeval condition of the world." But he goes on to say, "But since they propose also to be statements of faith they possess enduring theological interest." In other words to von Rad we do not have a description of what actually happened in Gen. 1, although the narrative purports to describe what took place. We might say that he understands at this point what the text says *prima facie*, but his posture toward Scripture prevents him from committing himself to the assertions of the account.

Turning finally to the Fall narrative in Gen. 3 it is much the same story. The historicity of the Fall is not even considered by von Rad. We have here merely a beautiful Jahwistic piece, going back to Solomonic times, having certain aetiological features and taking over and demythologizing many Oriental materials. It is too didactic for myth; again in doctrine. The story acquits God of all responsibility for sin. The troubles of life have their root in man's estrangement from God.

A number of conclusions may be drawn from the foregoing representative selection of examples of Approach A to Gen. 1-3:

1. There is a strong emphasis upon the long development of the creation story either from neighboring mythology or Jewish mythology (Cassuto).

---

10. von Rad, Gerhard, *Genesis*. London: SEM Press, 1961.

No mention, no consideration is given the possibility that we have in this account a divine revelation.[11]

2. There is a strong emphasis usually on the polemical nature of the account, against polytheism, false cosmologies, etc. This tends to vitiate the factuality of the account, since the purpose of the account is polemical. There is a non-sequitur here.

3. There is a disbelief that the account could possibly be descriptive of what has actually happened, or a rejection that the genre here employed allows for such an interpretation.

4. Often (except in the case of Cassuto) the interpretation is tied very closely to the documentary hypothesis, implying that there are divergent (contradictory) theologies of creation in Gen. 1-2, and that interest in the doctrine of creation came late to the Israelites or that it was not important to them. Here we see how very important isogogics is for exegesis.

5. There is much form criticism employed in this approach. The idea is that the Hebrew form of literature is derived from that of contemporary cultures (myth, legend, saga, epic, etc.).

6. Most important of all, there is much emphasis in this approach upon the profound nature and beauty of the account, upon the deep reflection and insight of the author (whoever he was), but never (except for Danielou) that he was a spokesman of God, that he bore a revelation from God, doctrine which was true, forever and binding. It is only that he was a clever, insightful, "inspired" child of his time.

2. Approach B

This approach accepts Genesis 1-3 in the traditional way, as an account of how things really happened at creation and at the time of Fall. The account is not taken as myth or saga, etc. but as a history, a revelation of actual events, giving us satisfactory *information* concerning prehistoric times and *Urgeschichte*.[12] To quote Leupold: "[The account] goes back beyond the reach of available historical sources and offers not mythical suppositions, not poetical fancies, not vague suggestions, but a positive record of things as they actually transpired and at the same time, of matters of infinite moment for all mankind." This interpretation insists that the Biblical account is utterly superior to the other cosmogonies of the day and is therefore not a derivative of any of them, although Moses may have been

---

11. An exception is found in a new book by Jean Danielou, SJ., *In The Beginning . . . Gen. I-III*, tr. by Julien L. Randolf. Dublin: Helicon Press, 1965. Danielou follows approach A on most points, but at the same time continually speaks of a revelation of actual history. His might be considered a mediating approach.

12. This is the position roughly of Leupold, H. C., *Exposition of Genesis*, Columbus, Ohio: Wartburg Press, 1942, p. 25 ff; Edward Young, *Westminster Theological Journal*, XXV, I. 1 ff; Procksch, Otto, *Die Genesis* (at least in reference to Gen. 2); Moeller, H., *Biblische Theologie der Alten Testaments in heilsgeschichtlicher Entwicklung*, Zwickau, 1938; Heinish, *Theology of the Old Testament*, Collegeville, Minnesota, 1950.

aware of these accounts and used aspects of them. Such an approach in no way implies that metaphors, anthropomorphism and other figures of speech are not employed, e.g. God speaks, walks in the garden. In Gen. 2:7 God does not necessarily act precisely as a potter; yet we cannot say that He did nothing. For instance, when God spoke something happened; this means He did speak.

This approach too has variations. For instance, although both Heinish and Moeller hold the account to be descriptive, they do not hold to a strictly chronological account as do Young and Leupold. Again, Franz Delitzsch denied a literal six-day creation while still insisting that the Gen. 1-2 narrative was chronological.

This approach does not object (usually) a priori to borrowings of mythical phrases or thought forms, but it cannot grant that there is wholesale borrowing of entire genres. Approach B insists that we have in the account a revelation of God, not merely a poetic insight of a succession of Hebrew minds. And we have a descriptive account.

Approach B manifests basic theological concerns. It is contended that such an understanding of the pericope is fundamental to a full understanding of our doctrine of sin and redemption (Law and Gospel). This approach insists that the Genesis account of creation and the Fall agree with the rest of Scripture (e.g. Rom. 5). Thus, theologically one might insist upon a *created* universe with a transcendent God (against all forms of pantheism and naturalism), a created human man and woman (against evolutionism and polygenesis), a man created in a state of perfection, and an actual, historic Fall (against all mythological or other explanations of man's present sinful condition). This interprets Genesis 1 and 2 in terms of Law and Gospel.

3. Conclusion

We should have no problem seeing that approach B to Gen. 1-3 agrees with all the hermeneutical principles and with the exegesis of historic Lutheranism, and not approach A. What is possibly not so apparent is the great cleavage between the modern approach (A) and that of our Confessions. Modern exegetes are, for the most part, reading the Scriptures from an entirely different viewpoint, with an entirely different set of presuppositions and hermeneutical rules, from our Lutheran Fathers.

And we must not suppose that this modern approach is confined to a few German scholars who have no truck with the Lutheran Confessions anyway. Not at all. The approach is common in even the conservative confines of American Lutheranism. To cite just one clear example: Prof. Carl Losen of Luther College, a formerly conservative Lutheran school which wished to be considered Confessional, in an article entitled "The Historical-Critical Method and the Old Testament"[13] presents the view of von Rad in a nutshell. Prof. Losen wishes to apply the so-called historical-critical method to the Old Testament. This is the only objective way, he says. But he completely ignores

---

13. This essay is found in *Theological Perspectives, A Discussion of Contemporary Issues in Lutheran Theology,* issued by members of the department of religion Luther College, Decorah, Iowa: Luther College Press, no date, pp. 24-33.

our Confessions and the fundamental principles of hermeneutics ennunciated there. He ignores the analogy of Scripture (that Scripture interprets itself) and the principle that Scripture is God's Word and revelation, and he flatly denies the unity of Scripture and its inerrancy. Clearly his approach has little in common with Luther, Melanchthon and Chemnitz and the other theologians who wrote our Lutheran Confessions.

III. Modern Historicism and Exegesis: A Case Study: "Form Criticism"

Having seen that modern theologians in many cases are reading the Scriptures from a posture quite different from that of our Lutheran Confessions and Fathers, let us now become more specific. Let us *first* examine how the recent preoccupation with history has affected exegesis today. And let us *second* examine some really new approaches to the interpreting of Scripture.

Because Christianity is a historical religion and because the Bible was written by men who lived at a certain time in history and in a definite culture, modern theologians tell us that Scripture must be read historically. So far we would scarcely disagree. But most modern theologians go on to say that to read Scripture from a historical perspective means to read Scripture as a book historically conditioned and therefore subject to the same historical analysis and criticism as other human writings. Such an approach, except as practiced by certain Roman Catholic and conservative Protestant theologians, ignores or denies the divine origin of Scripture and assumes that Scripture contains contradictions and errors which can be historically pointed out and analyzed. This modern historical method as applied to Scripture has produced many results. In the case of the four Gospels it has resulted in the so-called quest for the historical Jesus. Assuming that the Gospels were not primarily history or records of events, but rather doctrinal and propaganda documents, our modern theologians attempted to go behind the Christ presented in the Gospels to find the real Jesus of history. Such a quest, renewed again and again, proved to be quite fruitless. If the Gospels themselves do not offer us reliable history and records of events — and they are the only records we have of Jesus — then any quest for the "real" Jesus of history is doomed to failure from the start, and we find ourselves caught in the dead end of scepticism. Still scholars persist, by sifting the true from the false in the Gospels, the authentic from the unauthentic, in their hopeless quest; and this because they could not trust the only good source of information they have, the Gospels themselves.

A. Form Criticism Examined

Closely related to the quest for the historical Jesus and also a result of historical criticism is the method, literary in nature, known as form criticism. Form criticism, according to Bultmann, one of the chief practitioners of the method,[14] is the attempt to isolate and analyze the various types of traditional

---

14. See, e.g. "The New Approach to the Synoptic Problem" in *JR* III, (1926), p. 337 ff.

materials dealing with Christ's life and message. These forms, or types, are the following:

a. *Miracle Stories.* These are stock stories taken over from Hellenistic miracle narratives and having the same basic structure throughout.

b. *Apothegms.* These are hero sayings, or controversial utterances, often given in the form of a counter response to a question or in the form of a brief parable. These sayings are mostly unauthentic, according to Bultmann. The context and setting is always fictitious. For instance, the story of the disciples not fasting (Mk. 2:23-26; 7:1-8) was made up by the later church and words put into Jesus' mouth to justify the action of the disciples.

c. *Parabolic Saying.* The parables are often put into different settings by the evangelists and not understood by the evangelists. Most of them cannot be traced back to Jesus and were merely "worked over under the faith of the community." Often the original meaning was utterly changed.

d. *Proverbs.* Such aphorisms, Bultmann says, are not characteristic of Jesus and are therefore the most unauthentic of all.

e. *Apocalyptic Sayings.* These are partly authentic, but usually later additions and supplementations were made.

f. *Legal Sayings.*

One of the obvious results of this form criticism is that we have in the Gospels various levels or strata of material concerning Jesus' life and words, 1. Some of his words recorded are authentic and some of his deeds recorded uncolored by the Easter "experience" of the early Church. 2. The second layer of material was provided by the earliest Palestinian Christian community. These Christians modified the traditions they had received in the light of the Easter "faith." 3. The Hellenistic Christians translated these earlier traditions into Greek, and added new sayings which they erroneously attributed to Jesus, and they reapplied other traditions to new situations. All was done in good faith. 4. The contribution of the evangelists themselves.[15] Now if such conclusions are correct, then the New Testament gives us very little accurate, information about Jesus. And this is exactly the conclusion of Bultmann. We cannot know with certainty that any thing pertaining to Jesus' message is certain, he says. And we know only little about His life. His baptism by John and His crucifixion were no doubt historical, although the accompanying circumstances to these events are the result of mere "pious fancy." This is the case with the weeping women who speak to Jesus when He carries His cross, the death of Judas, the washing of Pilate's hands. These are embellishments to enhance the death of Jesus as a world-transforming catastrophe! Again the resurrection is a fiction composed "under the influence of devout imagination" and it shows "how active the Christian imagination has been." The transfiguration was just another (confused) resurrection narrative. Other pure legends are Jesus' entrance into Jerusalem, Peter's catch of fishes, the miraculous birth of Jesus and the great commission.

---

15. This is one accepted conclusion of the form critics, according to R. Fuller, *The New Testament in Current Study*, New York: Charles Scribner's Sons, 1962, p. 70ff.

Now what about these conclusions which are of course Bultmann's and not those of all form critics? They are quite convincing and consistent, *if* we agree with the assumptions which lie behind form criticism. And what are these assumptions? For Bultmann they are the following:

a. *A Naturalistic World-View.* Bultmann does not believe that the "mythical" cosmology, soteriology, eschatology or sacramentaology of the New Testament are true; these cannot be accepted by modern man with his mastery of the world and his advance in knowledge. Therefore the miracles in the New Testament could not have happened; they must be fictions or borrowings from Hellenistic myths.

b. *An Evolutionary Theory of the Development of Doctrine.* Bultmann (and with him at this point the other form critics) simply take for granted that Scripture contains discrepancies, contradictions (e.g. between the four evangelists) and errors. Without this assumption there could be no form criticism; and we would be back in the precritical days. This means that the theology of Paul and John, for instance, will differ, representing merely their own insights into God, the world, and human existence, insights taken often from their thought world, their culture, but also from foreign cultures. The *possibility* of God directly revealing theology to the evangelists and apostles is perhaps granted by certain practitioners of form criticism, but it is never made a viable hypothesis for understanding and interpreting a text. Thus, we see the inerrancy and the verbal inspiration of Scripture rejected and therefore invalidated as principles to be observed in interpreting scripture.

c. *The Absolutizing of the Historical Method.* It is assumed that the Bible must be read and assessed according to the same canons of historical science as all other writings. This simple postulate of Bultmann's is shared by most of Biblical theology today. Lip service may be paid at times to the so-called "divine side" of Scripture but the historian studies the Bible as a human document arising out of its own cultural and religious climate, not as the Word of God. We must go into this presupposition a little more closely as it is advanced by Bultmann.

Bultmann absolutizes historical science as a principle of hermeneutics. He insists that we must approach Scripture with no dogmatic presupposition.[16] We must not assume Jesus' Messianic self-consciousness. We cannot assume that Matthew and John were Jesus' disciples and therefore basically reliable witnesses of things and events. Any such assumptions must themselves be subjected to historical criticism. For to Bultmann the one great principle of hermeneutics is the historical method. He says, "The one presupposition that cannot be dismissed is *the historical method* of interrogating the text. Indeed, exegesis as the interpretation of historical texts is a part of the science of history."

And what is this historical method of Bultmann's? It is not merely finding the historical background to a text, studying contemporary literature and historical conditions at the time of the writing of the text. No, listen to what

---

16. Cf. Bultmann, *Existence and Faith,* selected and translated by Schubert M. Ogden. New York: Meridian Books, Inc., 1960. From the chapter "Is Exegesis with Presuppositions Possible?" p. 289.

100

he says: "The historical method includes the presupposition that history is a unity in the sense of a closed continuum of effects in which individual events are connected by the succession of cause and effect." He is saying that the historical method assumes a closed universe, outlaws miracles and any divine intervention into our space and time. Listen to him again as he goes on: "This closedness means that the continuum of historical happenings cannot be rent by the interference of the supernatural, transcendent powers and that therefore there is no 'miracle' in this sense of the word." This is indeed quite a hermeneutical principle of Bultmann's. No statement and affirmation of Scripture, no theological doctrine can run against the conclusions of the historian — and the historian cannot believe in supernatural events.

But there is something even more desperate in Bultmann's approach to Scripture. The conclusions of historical science, he says, can never be any more than contingent and probable. And so all Scripture is at the mercy of what can only give contingent and probable answers.

B. Form Criticism Criticized

Now it is easy enough for us to criticize Bultmann and his form criticism and use of the historical method. He has denied the Christian faith. But what about form criticism itself as an example of the historical method? Certainly not all who employ the method go all the way with Bultmann. Here I would like to make several comments by way of criticism.

1. It is a question whether without the three postulates of Bultmann, viz. a) a naturalistic world view, b) a developmental theory of the evolution of doctrine, and c) the insistence that Scripture is in every way like other literature and therefore subject to all the canons of historical science — it is a question whether without these postulates the form critical enterprise could ever have gotten under way. In other words, take away these basic postulates and you have a method with no basis, a superstructure with no foundation. Deny these postulates, and there seems to be little purpose in going behind the Gospels, little purpose in form criticism. And as Christians we must deny these postulates which are destructive of our faith.

2. It might be said that form criticism cannot be harmful since it is only a method (like the scientific method). A method stands for no conclusions, and therefore form criticism need not affect Christian doctrine. Such a view is both naive and contrary to the facts. *First,* a method, as I have just said, can be no better than the presuppositions and postulates which underlie it. The reason we accept the scientific method today is simply because we accept the postulates of induction and empiricism which underlie it. *Second,* the form critical method *as consistently applied to Scripture* has led to the most disastrous results for the Christian faith. On the basis of his critical research Bultmann says,[17] "I do indeed think that we can know almost nothing concerning the life and personality of Jesus, since the early Christian sources show no interest in either, are moreover fragmentary and often legendary; and other sources about Jesus do not exist." His conclusions

17. *Jesus and the Word,* p. 8.

drawn from a rigorous application of the method, are that what we have in the Gospels about Jesus is a totally "fantastic and romantic" picture. Why should any Christian wish to follow a method which will only lead him into scepticism and unbelief?

3. But perhaps Bultmann is typical only of the radical wing of form critics, and it is unfair for me to condemn the method because of his excesses. After all, the method is also employed by humble Christians in a modest way. This may well be. The two great British exponents of the method, C. H. Dodd and Vincent Taylor still wish to hold to the chief doctrines of our Christian faith; they believe in miracles, and they hold that the Gospels can be read as historical documents as well as preachment. Dodd believes, for instance, that historical memory still controlled many stories concerning Christ so that we are presented relatively reliable facts, e.g. the events of Jesus' birth, the flight into Egypt, Judas' betrayal, and of course the resurrection. But the story of the coin in the fishes mouth (Matt. 17:24) is a later accretion. The blind man of Bethsaida, the dumb man of Decapolis and the story of the Gadarene swine are probably not historical (because they are similar to non-Christian popular tales).

Now it might seem that Dodd and other more conservative practitioners of the form critical method have turned Bultmann's historical method against him and used the method to prove the historicity and authenticity of at least many events in Christ's life. But against this more moderate use of the method I would like now to bring three arguments.

a) There is no good reason for Dodd on historical grounds to affirm the probability of the events connected with Christ's birth, for instance, and to deny the probability of some of the lesser miracles of Christ's ministry. There were in the days of Christ many popular tales of miraculous births. Why then should Christ's miraculous birth be authentic according to Dodd's principles? This reveals one of the great weaknesses of form criticism: there are no controls. To deny the actuality of some miracles and not others recorded in Scripture is an arbitrary business. If a method cannot be applied rigorously and consistently, should it be employed at all?

b) The conservative practitioners of form criticism are at least, like Bultmann, elevating historical science above the Scriptures. The German Lutheran, Ernst Kasemann, and others like Dodd, have used the historical method to prove the authenticity of Christ's words and deeds. This seems like a noble apologetic venture until we learn that on this view all sayings of Jesus recorded in the New Testament which reflect the post-Easter situation must be eliminated as unauthentic, as well as all material which can be paralleled in contemporary Judaism. But apart from the rather sterile results of this new approach, we perceive here the huge concession, that the historical method is adequate and capable of verifying with a degree of certainty what the Scriptures affirm, *or discounting what the Scriptures affirm*. Thus the research of man sits in judgment (whether to vindicate or to eliminate) over the witness of spokesmen of God.

And this leads to my third argument against the "moderate" use of form criticism.

c) There is at least one Bultmannian presupposition present with every form critic. It is that the Gospels, and indeed all of Scripture, do not offer us straight history, but rather preachment, doctrine, kerygma, propaganda. The argument then goes: since the Gospels are not strict chronicles of events, since they do not offer us a strict biography of Jesus, they are therefore not interested in history as such. And *therefore* the events of Jesus' life recorded therein may not have happened at all, but may merely be later interpretations, accretion, supplementation by the early Church. And it is the task of the interpreter to separate the event from the later interpretation. Let me offer an example of this position as it is presented in American Lutheran circles. Dr. Warren Quanbeck says:[18]

> The four Gospels, then are liturgical and propaganda materials of a missionary movement. This is not to say that they have no historical value, but that any use of them by the biographer or historian should be in the light of their special purpose *in the life of the Christian community* [my emphasis. Note "in the life of the Christian community," not ("in the life of the author, the evangelist, the eye-witness.") The implication is that the Gospels are the product of the Christian community, not of inspired evangelists.] . . . There are three levels of material in the Gospels. Part of it goes back to Jesus himself; part of it has been modified by the special interests and concerns of the early Christian community [sic] and a third part is contributed by the evangelist himself in his selection, arrangement, and editing of the materials. It is frequently fairly easy to identify the editorial work of the evangelist, but more difficult to distinguish between the words of Jesus and the form given to them in the preaching and worship life of the Churches. The Gospels do not confront us as books fallen from heaven, every word of equal authority and every word binding in a legal sense [notice the irrelevant thesis here]. The Gospels have developed in history and show the marks of their development.

If this position of Prof. Quanbeck appears to be relatively innocent and innocuous, let us see how the position works out in the practice as another ALC professor, Wilfred Bunge of Luther College, applies the principle.[19] After mouthing the usual introductory formulas of the form critics, that the New Testament was written in this world by real people, that it must be read in terms of its own day, that the Gospels are not "straightforward records of the life and teachings of Jesus," Prof. Bunge gets down to cases of specific application of the form critical method. Let me just mention a couple of examples of application which ought to make your hair stand on end. The "tradition" concerning the baptism of Jesus as reported in Mark 1:9-11 which speaks of the opening of the heavens, the descent of the Spirit and the voice from heaven, does not present objective events at all. But it is all a matter of theological "interpretation." "Those present saw Jesus baptized by John in the same way that many others were baptized by John. But the Church, as it

---

18. "Stewardship in the Teachings of Jesus" in *Stewardship in Contemporary Theology*, ed. T. K. Thompson. New York: Association Press, 1960, pp. 39-40.
19. See *Theological Perspectives, op. cit.* pp. 34-39.

looked back on this event after the death and resurrection of Jesus interpreted the event theologically." Another example. Mark 1:12-13 relates the temptation of Jesus. But "that the Spirit drove him into the wilderness, that he was tempted by Satan, and that the angel ministered to him — these are all theological interpretations." These things never really happened. Such examples illustrate where those wind up who would be even "conservative" exponents of the form critical method. At this rate why should the resurrection of our Lord not be a matter of interpretation and no objective event at all?

Now in the case of this young man at least all his excesses seem to result from his taking over uncritically just one of Bultmann's assumptions, viz. that our Gospels come from an anonymous primitive community which had no historical interests. I would now like to attack this gratuitous assumption which seems so prevalent today.

First of all, the early Christian community which is supposed to have given rise to the Gospels, is not anonymous, but it is well known to us through the witness of the apostles who were eyewitnesses of the life of Jesus and were leaders in the community. Peter repeatedly preaches and speaks as a representative and head of the apostolic group and the community (Acts 2:14-40; 3:12 ff.; 4:8-12; 5:29). At an early date Peter and John as apostles go to inspect the young churches, the communities (Acts 8:14-17). Later Barnabas does the same in Antioch. One simply cannot speak of a primitive Christianity apart from the guidance of the apostles.

Second, the evangelists and apostles were interested in history. Obviously they did not write history as it is written today. But their intent was to report faithfully the deeds and words of Jesus, historical facts. Again and again they refer to themselves as witnesses, witnesses of the events of the life of Jesus (Acts 1:22; 2:32; 3:15; 5:32; 10:39; 22:15; I Pet. 5:1; II Pet. 1: 16 ff.). And Jesus had said, "Ye shall be my witnesses" (Acts 1:8; Luke 24:48). And the apostles represent their message as *true* witness. John concludes his Gospel with the words, "This is the disciple which testifieth of these things and wrote these things: and we know that his testimony is true" (John 21:24). Of course, the evangelists were creative (they schematize, they do not offer us the *ipsissima verba* of Jesus, they adapt their message to their readers, etc., etc.). Of course they have a dogmatic bias. Who would not when he had seen the risen Christ? Of course, they were believing Christians and not merely objective historians. But faith and history do not oppose each other. How can one report a historical event if he does not believe it? And profound interpretation does not vitiate or cast doubt upon the reality and historicity of the event interpreted. A religious aim may well influence the presentation of facts, but this does not change the facts themselves. There is nothing wrong with facts being explained by one who has experienced them and been deeply affected by them.

The idea that the early Christian community and the evangelists were uninterested in history is a myth, concocted by men who have lost confidence in the authority of the New Testament witness to Christ. It is interesting to note that the latest scholarship has shown that the Jews of the Old Testament, like the evangelists and the people around them, had a keen interest in history. Donald Wiseman, Orientalist at the University of London and the British Museum, maintains that the early narratives of Genesis are to be considered "historical," even in a modern sense of the term up to the period of the Hellenistic historians and their successors."[20]

d. And this leads to my fourth argument against form criticism. It is difficult to see how the form critical program can be made compatible with the *sola scriptura* principle. The prime purpose of the program is to get behind the Gospels in order to know more certainly about the activity and message of Jesus. Thus the presentation in the gospels is assumed to be somehow unreliable, or at best unauthentic. This is certainly a debasement of Scripture as the *only* rule and norm of faith and life, as carrying with it in its very words God's authority.

The form critics are for the most part the first to agree with what I have just said that their method is not compatible with the old Lutheran *sola scriptura* principle or with the verbal inspiration and inerrancy of the Scriptures. They can see that to speak of the contents of the Gospels in terms of layers, levels, strata, erosion, distillation, reconstruction, conflation, supplementation, accretion, etc. does not leave much authority to the Gospels as such and is hardly conducive of confirming one in the old orthodox view of the Bible. R. H. Lightfoot speaks for the form critics when he says,[21] "So long as the view of inspiration prevailed, the four gospels could only be regarded as of equal value, historically and otherwise. It chanced, however, that just as their belief began to crumble, the discovery was made that one among the four gospels was quite definitely on a superior historical level . . . and the discovery that there were good grounds for finding in St. Mark a chief authority for the gospel of St. Matthew and St. Luke gave birth to the hope that in St. Mark's Gospel above all we might hope to discover the Jesus of History." It would appear, according to Lightfoot's implication, that only when one abandons the inspiration of Scripture can he become a full-fledged form critic.

But what about Lutheran form critics today who are also committed to the Lutheran Confessions and the absolute authority of Scripture? What do they do with their obvious predicament? I do not know what is being done in our Missouri Synod. Those who are enamored with form criticism either do not write on the subject or write in rather guarded language. For instance, in a recent *American Lutheran* article it is asserted that in the New Testament there is a "rich variety of theological systems and viewpoints," and this even within one Gospel, like Luke. There are also "several theologies" of the Lord's Supper, it is alleged. But all of this is said only to argue Lutherans into unionistic fellowship with those who have a different doctrinal position and hardly tells us much about the author's form criticism and how he would relate it to the authority of Scripture.[22]

---

20. See "Archaeology and Scripture," paper read at Boston Seminar. June 21. 1966, p. 14. Cf. Passim.
21. *History and Interpretation in the Gospels,* pp. 10, 12.
22. R. J. Gotsch, "New Testament Theology and Church Unity," *American Lutheran,* XLVIII (December 1965), p. 13 ff.

However, outside our circles Lutherans have been less circumspect, and seem for the most part to have taken two courses.

The *first* course of action is for the Lutheran form critic simply to ignore the authority of Scripture as he applies his method. If the New Testament contains mistakes and errors, it is simply up to the historian to get to the bottom of things as best he can. I suppose the only authority which might be ascribed to Scripture in this case would be the authority of the oldest extant documents containing traditions concerning Christ. Let me offer one example of this course of action by Prof. Bunge.[23] Commenting on Acts 15:28-29, he says:

> It may very well be that some members of the church in Jerusalem did decide upon certain food law requirements for the Gentile Christians, and that Luke did not simply invent this letter which was to be sent to the Gentile churches. However, Luke is definitely wrong in saying that Paul agreed to these requirements. Here Luke's interest in the harmonious development of the early church apparently led him to smooth over a serious difference of opinion within the church.

And then Prof. Bunge tells us that the historico-critical method must be used in discerning what really did happen.

The *second* course of action for the Lutheran form critic is to re-define the authority of Scripture in a way which makes it somehow compatible with form criticism. This rather popular course is that of Prof. Quanbeck. He says:[24]

> The authority of the Gospels does not lie in the stratum which can somehow be demonstrated to be original, a sort of red-letter edition of the words and works of Jesus, from which they take their name — the *gospel*. It resides in the message which they bring, and from which they take their name — the *gospel*. It is the gospel which is authoritative as it communicates the good news of what God has done in Christ for us. Had we in our possession one indubitably genuine stenographic transcription of the words of Jesus, say on the subject of house construction, it would have no binding force upon modern housing contractors nor be much more than a curiosity to the church. The church is the community called into being by the gospel, and it is the gospel in the Gospels which is authoritative, with an authority not of a law code but of the personal God who addresses us in it.

Now Prof. Quanbeck has not said a thing about the authority of Scripture (*sola scriptura*) or the New Testament in the traditional sense of our Lutheran Confessions, he has not said a thing about Scripture as the one source and norm by which all teachings and teachers in the Church must be judged. Rather he has spoken of the transforming power of the Gospel in the life of the Church, a power which resides in any evangelical sermon or hymn, a power which could be active in the Church even if there were no Bible present. And this he calls the authority of the Gospels. The absolute authority (*autopistia*) of Scripture, that all Scripture is worthy of our acceptance

---

23. *Op. cit.*, p. 42.
24. *Op. cit.*, p. 40.

simply because it is a *Scriptura divinia,* that whatever Scripture asserts God asserts and should be believed — this position which was so fundamental to our Confessions as they read and apply the Scriptures is jettisoned by the new definition, or at best ignored.

And so my brief criticisms of modern historicism as it applies to the form critical method comes to an end. One can easily perceive that few of the fundamental assumptions and norms of the old Lutheran hermeneutics will stand when this new method is put into operation. But most important of all: the inspiration, authority and inerrancy of Scripture cannot be made to harmonize with the method. I have never found a Lutheran who has even tried to harmonize our Confessional high view of Scripture with the form critical method. This should indicate that the popular hermeneutical approaches to our day present a rather dark picture to those of us who wish to remain loyal to the Lutheran Symbols and their reading of the Scriptures.

But an even more dismal picture emerges now as we proceed to study and describe two specific new and popular approaches to the interpreting of Scripture: a) demythologization, and b) Midrash.

IV. New Approaches to the Interpreting of Scripture

A. Demythologization and Biblical Interpretation

By far the most devastating hermeneutical approach to our time to the New Testament is the demythologization program of Rudolf Bultmann. This program begins for Bultmann with modern man and his inability to accept the world view and events recorded in Scripture and with Bultmann's attempt, apologetic in nature, to preach to modern man what he thinks is palatable and still valuable in the New Testament. Let me quote him rather at length as he describes the problem and his enterprise, for his position seems quite clear:[25]

> The cosmology of the New Testament is essentially mythical in character. The world is viewed as a three-storied structure, with the earth in the centre, the heaven above, and the underworld beneath. Heaven is the abode of God and of celestial beings — the angels. The underworld is hell, the place of torment. Even the earth is more than the scene of natural, everyday events, of the trivial round and common task. It is the scene of the supernatural activity of God and his angels on one hand, and of Satan and his daemons on the other. These supernatural forces intervene in the course of nature and in all that men think and will and do. Miracles are by no means rare. Man is not in control of his own life. Evil spirits may take possession of him. Satan may inspire him with evil thoughts. Alternatively, God may inspire his thought and guide his purposes. He may grant him heavenly visions. He may allow him to hear his word of succour or demand. He may give him the supernatural power of his Spirit. History does not follow a smooth unbroken course; it is set in motion and controlled by these supernatural powers. This aeon is held in bondage by Satan, sin, and death (for

---

25. Hans Werner Bartsch, ed. *Kerygma and Myth,* tr. Reginald H. Fuller (New York: The Macmillan Company, 1957), p. 4 ff.

"powers" is precisely what they are), and hastens toward its end. That end will come very soon, and will take the form of a cosmic catastrophe. It will be inaugurated by the "woes" of the last time. Then the Judge will come from heaven, the dead will rise, the last judgment will take place, and men will enter into eternal salvation or damnation.

This then is the mythical view of the world which the New Testament presupposes when it presents the event of redemption which is the subject of its preaching.

All this is the language of mythology, and the origin of the various themes can be easily traced in the contemporary mythology of Jewish Apocalyptic and in the redemption myths of Gnosticism. To this extent *the kerygma is incredible to modern man, for he is convinced that the mythical view of the world is obsolete.* We are therefore bound to ask whether, when we preach the Gospel today, we expect our converts to accept not only the Gospel message but also the mythical setting?

Bultmann's answer to this question is a resounding no. Listen to him as he goes on to make himself more clear.

The only honest way of reciting the creeds is to strip the mythological frame work from the truth they enshrine — that is, assuming that they contain any truth at all which is just the question that theology has to ask. No one who is old enough to think for himself supposes that God lives in a local heaven. There is no longer any heaven in the traditional sense of the word. The same applies to hell in the sense of a mythical underworld beneath our feet. And if this is so, we can no longer accept the story of Christ's descent into hell or his Ascension into heaven as literally true. We can no longer look for the return of the Son of Man on the clouds of heaven or hope that the faithful will meet him in the air (I Thess. 1:15 ff.). . . .

The mythical eschatology is untenable for the simple reason that the parousia of Christ never took place as the New Testament expected. . . .

The same objections [that it is incomprehensible and abhorrent] apply to the *doctrine of the atonement.* How can the guilt of one man be expiated by the death of another who is sinless — if indeed one may speak of a sinless man at all? What primitive notions of guilt and righteousness does this imply? And what primitive idea of God? The rationale of sacrifice in general may of course throw some light on the theory of the atonement, but even so, what a primitive mythology it is, that a divine Being should become incarnate, and atone for the sins of men through his own blood! . . . Moreover, if the Christ who died such a death was the pre-existent Son of God what could death mean to him? Obviously very little, if he knew that he would rise again in three days! . . .

The *resurrection of Jesus* is just as difficult if it means an event whereby a supernatural power is released which can henceforth be appropriated though the sacraments . . . Quite apart from the incredibility of such a miracle, he [modern man] cannot see how an event like this could be the act of God or how it could affect his whole life.

Such a long citation suffices to show what Bultmann's position is and just what needs to be demythologized according to his program. Apart from a good deal of crass caricature as to what the New Testament really teaches, one is struck by Bultmann's frankness and honesty — and by the consistency of his position. "The mythical view of the world must be accepted or rejected in its entirety," he says. Everything offensive to modern man must be stripped away.

And what is left for us to preach? What is the kerygma which we can sift from all this mythology and offer modern man? By the message of Christ's death and resurrection (which did not happen objectively) we can offer modern man a better understanding of himself. Modern man can now somehow be enabled to put off the old unauthentic existence and live authentically.

It is no wonder that Bultmann's many critics have repeatedly accused him of stripping away the entire message of the New Testament. Nothing more remains. He has demythologized Christianity completely.

Now it is not my purpose here to criticize Bultmann's entire program of demythologization together with its ethereal existentialistic basis. His inadequate understanding of modern man, his false conception of myth, his misuse of the historical method to serve scepticism — these gross faults have all been clearly pointed out by his critics.[26] What I would like to point out is that his program which fits tongue in groove with the radical historicism of the form critical enterprise actually *contradicts all traditional hermeneutics at every point*. Beginning with the premise that Scripture is filled with myths, inaccuracies, conflicting theologies, outright contradictions and palpable errors, Bultmann is incapable of adhering to any of the hermeneutical principles of Lutheranism or historical Christianity. e.g. the divine origin of Scripture, the authority of Scripture, the unity of Scripture, the analogy of Scripture, the clarity of Scripture. But most remarkable is that Bultmann is no longer interested as an exegete in *finding the literal sense* of Scripture, the plain meaning intended by the writers. What John or Matthew or Paul *intended* to present as fact is erroneous, myth. And this cannot be taken seriously. The modern exegete must demythologize. What is this if it is not some sort of new allegorical method, a new esoteric, spiritualized exegesis? Thus Bultmann has undermined the entire exegetical enterprise as it has been understood since the time of the Reformation.

Let us make this point crystal clear, Biblical exegesis like all other literary criticism, seeks to find meaning in literature by discerning the literary form, or genre, indicated and intended by the author of the text under study. Now, the intended genre of the apostolic writings as they witness to God and His activity among men is *ex professo* not mythology. But Bultmann insists that it is. Refusing to read these writings as they were meant to be read and finding a new existential meaning which is not in the text, Bultmann turns the New Testament into a waxen nose and makes a shambles of all legitimate literary analysis.

There is, I believe, a most important lesson to be learned here, a lesson

---

26. We might just refer to one excellent analysis by Hermann Sasse, "The Impact of Bultmannism on American Lutheranism, with Special Reference to His Demythologization of the New Testament," *Lutheran Synod Quarterly*, V, 4 (June, 1965), pp. 10-12 *passim*.

which could also be learned from the example of the modern approach to our Gen. 1-3 pericope. When one has abandoned the high doctrine of the infallibility of Scripture and no longer believes Scripture to be reliable in its claims and assertions, then the quest for the genuine, literal sense of Scripture, is no longer so important. For if there are errors in Scripture, then the interpreter will wish somehow to avoid the implications of the literal sense of Scripture and find a "new" meaning which will be more congenial to his world view or more "relevant" to his day.

Believing in the authority of the Bible means that we not only seek and find the intended, literal sense of Scripture, but also that we accept it.

If Bultmann is the father of the notorious demythologizing enterprise, he is not the only theologian to find myths in Scripture, and thus to impose interpretations upon Scripture which are external to the text. We might mention here the example of Millar Burrows, prime mover in the translation of the RSV. Operating on the assumption that verbal inspiration is impossible, that the inerrancy of the Bible must be left behind, that the Bible is filled with errors and contradictions, and that we must decide what in the Bible is true and false,[27] Dr. Burrows has the following to say about specific stories in the Bible, their genre, truthfulness and authenticity. Both Old and New Testament are filled with myths, he says. The creation, the Fall and the flood are myths. The miracles are legendary. The angels and Satan are myths. We cannot tell if the patriarchs really lived or if they are legendary. Job, Ruth, Jonah, Esther, Daniel are fiction. Micah is a forgery. There is much myth in Paul's theology and that of his contemporaries. The idea "Son of God" is a mythical idea which does not mean that Jesus is the Son of God anyway.

Now it is safe to say that Dr. Burrows *knows* that in every case he is running counter to the clear *intent* of the periscopes under consideration. But like Bultmann, he is not interested in the basic task of traditional Christian exegesis, finding the plain, genuine meaning of the text.

What is the result of reading Scripture in this fashion, of interpreting every supernatural event recorded therein as myth? Well, to say the least, Christianity is stripped of its roots in history, becomes, to cite a term of Nils Dahl's,[28] a sort of "kerygma-theological Docetism," representing no more than human insights into God or human existence. It is little wonder that the next step in hermeneutics which we are now encountering is the so-called "New Hermeneutic" of Fuchs and Ebeling whereby the exegete no longer interprets the Word of Scripture, but is in a sense himself interpreted by the Word, thus eliminating the possibility of all objective Biblical hermeneutics.[29]

---

27. For what follows see Millar Burrows, *An Outline of Biblical Theology.* (Philadelphia: The Westminster Press, 1946), pp. 24 ff.; 113 ff.
28. See his chapter "The Problem of the Historical Jesus" in *Kerygma and History,* tr. and ed. by Carl E. Braaten and Roy A. Harrisville, (Nashville: Abingdon Press, 1962), p. 161.
29. For a good analysis of the "New Hermeneutic," its obscurity, its lack of objectivity, its making the text of Scripture say what we want it to say, see John Montgomery, "Lutheran Hermeneutics and Hermeneutics Today," in *Aspects of Biblical Hermeneutics,* p. 82 ff.

And what is the result in practice? Well, as one honest German pastor said, who can preach on myths, specially at Christmas and Easter time?

B. Midrash and Biblical Interpretation

A rather common view today is that the Old and New Testaments present certain stories in the literary form of midrash. Midrash among the Rabbis during the period of normative Judaism after Christ was merely the (often quite fanciful) interpretation and application of a certain Biblical narrative to illustrate a definite point. Sometimes the Biblical story would be mixed with pure fiction. Something rather like this is suggested by modern commentators as they interpret this New Testament. In other words, they say that the Biblical author sometimes made up stories to stress a certain point. Let me offer a couple of examples of this.

C. S. Mann[30] believes that the Birth Narrative of Jesus has this form. These are his conclusions, arrived at as a result of a number of prioris. 1) The virgin birth is not a part of the original apostolic message. Matthew and Luke were written late (note the form critical conclusions at work); and no doubt they are merely employing similar stories of that day which stress divine paternity of important figures in history (Romulus, Sargon, Cyrus, Plato, etc.). Note the presupposition also concerning the evolution of Biblical theology, borrowing, etc. 2) The star, or planet, was also often said in those days to herald an important birth, e.g. Mithridates, Alexander Severus, et al. Murders and the slaughter of infants were also in the folklore of those days common concomitants to the birth of a celebrated person (no evidence is given of this). 3) Matthew was so intent upon tying up the birth of Jesus with the Old Testament details and figures that he spends little time on the most central points of the birth event. This indicates his purpose — and I quote Mann at this point: "The acceptance of Mary of her vocation to be the mother of the designated Messiah links the whole nativity story in Matthew with the demands of God for obedient faith under the Old Dispensation." It is as easy as that. Mann's conclusion is the following: "It is hardly possible to avoid the conclusion that Matthew's account of the visit of the magi to Bethlehem was *meant to be read* as a parable." He then offers additional evidence for his thesis. 1) Josephus does not tell us of the massacre. And he would have ordinarily told us. 2) The details of the magi-saga are common stock in the legendary literature of that day. 3) The magi were not priests, but dealers in black magic, omens and soothsaying — a terrifying occupation in those days. Matthew's point, then, in telling this story is that with the coming of Christ all such sinister work is shattered and demolished. Thus the story has nothing to do with Christ's manifestation to the heathens. Like the book of Jonah, it is pure parable.

One cannot fail to see the arbitrary and speculative nature of such conclusions. The story just couldn't have happened as Matthew tells it. There-

---

30. "The Historicity of the Birth Narratives," in *Historicity and Chronology in the New Testament* (London, 1965).

fore we assume, according to the presupposition of development, that all the major points *must* have been borrowed: the virgin birth, the magi, the star, etc. Once again, Matthew and Luke are considered to be artists rather than witnesses (e.g. Luke takes the entire birth story from I Sam. — the Benedictus and the Magnificat). And it is anybody's guess what an artist who can fabricate at any point has added and what he has not, — and what he really has in mind.

Another scholar who finds midrash in the New Testament is Robert Grant.[31] In I Cor. 10:1 ff. Paul says that the Israelites of the Old Testament all drank of the spiritual Rock that followed them, and that Rock was Christ. Grant says that Paul here is alluding to the three times that a miraculous gift of water was given the Israelites from a rock during their wandering in the wilderness (Ex. 17; Num. 20 and Num. 21:6 ff.), and he says that Paul is giving these stories a Christian interpretation. An old Hebrew midrash has it that the very same rock followed the Israelites and many times gave them water. Paul is following this midrash arbitrarily and innocently following rabbinic interpretation.

Now in reply to such fanciful exegesis we can say the following: There is no evidence that Paul has an old midrash in mind at all, or that he ever followed Jewish midrashim (which can first be traced only to a time later than Paul). Paul is not implying that some rock followed the Israelites in the wilderness. Rather he is using an analogy: just as the Israelites drank water from that rock in the wilderness, they also drank spiritually from a spiritual rock which came after them, viz. Christ. The rock in the Old Testament is a type of Christ. Grant assumes that when there is some similarity between Paul's use of an Old Testament story and that of the Rabbis, Paul is copying. He seems more interested in trying to account for Paul's exegesis than in what Paul is saying.

May I make the following comments concerning the two examples of midrash or parabolic interpretation. There seems again to be not sufficient interest in the genuine, literal meaning of the text of Scripture. It is not so much the question of what does the text say; as to why was it said; what was the origin of the idea, etc.? The possibility that what Matthew and Paul say is the result of a revelation from God, that they speak as witnesses of real events, does not occur to these exegetes. No, the exegete must account for the story being told as it is. This attempt to discern the motives and psychology of the Biblical writer can really end up almost anywhere, and obscurity is bound to be cast upon a text which might otherwise be quite clear. We have seen this in the case of much modern exegesis of the creation and Fall accounts.

It is interesting to compare Mann and Grant with Bultmann. In the case of Bultmann the New Testament authors mean well but are limited by their day and thus mistaken. In the case of Mann and Grant the New Testament authors have a definite tendenz and manipulate facts for the sake of a higher purpose. The traditional understanding of the inerrancy of Scripture was that the Biblical writers were not deceived and did not de-

---

31. *The Bible in the Church*, pp. 22-23.

ceive others, but are reliable witnesses of the facts they tell. Bultmann denies the former aspect of inerrancy; Mann and Grant deny the latter; and all deny that the New Testament writers are reliable witnesses of real events.

V. Conclusion

I suppose that many of you feel by now that I have painted a terribly dark picture of modern hermeneutics. But I believe the picture is just this dark. This does not mean to deny that there is a great and increasing number of first rate exegetes in our Synod and outside who read the Sacred Scriptures from the posture of our Confessional Lutheran hermeneutics and with complete confidence in the authority of the Word. We all know this to be true. And it is most gratifying to see so much solid Biblical study offered by such evangelical scholars. But for me to have dwelt on the hermeneutic of these evangelical theologians who are following the old paths would have been to repeat what was said in the former part of my paper, and this was not my assignment.

So allow me to try to make some cogent and edifying remarks by way of analysis and conclusion to all the foregoing.

From all that has now been said one definite conclusion should now be quite clear: poor and sloppy hermeneutics is very often the result of a poor attitude toward the sacred Scriptures. I think that many theologians have failed to see this. They wish to follow some scholar's newest hermeneutical hypothesis or ride the newest exegetical hobby-horse. And they do not or they wish not to see that a low, sub-Christian view of Scripture underlies this. Naively and mistakenly they suppose that they can believe that Scripture is the Word of God but treat it as merely the word of man. This, I believe, is particularly true in our circles where the strictest view of Biblical authority has always been maintained and such terms as "verbal inspiration" and "inerrancy" have virtually become shibboleths.

However, a number of younger Lutheran theologians in our country have seen the close relation between bibliology and hermeneutics. They perceive that the doctrines of Biblical inspiration and inerrancy must be utterly rejected, if they are to read Scripture with the degree of elbow room and freedom which the newer hermeneutics dictates. For this reason men in rather conservative Lutheran circles are now in increasing numbers leveling attacks against the inspiration and inerrancy of Scripture.

These often bitter attacks are usually two pronged, consisting A) of a caricature of the orthodox position, and B) of irrelevant or specious arguments for the non-inspiration and errancy of Scripture. Let me give some examples of this, and you will readily see how hermeneutics plays a part also here.

A. Typical Misrepresentations of the Inspiration and Inerrancy of Scripture

1) *The old doctrine of verbal inspiration is a mechanical dictation theory which dehumanizes the writers of Scripture and does not allow for the many obviously human features of the biblical writings.*

This old stock argument which is supposedly based on sensitive hermeneu-

113

tics is advanced in a most blunt but typical form by Werner Elert.[32] In a discussion entitled, "The Inadequancy of the Inspiration Doctrine," after conjecturing without any basis that the Lutheran doctrine was borrowed from Calvin and Trent (of all things), Elert contends that the classic Lutheran doctrine of inspiration is unable to explain Paul's forgetfulness in I Cor. 1:16, his distinction between his own command and the command of the Lord (I Cor. 7:12), and his reference to his own personal judgment (I Cor. 7:40). Nor is the old Lutheran doctrine compatible with the fact that Luke investigated sources before writing his Gospel (Luke 1:3). And all because it was a theory of dictation which, Elert says, borders on blasphemy. Now, such a charge is utterly unfounded. The old Lutheran doctrine of inspiration was set forth with a clarity which defies misunderstanding; and the doctrine stated that the Holy Spirit used all the endowments and peculiarities of the writers (yes, even forgetfulness) as He inspired them to write.

2) *The doctrine of verbal inspiration and inerrancy is an a priori, an unfounded assumption that God's Word must possess such and such a character; it is not the result of exegesis, but a postulate imposed upon Scripture.*

This is the allegation of another young ALC theologian, Gerhard Forde.[33] Prof. Forde's charge is as unfounded as Elert's. What orthodox Lutheran theologian ever treated Scripture in such a cavalier fashion as Prof. Forde describes? Certainly the myriads of theologians through the centuries who called Scripture inspired and infallible did not say so just because they assumed that thus it must be. Rather they went to the Scriptures as committed Christians to see what the Scriptures said about themselves. And they found their answer. God speaks to man in the Scriptures, through His inspired spokesmen prophets and apostles who are His men, under His control, and who as witnesses through whom He speaks tell the truth always, just as God has commanded all men to do when speaking in His name (Rom. 9:1; II Cor. 11:31; Gal. 1:20; I Tim. 2:7; John 21:24; I John 1:1-5a; II Pet. 1:15-18).

3) *Inerrancy means that the Scriptures describe all things with absolute precision.* This is the position of Dr. Robert Scharlemann,[34] and therefore he feels called upon to reject the doctrine of inerrancy. He points out the reverse order of the Greek word *houtos* in the three accounts of the inscription on the cross of our Lord (Luke 23:28 has it last and Matt. 27:37 has it first), and his conclusion is that either Matthew or Luke is in error. This seems to be the most desperate caricature of all. Again the theologians professing belief in the inerrancy of Scripture have been aware of the different formulations of the words on the cross and still felt confidence in the veracity of Scripture. St. Augustine pointed out, when discussing such

32. Werner Elert, *Der Christliche Glaube*, Berlin, 1940, p. 169 ff.
33. See *Theological Perspectives*, p. 50 ff. A similar view is propounded by Rev. Robert Hoyer (*The Cresset* [October, 1965], p. 18). He claims that our doctrine of an inerrant, verbally inspired Bible is the result of our yen to have an absolutely certain foundation for our faith. But the doctrine of an errorless Bible is impracticable, he says, because we, the readers of Scripture, err anyway.
34. *The Lutheran Scholar*, XX, 2 (April, 1963) p. 36.

problems between the Synoptic Gospels (if they are problems at all), that it is *what* was said or written that the evangelists preserve for us, *not the exact words* (which in this case were written in three different languages).[35] If a sign said "No Smoking" and my three-year-old daughter asked me what it said, and I replied, "It says 'Don't Smoke'," I should hardly think anyone would want to accuse me of error. Why should anyone wish to demand such impossibly stringent requirements of the Scriptures before he will grant that their witness is true? Such a conviction would seem to be the result of reading Scripture in a fundamentalistic, atomistic way.

B. Typical Arguments for the Non-Inspiration and Errancy of Scripture

1) *Scripture is written in human language. Human language is relative and therefore fallible.* This is the a priori hermeneutical assumption of Warren Quanbeck that "since human language is always relative, being conditioned by its historical development and usage, there can be no absolute expression of the truth even in the language of theology. Truth is made known in Jesus Christ, who is God's Word, his address to mankind. Christ is the only absolute."[36] The editors of *Dialog* magaine echo the same sentiments in even more dogmatic form:[37] "This voice [of the Gospel] is a human voice and therefore liable to err." The alternative to this position which is the doctrine of inerrancy is to "deify" Scripture according to these theologians, and to "prohibit treating it as a book." I think it is safe to say that the sort of emotional and irrational *non sequitur* and irrelevant thesis manifested by such argument is hardly the result of the study of language or of sensitive hermeneutical insight.

2) *The Bible is not interested in objective history, accuracy of presentation; therefore, we must expect to find errors present.* We have already heard this argument, and have shown that the major premise is quite false. The Bible is most interested in history, and accuracy of presentation.

A corollary of this argument is advanced by Prof. Forde. He says the Bible is inspired only by reason of its content; and so our preaching would be inspired for the same reason. According to this view, errors just don't matter. The theory (purely a priori in nature) is that all errors in Scripture must be small ones. And how do we know that the errors are only small ones? By faith, born of the Law-Gospel experience. But such an esoteric answer to such an important question is both arbitrary and silly. Silly, because the facts and teachings presented in Scripture are, for the most part, interconnected, like the stones of a building. If one or another stone is removed, the entire edifice begins to shake. Dr. Forde has failed to see the unity of Scripture and the fundamental importance of this hermeneutical principle.

3) *Revelation is not propositional in form, it is not dianoetic and informative; it is rather God Himself confronting us, and this alone is truth, not*

---

35. *De consensu evangelistarum*, 2, 66 (*PL* 34, 1139).
36. *Theology in the Life of the Church*, ed. Robert W. Bertram (Philadelphia: Fortress Press, 1963), p. 25.
37. *Dialog*, 2, Autumn, p. 272.

the propositions of Scripture. Since God's revelation is personal confrontation, we do not need an inerrant Scripture. This . view which can be traced directly to the *Schwaermerei* of Karl Barth is taken over by a number of young Lutheran theologians. For instance, the editors of *Dialog* magazine, after calling the orthodox view of Biblical inerrancy "pagan," argue, that Christ is absolute truth (they never bother to explain what in the world this means), all ideas or statements in reference to Him can only be relatively true, i.e. probable and liable to error. Listen to the argument:

> For faith, Jesus Christ, a *person,* and the event in which He confronts us [this is the neo-orthodox, Barthian idea of revelation], is absolute truth. Therefore [sic], absolute truth can never be predicated of our ideas, because we are not Jesus Christ, and because, if absolute truth is personal, then it is not predicated of *ideas* at all. If *Jesus Christ* is the Truth, then all idea truths, even theological propositions read straight from the Bible, are only relatively true.[38]

Now what is being said here? Obviously the infallibility of Scripture is being rejected, and it appears that some sort of substitute position is being offered. But actually what we have here are a series of unverified declamations, unexplained definitions and undefined terms which are quite without meaning. What is meant by "absolute truth"? How does this differ from just plain truth? In what sense is Christ, who is a person, and the event in which He confronts us, truth? What is the relation of such a "truth" to the truth of assertions about Christ? And why, if Christ, the person, is called absolute truth, should all statements in Scripture about Him be necessarily only relatively true, i.e. probable and fallible? Take such statements as "God is Love," (I John 4:8) or "Christ Jesus came into the world to save sinners" (I Tim. 1:15). In what sense is the *truth* of such statements relative? And finally, how do we know that Christ and His event in our life is absolute truth, if all ideas and affirmations about Him in Scripture are only relative?

Harris Kassa, Professor at Luther College, tries to create a climate of prestige for this unintelligible existentialistic jargon by linking it with Luther.[39] It was only later during the period of orthodoxy, he says, that Lutheranism lapsed into a "fateful and fundamental" legalism by holding to a "nomistic-intellectualistic" conception of revelation and teaching the inerrancy of Scripture. It is the tragedy of Midwest Lutheranism, living in a foreign-language ghetto, that it repristinated the doctrine of the absolute inerrancy of Scripture. But now, says Prof. Kassa, we are emancipated from this by a rediscovery of Luther's dynamic concept of revelation. Poor Luther! The greatest antagonist against the *Schwaermer* has now become one of them, teaching a doctrine of non-objective, non-verbal, non-doctrinal, non-cognitive revelation. But Prof. Kassa is right on one point. If God's revelation to man is nothing more than a divine-human confrontation without the imparting of information, then there is indeed no need for an inerrant Scripture — or of serious hermeneutics either.

---

38. *Dialog,* 2, Winter, p. 7.
39. *Theological Perspectives,* p. 15 ff.

4) *The Lutheran Law-Gospel approach to theology is opposed to the verbal inspiration and inerrancy of Scripture.* This is again the contention of Prof. Forde.[40] He insists that we preach Law and Gospel to make people Christians and do not appeal to the inspiration of Scripture (the Law-Gospel method as opposed to the verbal inspiration method). Such an argument seems to lack all cogency. Of course I have never begun with the inspiration of Scripture when talking with an unbeliever and trying to convert him. But surely the inspiration and truthfulness of Scripture is not thereby vitiated or rendered unimportant. Christians did not invent the theory of inspiration to support Christianity, as Forde implies. Rather all have arrived at the doctrine of inspiration in the same way as they arrived at every other article of faith, by drawing it from Scripture itself.

Now what shall we say by way of comment to these sundry attacks against the orthodox doctrine concerning the sacred Scriptures and what has all this to do with modern developments in hermeneutics?

Certainly one of the remarkable aspects of what I have just attempted to describe is the zeal, acrimony and unfairness with which the enemies of verbal inspiration and Biblical inerrancy attack these doctrines. If these doctrines are so out of date, so legalistic, so contrary to facts, why the endless barrage of arguments against them? And why are the doctrines in almost every case caricatured and misrepresented? If they are so patently untenable, why not represent them fairly and correctly when repudiating them, and be done with it?

I think we can answer these questions by saying that there are still a great many Christians who hold to the verbal inspiration and absolute infallibility of Scripture. And these attacks are meant for us to read. Moreover, these attacks may represent a certain amount of insecure bombast, whistling in the dark. For there is still great power and attraction in the old doctrines; after all, they are the doctrines of the Scriptures themselves and of the Church catholic for centuries.

But why should it be so important for our modern theologians and exegetes that the Scriptures contain error? Why this almost fantastic desire to prove Scripture at fault? The reason usually given is plain honesty. Intellectual honesty requires it of us, it is said. But apart from the fact that such an explanation is utterly gratuitous — who would ever claim to argue a case from motives which are not honest? — we might ask if the real explanation is not usually something quite different. Is it not really because the theologian and exegete wants the freedom and elbow room in interpreting the Scriptures which he thinks is dictated by modern developments in hermeneutics, by the historical method, by form criticism, etc.? And verbal inspiration and inerrancy do not allow for this.

One interesting feature of the new trends in hermeneutics is the almost complete failure to ask from the Scriptures themselves the principles and rules of Biblical interpretation. We are told that we must now read Scripture on

---

40. *Ibid.*, p. 59 *passim*. This appears to be the position of Prof. Walter Bouman too (see *op. cit.*). It is a position which owes a good deal to Werner Elert, I think.

its own terms according to the stylistics and genres contained in Scripture itself. Good. But what about reading Scripture on its own terms when it speaks of its own divine origin and authority, when it speaks of man's (the interpreter's) sinfulness and proneness to intellectual pride and error, when it speaks of the necessity of prayer and the guidance of the Spirit in reading God's Word, when it speaks of Christ as its nucleus, soul and center and of faith in Christ as necessary for all edifying Bible reading. These are the great and living *Biblical* principles of Bible reading, ignored, for the most part, by the new hermeneutics. And so long as this situation obtains there will remain, I think, two different ways of reading the Scriptures, the old evangelical way as evidenced in our Lutheran Confessions, and the new way as evidenced in the various approaches of the modern historical-critical method. And a great cleavage remains between these two ways. It is as serious as that!

Now what about our Synod and its place in this controversy which rages? I think we are in a state of confusion and perhaps bewilderment as these two different approaches and ways of reading Scripture impinge upon us. And although some individuals are proposing this approach or exegesis and others that, where is the prophet to tell us just where we will be in ten years or twenty?

I hope I have made it clear which direction I would like Missouri to take in the coming critical years. With this in mind let me list three dangers or problems which I think are somewhat peculiar to the Missouri Synod in the present crisis. And then I will conclude with a word of exhortation.

1. It seems that there is a certain amount of embarrassment, if not downright reaction, in our Synod against its past. Our accomplishments under God in evangelism are often ignored or played down, and our fathers, men like Walther and Pieper and even Stoeckhardt, are criticized and even panned. In other conservative circles these great theologians are greatly respected (I met a man in Norway who was converted by reading Pieper's dogmatics), but so often we do not seem to appreciate them *and the relation between their theology and the great evangelical outreach of our Synod in its past history.*

2. There is today in our Church as much as anywhere a fawning, almost servile attitude toward what is called scholarship and a reluctance, even fear, of questioning the "assured results" of what is called modern scholarship and going against the stream. Whereas Stoeckhardt, and Ludwig Fuerbringer and Walter Maier aggressively attacked the documentary hypotheses of their days, we seem afraid to do so today. We seem incapable of distinguishing facts from hypotheses and interpretations; and we are timid (if not altogether silent) in exposing the clay feet, the sub-Christian presuppositions, of much modern Biblical scholarship. Prof. Franzmann has correctly pointed out that this hierarchy of the "scholars" has taken on a sort of cultic aspect. Twenty years ago when I was a seminarian the kindest compliment you could pay a theologian was to call him either pious or orthodox; now we praise him by calling him scholarly. Now we know that scholarship is a gift of God. But we also know that scholars have been wrong again and again and again. Scripture is a gift of God, too, and Scripture has never been wrong.

3. There is in our circles today what I might call a subtile unionism. Influenced by the pervasive ecumenism of our day, we have become friendly with Christians and especially Lutherans outside our fellowship — and such friendliness is good. But there is also an aversion to point out false doctrine when we observe it in the teaching of our new friends. There is another more serious side to this subtile unionism. In the old days our doctrine of church fellowship forbade us to worship or do church work with those who taught doctrine contrary to the divine Word. Among other things, the reason for this was to protect our members from the poison of false doctrine. But there is one area where even the strictest separation cannot protect a church. You cannot stop people from repairing to the written word. And the written word is powerful. Missourians may have stayed out of range of Barth's pulpit or lecture podium but they had no compunctions against reading his books. Today, laymen and students in particular are overwhelmed by an inundation of theological writings. Our problem is first what to read, and second to read everything critically. Students especially are in need of guidance to read and study all new theological contributions critically under the Scriptures and the Lutheran Confession. In all this we can only try to help each other.

What can we do in the face of all the new hermeneutical developments and in the face of our own weaknesses and the problems which face us? What reply can be given such searching questions except to go back to the divine word? It is not enough to talk about the Bible and mouth orthodox expressions. We must go to the Bible again and again, searching out its message, knowing that it carries with it God's power, it is its own best defender, it will surely authenticate itself to us. Therein we meet our Lord Jesus Christ. We must never forget that the only reason for any discussion of Scripture or hermeneutics is that the Christ of Scripture might be made more real to poor sinners. And when this happens, when we meet Christ in the Scriptures and learn to trust and love Him, the Bible ceases to be something to speculate about and criticize and disect, it becomes God's Word of comfort and truth to us. And the only possible response I can make to the Christ of Scripture is in the words of the hymnist:

> Speak, O Lord, Thy servant heareth,
>   To Thy word I now give heed;
> Life and spirit Thy word beareth.
>   All Thy word is truth indeed;
> Death's dread power in me is rife;
> Jesus, may Thy word of life
> Fill my soul with love's strong fervor,
> That I cling to Thee for ever.

> Lord, Thy words are waters living,
>   Where I quench my thirsty need,
> Lord, thy words are bread life-giving,
>   On Thy words my soul doth feed;
> Lord, Thy words shall be my light
> Through death's vale and dreary night;
> Yea, they are my sword prevailing
> And my cup of joy unfailing.

Precious Jesus, I beseech Thee:
　　May Thy words take root in me;
　　May this gift from heaven enrich me,
　　　　So that I bear fruit for Thee;
　　Take them never from my heart
　　Till I see Thee as Thou art,
　　When in heaven, in bliss and glory,
　　I shall see Thee and adore Thee.

Something which has always puzzled me is that the critics of Scripture often search it and master its contents with a zeal which shames us who have the highest and noblest view of it. Why should this ever be? Perhaps the scholars overawe us with their erudition and their sometimes difficult to answer criticisms of the Scriptures. But no scholar ever made a discovery or statement which set aside one single Bible verse. No, we have nothing to fear from reading Scripture, but everything to gain. Of course, we meet with problems, sometimes insurmountable ones. But such difficulties do not shake our confidence in the reliability of the Word; they only drive us deeper into it.

So let us build on the foundation of the apostles and prophets, on the authoritative and inerrant written Word of God, and let us resolve to dig deeper and deeper into this word of eternal life which, as Luther said, is like the swaddling clothes of Jesus; and we will not fail to find the Savior lying there. This is the only answer to our present dilemma and to every problem facing us. Doing this we will not only be strengthened and comforted ourselves, we will not only remain an orthodox Church and a bastion against theological liberalism and heterodoxy in every form, but we will surely become a great blessing to our lost and confused world which needs a sure and certain message of a Savior so desperately.

Part Two

**Biblical Interpretation and Ecumenicity in Light of
Luther and the Confessions**

VII.

LUTHER'S *SOLA SCRIPTURA*

Lewis W. Spitz, Sr.

Fifty gulden (about $470) to make Martin a doctor of theology was doubtless one of Elector Frederick's wisest investments — much wiser than the generous amount he spent for his prodigious collection of sacred relics. The payment of this fee guaranteed his Electoral Grace a tremendous benefit to his beloved University of Wittenberg. To obtain this sum of money for the promotion of his brilliant friar, Vicar John Staupitz had to assure the Elector that Luther would fill the chair of *lectura in Biblia* of the theological faculty for the remainder of his life. Frederick had every reason to congratulate himself on his investment as he beheld the enrollment at the university increase with students coming to Wittenberg from far and near in order to hear the lectures of the new doctor. Tired of the dry husks of scholasticism, they turned eagerly to feast on the Bread of Life served by Luther in his lectures on the Bible. For Luther his promotion later proved to be a source of comfort. By accepting the doctorate he had pledged himself to remain faithful to the Scriptures under all circumstances. No human authority could move him to relent.

Luther's road from a dual authority, Scripture and tradition, to the sole authority of Scripture was a long one. Already at the age of 14 he purchased a postil, probably containing 500 Biblical pericopes. At the same time, or shortly after entering the University of Erfurt, he saw a complete Latin Bible. In the "Georgenburse" at Erfurt, a hospice for students, in 1501, he daily heard a chapter from the Bible read and sometimes took his turn in reading a chapter at table. Upon entering the cloister in 1505 he received his own Latin Bible, a copy bound in red leather, which he eagerly read from day to day. When he was transferred to Wittenberg in 1508, he was obliged to leave his copy in the cloister in Erfurt, but found other copies in Wittenberg, which as an Augustinian he was obliged to use daily. Thus he was prepared for his task as a *Baccalaureus Biblicus,* which he assumed in 1509.[1] But all of this was merely preliminary; his life's task as an expositor of Scripture began with his promotion to the chair of *lectura in Biblia.*

It would have been strange indeed if the Occamist emphasis on the authority of Scripture had left no mark on Luther at the University of Erfurt. But Luther became more submissive to Biblical authority than Occam, who

---

1. M. Reu, *Luther and the Scriptures* (Columbus: The Wartburg Press, 1944), pp. 7, 8.

subordinated the authority of Scripture to that of the church. Luther rejected such ecclesiastical restrictions. His study of church history convinced him that councils and popes had erred. Replying to the *Dialogue Concerning the Powers of the Pope,* prepared by Silvester Prierias in 1518, Luther insisted that only the Holy Scriptures were without error. Cajetan at Augsburg and Eck at Leipzig compelled him to take his stand firmly on the Bible. There he stood before Emperor and Diet. He could not do otherwise. His heroic words still thrill the hearts of God's people: "Unless I am convinced by the testimonies of the Holy Scriptures or evident reason [*ratione evidente*][2] (for I believe neither in the pope nor councils alone, since it has been established that they have often erred and contradicted themselves), I am bound by the Scriptures adduced by me, and my conscience has been taken captive by the Word of God, and I am neither able nor willing to recant, since it is neither safe nor right to act against conscience. God help me. Amen."[3]

In his heroic declaration Luther used both terms — "Scriptures" and "Word of God." For him the Scriptures were the Word of God, though he well knew that "Word of God" is a broader term than "Scriptures." He knew that not all of God's words were recorded in writing. He also knew that Christ is the Word. Critics of Luther, like Adolph Harnack, deplore the fact that Luther placed Scripture and the Word of God on the same level. Harnack complains that besides adhering to the Word of God there was for Luther an adherence to the outward authority of the written Word, though, he adds, this was occasionally disregarded by him in his prefaces to Holy Scripture and elsewhere as well. Equating Word of God and Holy Scripture is for Harnack a remnant of Roman Catholicism which, he holds, has had disastrous results for Protestantism. Harnack laments that the requirement of ascertaining the pure sense of Holy Scripture was simply deprived of its force by regarding Scripture as the verbally inspired canon.[4] According to Harnack, Luther was involved in a flagrant contradiction, for while Luther, he says, criticized Scripture itself, he certainly, on the other hand, set up the letter as the Word of God, insofar as he adopted without testing the Rabbinic-Catholic idea of the verbal inspiration of Holy Scripture.[5]

Wilhelm Walther, professor of theology in Rostock, came to the defense of Luther against the criticism of Harnack and of others. In a scholarly essay, based on Luther's own writings, entitled "Der Glaube an das Wort Gottes," he insisted that Luther in his evaluation of Scripture never admitted any error in the divine Word. Therefore he challenged Lutherans ánd others: "Back to Luther!"[6] Others, like Karl Thimme,[7] have been persuaded by a few isolated expressions of Luther that the Reformer, despite his profound

---

2. For Luther's concept of reason see Bernhard Lohse, *Ratio und Fides* (Göttingen: Vanderhoeck & Ruprecht, 1958).
3. W 7, 838. "W" and "W-T" refer to the Weimar edition of Luther's Works.
4. *History of Dogma* (London: Williams & Norgate, 1899), VII, 246 f.
5. *Ibid.,* p. 235.
6. *Das Erbe der Reformation im Kampfe der Gegenwart.* Erstes Heft (Leipzig: A. Deichert'sche Verlagsbuchhandlung Nachf. [Georg Böhme], 1903).
7. Karl Thimme, *Luthers Stellung zur Heiligen Schrift* (Gütersloh: Druck und Verlag von C. Bertelsmann, 1903).

reverence for Scripture, did not regard it as inerrant in all its parts. In weighing these contradictory opinions one must keep in mind that Scripture was for Luther the written Word of the infallible God.

Commenting on I Cor. 15:3-7, Luther exalts the written Word. He had his troubles with the enthusiasts, who despised Scripture and public preaching and looked for other, private revelations instead. He says: "Observe how he [Paul] again extols and exalts Scripture and the witness of the written Word by using and repeating the phrase 'according to the Scriptures' in this manner. . . . There you hear St. Paul adducing Scripture as his strongest witness and pointing out that there is nothing stable to support our doctrine and faith except the material or written Word, put down in letters and preached verbally by him and others; for it is clearly stated here: 'Scripture, Scripture'."[8]

Luther's *sola Scriptura* implies the divine authority, efficacy, perfection or sufficiency, and perspicuity of Holy Scripture, but above all Christ as the center of it all. For Luther there is no *sola Scriptura* without *solus Christus*. Werner Elert shows that for Luther the divine properties of Scripture are based on the fact that for him the Bible is Christocentric.[9]

Luther's appeal to the sole authority of Scripture at the Diet of Worms demonstrates how far he had advanced from the medieval position of Scripture and tradition.[10] Even his *ratione evidente* does not conflict with his complete reliance on the authority of Scripture, for Luther is here referring to the *usus rationis ministerialis*. In his "Open Letter to the Christian Nobility," doubtless one of the writings he was asked to retract, he had mentioned various grievances that were matters of the secular domain and therefore belonged to the realm of reason rather than to that of Scripture.[11] This distinction is stated clearly by Luther in these words: "Let the Holy Spirit Himself read this Book to His own if He desires to be understood. For it does not write about men or about making a living, as all the other books do, but about the fact that God's Son was obedient to His Father for us and fulfilled His will. Whoever does not need this wisdom should let this Book lie; it does not benefit him anyway. It teaches another and eternal life, of which reason knows nothing and is able to comprehend nothing."[12] More specifically, the reader should find the Cross of Christ in the Bible.[13]

Luther's emphasis on Christ and the Cross explains his comparative evaluation of the various books of the Bible. A book of the Bible is precious to him to the degree that it exalts Christ Crucified. This is another way of

8. W 36, 500.
9. *Morphologie des Luthertums* (München: C. H. Beck'sche Verlagsbuchhandlung, Second Ed., 1952), I, 167.
10. For a scholarly presentation of this position see George H. Tavard, *Holy Writ or Holy Church* (New York: Harper and Brothers, c. 1959). In his chapter on Luther Father Tavard unfortunately departs from his scholarly objectivity.
11. See n. 2, *supra*.
12. W 48, 43.
13. W 1, 52. See also Theodosius Harnack, *Luthers Theologie* (Erlangen: Verlag von Theodor Blaesing, 1862), I, 55 ff.

saying that he evaluates a book in the light of *sola fide* and *sola gra*.
Accordingly James troubled him most, but he would not burden the conscience of others with his private opinion of this book. In placing Hebrews, James, Jude, and Revelation at the end of the New Testament canon
as books which were not quite on the same level with the other books, he
was not manifesting a more liberal attitude towards the Bible but simply
resorting to the church's practice of distinguishing between the *homologou-
mena* and the *antilegomena*. But even there he was rather conservative, for
II Peter and II and III John he included in the number of protocanonical
books.

In Luther's mind there was no doubt regarding the efficacy of the Word.
He declared: "Where the heart is idle and the Word does not ring out, the
devil breaks in and has done damage before we are aware of it. On the
other hand, such is the power of the Word if it is seriously contemplated,
heard, and used that it is never without fruit. It always awakens new
understanding, pleasure, and devotion and purifies the heart and thoughts.
For these are not inert or dead but active and living words."[14]

In view of Luther's *sola Scriptura* one may ask the question: Did Luther
believe in the verbal or plenary inspiration of the Bible? Adolf Harnack believed that he did; others disagree. Karl F. A. Kahnis believed he had discovered in the course of the Reformation a movement from liberty to
authority. Luther, he held, stood for liberty. Kahnis' understanding of that
liberty rules out a plenary inspiration of the Bible. Kahnis named some instances which, he thought, confirmed his opinion, but offered no adequate
collection to support it. He believed that the "more liberal" attitude of the
Reformers still influenced the second and third generations after them.
Chemnitz, Selnecker, and Gerhard, he thought, were still somewhat reserved
with regard to the doctrine of inspiration.[15]

Reinhold Seeberg gathered a larger collection of remarks by Luther which
supposedly indicate a more liberal attitude toward Scripture. Some of these
refer to the extent of the canon, others to passages in canonical books.
Typical quotations from Luther's writings which are said to reveal Luther's
critical attitude toward Scripture, like the following, do not prove what Seeberg and others try to prove with them. Luther is quoted as saying: The
books of the Kings are more trustworthy than the Chronicles; the prophets
often erred when they prophesied of worldly events;[16] the later prophets
built hay, straw, wood, and not silver, gold, and precious stones; the allegorical explanation of the name Hagar, in Gal. 4:25, is too weak to prove
the point.[17]

Taken out of the total context of Luther's profound respect for the

---

14. W 30 I, 146.
15. *System der Lutherischen Dogmatik* (Leipzig: Dörffling und Franke, 1868), III,
    142 ff. For a careful study of the position of the 17th century Lutheran dog-
    maticians see Robert Preus, *The Inspiration of Scripture* (Mankato: Lutheran
    Synod Book Company, 1955).
16. Reinhold Seeberg, *Text-Book of the History of Doctrines* (Grand Rapids:
    Baker Book House, 1952), II, 300 f.
17. Kahnis, op. cit., p. 143.

authority and integrity of Scripture, these remarks could be interpreted, as these writers have done, in a manner reflecting a modern, liberal attitude toward Scripture. However, in view of Luther's respect for Scripture as the authoritative Word of God, who cannot err, it is more generous and in accord with charity here to apply to Luther his explanation of the Eighth Commandment, that we defend our neighbor, speak well of him, and put the best construction on everything. If that is done, the passages quoted to prove Luther's more liberal attitude, to quote Luther, are too weak to prove the point.

Luther's opinion concerning the respective value of Kings and Chronicles should be quoted in full. He said: "The writer of Chronicles noted only the summary and chief stories and events. Whatever is less important and immaterial he passed by. For this reason the Books of Kings are more credible than the Chronicles."[18] Nothing is said here about errors in either. Regarding the "hay, straw, wood" statement writers have not been sure of their interpretation of Luther. Following Walther, Reu refers these remarks not to later prophets but to nonprophetic commentators. Thimme is quite certain that Walther is wrong.[19] Julius Koestlin, Thimme regrets, changed his opinion from the liberal view in his first edition of *Luther's Theology* to the opposite view in the second edition.[20] Regarding Seeberg's remark that Luther attributed errors to the prophets when they prophesied of worldly events, Luther should again be quoted. Commenting on Gen. 44 Luther said: "There is a common proverb among theologians which says, 'Spiritus Sanctus non semper tangit corda prophetarum,' 'The illuminations of the prophets were not continuous or perpetual.' "[21] Here one may think of Nathan, who on his own encouraged David to build a temple, but in the following night was instructed by God to tell David not to build one (II Sam. 7:1-17), or of Elisha, who did not know that the son of the Shunammite had died, because the Lord hid it from him (II Kings 4:27). As to the argumentative value of allegory, would anyone today disagree with Luther, who held that allegory *in acie minus valet?*[22]

Luther certainly did not accept a mechanical inspiration theory; he recognized fully the human elements in Scripture. But he insists that the Holy Spirit speaks when Isaiah and Paul speak.[23] He says: "In this article of the [Nicene] Creed which treats of the Holy Ghost we say: 'Who spake by the Prophets.' Thus we ascribe the entire Holy Scripture to the Holy Spirit."[24] In view of these and countless similar statements, one must agree with Dr. Theo. Engelder, who says in his *Scripture Cannot Be Broken*: "It is one of the mysteries of the ages how theologians who claim to be conversant

---

18. W-T I, 364.
19. *Op. cit.*, pp. 59 ff.
20. *Ibid.*, 60. Actually, Luther distinguishes between ordinary students of Scripture and prophets who were inspired by the Holy Ghost. W 54, 3.
21. W 44, 575.
22. W 43, 12.
23. W 48, 102.
24. W 54, 35.

with Luther's writings can give credence to the myth that Luther did not teach Verbal, Plenary Inspiration."[25]

The sufficiency of the Bible, according to Luther, implies its perspicuity. He says: "No clearer book has been written on earth than the Holy Scripture. It compares with other books as the sun with other lights. . . . It is a horrible shame and crime against Holy Scripture and all Christendom to say that Holy Scripture is dark and not so clear that everybody may understand it in order to teach and prove his faith. . . . If faith only hears Scripture, it is clear and plain enough to enable it to say without the comments of all fathers and teachers: That is right. I, too, believe it."[26] Luther does not deny that there are dark passages in Scripture, but he says they contain nothing but precisely that which is found at other places in clear, open passages. Whoever cannot understand the dark passages, he advises, should stay with the clear ones.[27] Lack of faith indeed makes the whole Bible a dark book. "To read Holy Writ without faith in Christ," he says, "is to walk in darkness."[28]

Luther has been credited with giving the people the open Bible. He gave them the Bible in their own language in a style very much improved over that of previous editions in the vernacular. But more important is the fact that he proved Glapion, the father confessor of Charles V, wrong, who said that the Bible was like a waxen nose. Nicholas Lyra's *quadriga sensuum Scripturae*:
Littera gesta docet; quid credas allegoria; Moralis, quid agas; quo tendas, anagogia indeed gave Scripture a waxen appearance. Luther at one time thought highly of Lyra. It has been said: *Si Lyra non lyrasset, Lutherus non saltasset.* That is doubtless an overstatement. Be that as it may, Luther got away from the *quadriga*, and held that *sensus literalis unus est.*[29] Allegories merely adorn, says Luther, but prove nothing.[30] In his commentary on Deuteronomy he added brief allegories almost for every chapter. This he did, he said, not because he attached great importance to them, but he wanted to forestall the silly attempts at allegorical interpretation that some make.[31]

In conclusion we turn again to Luther's emphasis on *solus Christus.* Only in the light of that emphasis can his *sola Scriptura* be fully understood. Luther says: "For the sake of Messiah and God's Son Holy Scripture was

25. (St. Louis: Concordia Publishing House, c. 1944), p. 290.
26. W 8, 236.
27. W 8, 237, 239.
28. W 44, 790.
29. David Löfgren, *Die Theologie der Schöpfung bei Luther* (Göttingen: Vandenhoeck & Ruprecht, 1960), pp. 220 ff.
30. In his lectures on Genesis, 1535-45, he said: *Postremo quaerendae erant hoc loco allegoriae. Sed ego iis non perinde delector, ac Origenes aut Hieronymus. Non curo eas, nisi quatenus ornant historicam sententiam, quae ex simplici historia colligitur. Atque ibi sunt veluti flores interspersi, sed nihil probant: id quod de figura Augustinus dixit.* W 43, 490.
31. W XIV, 500. For an interpretation of Luther's use of allegory see Hans Wernle: *Allegorie und Erlebnis bei Luther* (Bern: Francke Verlag, 1960).

written, and for His sake everything that happened took place."[32] He sums up the message of the Bible in these words: "The entire Bible does nothing else than give a person to understand what he was, what he now is, what behooves him, and what his works are. It informs him that he is completely undone. Secondly, it tells what God is, what pertains to Him, and what His works are, and especially the mercy in Christ. It leads us to understand Him, and through His incarnation it conducts us from earth to heaven, to the Godhead. May God the heavenly Father grant all of us His grace and mercy to this end, through Christ, our dear Lord and Savior. Amen. Amen. Amen."[33] There is no better way to conclude a study of Luther's *sola Scriptura*.

32. W 54, 247.
33. W 48, 272.

VIII.

LUTHER AS EXEGETE[1]

Douglas Carter

In the era of the 16th-century Reformation it was given to Martin Luther to fill a role unique in its range. He was a controversialist who joined issue with the regnant theology of his day; a reformer who brought about such a renewal of the church as many of his contemporaries and predecessors had dreamed of; the reorganizer who changed the ecclesiastical map of Europe; a pastoral administrator; a spiritual director; and a writer of great versatility whose published works run to more than 50,000 pages in the Erlangen edition. His own church he gave not only a translation of the Bible, but also its catechism, its first vernacular liturgy, and the beginning of its hymnody, and through his sermons — read far and wide in churches and households — its distinctive piety and ethos. When towards the end of his life he let slip the remark that God had led him like a blind mule, he was without doubt disclosing his own astonishment that he had been guided into such unpremeditated paths. For at the beginning of his career, when many voices were calling for a removal of abuses in the church, the only reform that Luther foresaw as desirable was a reform of theological education based on the Bible, and liberated from the heavy hand of the scholastic theologians, whom he considered to be deeply infected with philosophy, rationalism, and moralism. In short, he hoped for a revival of Biblical theology. From the age of 29 he held the chair of Biblical exegesis in the University of Wittenberg, and from time to time he shared the preaching duties at the town church (where there was a sermon each weekday and three times on Sunday). The interpretation and application of Scripture was therefore his constant daily occupation. In this paper we shall attempt to examine what is distinctive in his approach to it.

We must begin by taking stock of the background.

1. The 15th century was an age when the Scriptures were read. On entering the monastery of the Augustinian friars at Erfurt, Luther was given a Bible and told that the statutes of the order required its members "eagerly to read, devoutly to hear, and zealously to learn" the Scriptures. Throughout Germany translations abounded and were freely circulated, 18 editions of a complete German Bible being published between 1466 and 1521. The study of the Bible amongst the laity, more common during the Middle Ages than

---

1. This article was originally presented as "The Reformation Lecture" in Luther-Tyndale Memorial Church, London, England.

Protestants have sometimes cared to admit,[2] had been greatly encouraged as the influence of the Brethren of the Common Life made itself felt through northern Europe[3] and the theological curriculum of the University of Paris shows how large a part the Scriptures played in the education of the clergy.[4] The spread of the new learning had given fresh impetus to Biblical studies by restoring to honor the philological study of the text in the original languages, while at the same time indirectly encouraging them by its criticisms of scholastic theology. Luther's contemporaries included Jacques Lefèvre d'Étaples (1455-1536), humanist, exegete, and Pauline scholar; John Reuchlin, the Hebraist (1455-1522): and Johannes Trithemius (1462-1516), Abbot of Sponheim, whose exertions made his Rhineland monastery illustrious as a center of Biblical learning.

2. In the theological schools, Scripture was recognized, at least in theory, as the unique authority in matters of doctrine.[5] Although the tendency to elevate tradition to the same level as Scripture, and to condition the interpretation of Scripture by tradition, had been growing throughout the Middle Ages, it was not until 1546 (two months after Luther's death) that the Council of Trent decreed by a significantly small majority that Scripture and tradition are to be received "with an equal affection of piety and reverence." It is true that at the beginning of the 16th century the accepted method of interpretation was to determine the sense of Scripture by what the fathers and other doctors of the church had said. Thus at the Leipzig disputation of 1519 Luther's opponent, Eck, based his argument for the papal supremacy on the text, "The Son can do nothing of Himself but what He seeth the Father do, for whatsoever things He doeth, these also doeth the Son likewise" (John 5:19), showing that St. Bernard of Clairvaux had deduced from this passage that there must be a hierarchy of order in the church. Nonetheless when Luther answered Eck by asserting that only the literal meaning of Scripture is adequate as proof in matters of doctrine, and

---

2. Official prohibitions of Bible reading by the laity belong mainly to the first half of the 13th century as emergency countermeasures against the Cathari and Waldenses. Even so, in a letter of 1237 to Germanos, Patriarch of Constantinople, Pope Gregory IX writes that "it is expedient that all should read or hear" the Scriptures.

3. Cp. Gerhard Zerbolt of Deventer, *De utilitate lectionis sacrarum litterarum in lingua vulgari.* They made a long-lasting impression on the popular spirituality of the Netherlands. Dutch Catholic devotional literature up to the end of the 17th century is so full of Biblical allusions as to have been all but incomprehensible to anyone unfamiliar with the Scriptures.

4. Speaking out of his vast knowledge of medieval spirituality, John Mason Neale describes the first characteristic of medieval sermons as "the immense and almost intuitive knowledge of Scripture which their writers possessed." He takes note that their citations are habitually drawn from every part of the Bible. *Mediaeval Preachers and Mediaeval Preaching* (London, 1856), pp. xxv ff. On the subject in general see B. Smalley, *The Study of the Bible in the Middle Ages* (2d ed.) (Oxford, 1952).

5. Notably by the exponents of the *via moderna.* Cp. Occam: Christianus de necessitate salutis non tenetur ad credendum nec credere quod nec in Biblia continetur nec ex solis contentis in Biblia potest consequentia necessaria et manifesta inferri. Dialogus, 411.

131

that the comments of the fathers do not determine the sense, he was in fact echoing St. Thomas Aquinas, who says: "Theology uses the authority of the canonical Scriptures as an incontrovertible proof, and the authority of the doctors of the church as one that may properly be used, but only as probable. For our faith rests upon the revelation made to the apostles and prophets who wrote the canonical books, and not on the revelations (if any such there be) made to other doctors."[6]

Luther's championship of the sole authority of Scripture in matters of faith was therefore nothing new, even though in his day it was passing out of fashion. It is, for example, defended very thoroughly in the writings of Gregory of Rimini, a 14th-century professor in the University of Paris, and General of the Augustinian Friars.[7] He is quoted extensively (and without acknowledgement) by Peter d'Ailly, a writer whom Luther studied closely. Gregory distinguishes between *theological principles* (by which he means truths explicit in Scripture) and *theological theses* (propositions necessarily deducted from Scripture), and concludes that these two make up the proper subject matter of Christian doctrine. In contrast to those theologians who affirmed that there are truths of doctrine which may be discovered by natural reasons alone, Gregory excludes all rational proof from the field of theology, maintaining that doctrine is rooted exclusively in the self-revelation of God, who speaks in the Bible. This self-revelation creates faith (not knowledge, which is acquired by the method of demonstration); and such faith excludes all doubt and error. After the Council of Trent, Gregory's work passed into oblivion. But he represents a type of theology studied in the order to which he and Luther belonged, and this goes to explain why Luther was so warmly supported by his fellow Augustinians in the early stages of his battle for the authority of Scripture. He and they thought the same thoughts and spoke the same language.

3. The age was not wholly insensitive to the critical problems arising from the study of the Biblical texts, nor was Luther. He discusses copyists' errors, takes note of the difficulties of O.T. chronology, and is aware of the synoptic problem and of problems raised by the language and thought forms used by the sacred writers when they speak of the creation of the world and of the last things. He distinguishes between permanent and temporary elements in the Old Testament and urges expositors to make themselves familiar with its historical framework. In his *Preface to the Prophets*, 1532, he underlines the importance of a knowledge of their times.

4. Luther shared with his contemporaries a belief in the plenary verbal inspiration of Scripture. Both he and they took seriously the affirmation of I Cor. 2:13 that there is a state of man radically different from that of the natural man, namely, that of the spiritual man who is led by the Holy Spirit

---

6. *Summa theol.*, I. I, 8. -- ED. NOTE: Cf. the recent article in this journal "Scripture and Tradition in the Council of Trent," by Richard Baepler, XXXI (June, 1960), pp. 341-362. For a presentation of the relation between Scripture and tradition by a modern Roman Catholic scholar see George H. Tavard, *Holy Writ or Holy Church* (New York: Harper & Brothers, c. 1959).

7. See Louis Saint-Blancat, *La theologie de Luther et un nouveau plagiat de Pierre d'Ailly* in *Positions Luthériennes*, April, 1956, pp. 61 ff.

and who "makes known the things that are freely given to us by God . . . not in words which man's wisdom teacheth but which the Spirit teacheth." As Lutheran theology developed after Luther's death, the doctrine of inspiration was highlighted and reflectively elaborated, for the theologians of that period realized that it is not possible to uphold the principle of the sole authority of Scripture if it is not undergirded by the doctrine of plenary inspiration. So did their Roman Catholic opponents, who consequently minimized and even denied it. But it is a mistake to suppose that the Lutheran dogmaticians of the age of orthodoxy were responsible for introducing the doctrine of plenary verbal inspiration into the Church of the Augsburg Confession and thereby departed from Luther's attitude to Scripture. This doctrine is plainly taught in a Saxon confession published as early as 1549 (three years after Luther's death) by Justus Menius, a close friend of Luther and the translator of his Latin writings. What is more to our point, it is enunciated clearly and copiously by Luther himself. In his *Commentary on Romans*, 1515-16 (one of his earlier works), he says that the Lord wills us to receive and believe every word, since He Himself has said it. In his *Short Confession Concerning the Holy Sacrament*, 1544 (one of his last works), he says of Scripture that "we either believe altogether or not at all. If a bell is cracked only a little, it has lost its ring." These two quotations can be matched by a host of others. The following are typical: —

> No one letter in Scripture is without purpose, for Scripture is God's writing and God's Word. (WA 50, 282)
> It is very dangerous to speak of divine things in a different way, and in words different from those which God makes use of. (WA 15, 43)
> It is our accursed unbelief and carnal mind which hinders us from seeing and appreciating that it is God who speaks with us in Scripture. . . . Instead, we think of it as the word of Isaiah or Paul or some other man. And so it comes about that the Bible is not God's Word to us, and bears no fruit, until we realize that God speaks to us thereby. (WA 48, 102)
> This is the speech of St. John, or rather, of the Holy Ghost. (WA 54, 55)
> Holy Scripture is God's Word written and, so to speak, lettered and fashioned in form of letters, as Christ the eternal Word is clothed in our humanity. (WA 48, 31, 4)
> What Paul declares, the Holy Ghost declares, and what is contrary to Paul's word is contrary to the Holy Ghost. (WA 10, 11, 139)

These are of course chance remarks. We can hardly expect more from him since no one at the time controverted the doctrine of inspiration. Taking them as they stand, and in the context of those traditional beliefs about the divine origin of Scripture which Luther never questioned, they undoubtedly add up to a belief in plenary verbal inspiration. Having said this we must go on to say that his view is free from all mechanical, docetic, or mantic notions, and has no affinities either with the idea, derived by some early Christians from Philo, that the sacred writers were unconscious automata, or with the type of fundamentalism professed by Jehovah's Witnesses. Far from playing down the human element in Scripture, Luther's view exalts it by confessing that God's revelation comes to us precisely through human words. This most characteristic human medium, essentially so fragile and fugitive, has been seized upon by God, so that through a condescension of the divine majesty it has become the fitting mode of His speech with us.

Scripture is therefore the Word of God, though the Word of God is not synonymous with Scripture. At this stage it becomes necessary for us to enquire more closely what Luther means by "the Word of God." He knew that to the Hebrew mind a word is action and event and that the most distinctive characteristic of the true God is that He speaks. Through His eternal Word He created the world, thereby setting the pattern for His future dealings with the world. In Jesus Christ the Word was made flesh: In Him God spoke the Word which redeems and creates. This same Word is continually recalled and enunciated in the church's proclamation. Scripture is this same Word in written form, necessary to sustain the oral proclamation and preserve it from error. God's Word comes to us therefore in twofold form, preached and written. The essential unity of these two forms is such that Luther can use the term in both senses almost in the same breath, as in the answer to the question on the first petition of the Lord's Prayer in the Small Catechism: "[God's name is hallowed] *when the Word of God is taught* in its truth and purity and we, as the children of God, also lead a holy life according to it. . . . But he that teaches and lives otherwise than *God's Word teaches,* profanes the name of God among us." Here "the Word of God" is that which is taught, and also that which teaches, i.e., both preaching and Scripture. At times Luther can give the impression of exalting the oral Word over the written. In an Epiphany sermon of 1522 he says that Christ wrote nothing, and the apostles little, and then not until they had first preached and convicted. This proclamation, then and now, is the Epiphany star and the angelic message pointing to the crib and the swaddling clothes. Eventually the N.T. books were written, as a last resort, "in order that some sheep should be saved from the wolves." He concludes: "to have Scripture without knowledge of Christ is to have no Scripture, and is none other than to let the star shine and yet not perceive it" (WA 10, I, (1), 628). And yet passages such as this are offset by others attaching supreme importance to the written Word. In theological controversy his main argument was always "It is written."

It has, however, been maintained that Luther's attitude to Scripture was in fact very free. Those who assert this point out that he speaks of errors in Hebrews, James, Jude, and the Revelation. His consistently disparaging opinion of James is only too well known. Yet the fact that he never felt obliged to modify his overriding belief in the plenary inspiration of the Bible shows that his criticism of these four books is a criticism of their canonicity, that is, whether they do indeed form part of the N.T. He knew that the fourth-century writer Eusebius had placed them in a class apart from the undisputed N.T. books and that his Catholic contemporaries Erasmus and Cardinal Cajetan also doubted their canonical status. His historical doubts were, moreover, reinforced by his failure to discern in three of these four books the consistent authentic notes of the apostolic testimony to Christ, which is to be found in the undisputed books. Questions of authorship apart, there is the "hard knot" of Heb. 6 and 10, apparently disallowing repentance after Baptism. Luther finds himself obliged to ask whether such passages can be undoubtedly canonical when to all appearances so sharply at strife with the gospels and St. Paul. There is St. James' strange silence about the Passion and Resurrection and the Holy Spirit; his stranger talk about the "law of liberty" and about Abraham's being justified by his works whereas the apostle teaches that he was justified without works. It is this epistle which moves Luther to exclaim: "Whatever does not teach Christ is not apostolic, even though St. Peter or St. Paul taught it; and whatever preaches Christ would be apostolic, even if Judas, Annas, Pilate, and Herod were to do it." His doubts about the canonicity of the Book of Revelation are based on the apparent incongruity of its style with what we are otherwise led to expect from an apostle; "for it befits the apostolic office to speak of Christ and His words without figures or visions." But he makes it clear that this is his personal opinion on a debatable point. Later he was less willing to defend this rather capricious judgment, and in the lengthy preface to Revelation of 1545 he is content to note in passing that Eusebius gives evidence for its nonascription to John the apostle and that he himself regards its canonical status as an open question. As for the Epistle of Jude, he believes it to be a nonapostolic abstract of II Peter and therefore it "need not be reckoned amongst the chief books which have to lay the foundation of the faith."

Luther's opinions about the N.T. antilegomena were neither incorporated into the Lutheran Confessions of faith nor followed unanimously by the theologians of the age of orthodoxy. That they are evidence of his having taken a subjective attitude toward Scripture cannot be admitted, unless it be a sign of subjectivity to raise the problem of the distinction between canonical and deuterocanonical or uncanonical writings and to suggest a solution. But if this be so, the same charge could be laid against Augustine for his ambiguous attitude to Hebrews, against Origen, who doubted the canonicity of James and Jude, and against Cyril of Jerusalem, Gregory Nazianzen, and Chrysostom, who doubted the canonicity of the Apocalypse. Luther's view of the canon must therefore be regarded as a critical and historical judgment, in no way modifying his firm belief that all canonical Scripture is inspired.

Luther's well-known saying that the Bible is the Word of God insofar as it impels toward Christ — *soweit Sie Christum treibet*[8] has been cited as further evidence that he freely discriminated between parts of the Bible to be taken very seriously, and others which are not, because they do not immediately have Christ for their subject. It is true that he singles out some books as specially important; that he esteemed St. John's Gospel chief of the four on the grounds of its being fullest of doctrinal teaching; and that he gave pre-eminence amongst the other N.T. books to the Pauline epistles, especially Romans, and to I Peter, because they are "the true kernel and marrow of all the books." This distinction does not, however, arise from a belief in degrees of inspiration, but from a practical recognition that some books are more directly useful than others in setting forth the divine Law and Gospel. And in affirming that Scripture is God's Word insofar as it impels

---

8. *"Treiben"* has the same derivation as the English verb "to drive."

towards Christ, he is laying down a principle of interpretation, not of selection. There is no part of Scripture which does not impel towards Christ.

> The whole Scripture exists for the sake of the Son. (WA Tr 5, 5585)
> For the sake of the Messiah, the Son of God, Holy Scripture was written, and all that came about happened for His sake. (WA 54, 247)
> It is beyond question that the whole Scripture points to Christ alone. (WA 10, II, 73)

For this very reason Genesis is God's Word, for as the Christian believer reads that book, the veil is taken away so that God's promises and His covenant and the faith of the patriarchs all become luminous in the light of Christ.

At this point we touch on a distinctive quality of Luther's interpretation of Scripture, and that is its Christological character.[9] That is not to imply that he alone in his generation sought Christ in the Scriptures. The characteristic spirituality of the time was strongly centered on the person of our Lord, as its devotional literature shows. Throughout Europe the *Vita Christi* of the Carthusian Ludolf of Saxony, first printed in 1474, was widely read,[10] along with Thomas à Kempis' *Imitation of Christ* and other products of the *devotio moderna*,[11] a school of spirituality distinguished by its love of the Bible and its emphasis on our Lord as the Christian's example. But from all this Luther parts company. As early as 1515/16 (Lectures on Romans) he says that the Gospel is "good news" because it "brings Christ." The same thought is found in *The Liberty of a Christian Man* (1520) and is further elaborated two years later in the introduction to the winter series of the *Kirchenpostille* when he warns against reading the Epistles and Gospels as though they were the books of the Law and interpreting Christ's work as no more than an example (WA 10, I, 8). "Beware of turning Christ into a Moses, as though He had nothing more for us than precept and example, like the saints." He goes on to speak of the two ways of interpreting Christ's work: "first as an example proposed to you for imitation, as St. Peter shows (I Peter 2:21) — but that is the least important side of the Gospel. . . . You must rise higher than that. This is the chief and fundamental thing in the Gospel, that before you take Christ for Example, you are to recognize and accept Him as God's Gift to you." "For the preaching of the Gospel is nothing else than Christ's coming to you, or your being brought to Him." When this happens, then rises the sun — *die allerliebste Sonne*, "which brings life, joy, activity, and every good thing." In other words, Christ is so to be preached that faith in Him is established. The end of such preaching is that the

---

9. Christ is the "punctus mathematicus sacrae scripturae," WA Tr 2, 439 (2383).
10. P. Pourrat, *Christian Spirituality*, London, 1924, II, 311 f. It was the most popular devotional book in the later Middle Ages. Re-issued more than 60 times in many different languages, it deeply impressed Ignatius Loyola and was used by him in the composition of his *Spiritual Exercises*. A modern ed. by L. M. Rigollot, Paris, 1870.
11. See J. Dols, *Bibliografi der Moderna Devotie*, Nijmegen, 1941.

hearers shall "put on" Christ and thus be born again and become new creations.[12]

How thoroughly and consistently Luther applies this canon of interpretation may be seen from his introduction to Genesis. In this book, he says, there are three kinds of material: (1) the divine proclamation of the Law, the necessary prelude to the good news of salvation; (2) the predictions and promises of God concerning the Savior — "this is by far the best thing in the book"; and (3) the examples of faith, love, and the cross in the holy fathers, Adam, Abel, Noah, Abraham, Isaac, Jacob, Moses, and so on, "by whose examples we learn to trust and love God," and also examples of the unbelief of ungodly men and of the wrath of God. We are shown how God does not overlook unbelief but punishes Cain, Ishmael, Esau, and the whole world in the Deluge; and these examples too are needful for us. Luther is here using in part the traditional scheme of exegesis, interpreting the narrative "literally," as it applies to Christ, and "tropologically," as it applies to the believer and his response to God. What is most noticeably new in his use of this old method is the firmness with which he binds the two together. This brings us to a second characteristic of his hermeneutical method, his insight into the proper dependence of faith on the person and work of Christ so that whatever the Bible has to say about saving faith is always to be referred to faith in Christ. This leads him to say, in a sermon on Gen. 3:15 (the seed of the women) that Adam was already a Christian before Christ was born. He had exactly the faith that we have, for time makes no difference. "Faith is the same from the beginning of the world to the end: therefore he received by faith what I have received. He no more saw Christ with his eyes than we have done, but he had Him in the Word, and so also we have Him. The only difference is that *then* it should happen, *now* it has happened. The faith is all the same. So all the fathers were justified by the Word and faith, as we are, and also died therein" (WA 24, 99, 31). And in a sermon for the first Sunday in Advent 1522 on the text from the liturgical Epistle, "Now is our salvation nearer than when we first believed," he says that these words have reference to the promise made to Adam. This promise was urged by the prophets, all of whom have written of the Redeemer's coming, His grace, His Gospel. Through this promise the O.T. saints had faith in Christ. *We* believe, though we were not alive at the time of His coming, and so *they* believed, though not alive at Christ's time. Elsewhere in the same sermon, referring to the liturgical Gospel for the day (the Palm Sunday entry into Jerusalem), he adds in the same vein ("The children who go before the Lord sing Hosanna like the patriarchs. We follow and sing the same song. There is no difference between us, except that they precede and we follow after." (WA 10, I (2), 21 ff.)

In these passages Luther is speaking of *faith* in the light of what the N.T. has to say about it, employing a further principle of exegesis, very fundamental to his method, the principle of the *analogy of faith*.[13] It was

---

12. WA 40, I, 540, 7 and 17 (on Gal. 3:27).
13. Rom. 12:6 "(let us prophesy) in agreement with the faith: χατὰ τὴν αναλογίαν της πίστεως."

137

his conviction that the form of Scripture is such that the whole of the Christian faith is revealed in passages which call for no explanation, and that the dark places of Scripture are to be interpreted in the light of these clear passages.[14] If there were times when he discovered that this exegetical key did not open the door, he drew the conclusion that God wished the door to remain closed. Such, for example, is the case with the doctrine of predestination. He is convinced that Scripture teaches universal grace on the one hand and particular election on the other; that God wills the salvation of all; that Christ died for all; that God elects only those who are eventually saved; that it is not in man to determine his own salvation; and that God predestines no one to reprobation. Therefore the solution of this problem belongs to the light of glory. At other times his key opened doors long closed. It helped him to lift the doctrine of creation from the level of natural theology. Viewing creation in the light of Christ, "by whom all things were made" (John 1:3), he was led to reaffirm that it is "through faith that we understand that the worlds were framed by the Word of God" (Heb. 11:3) and that Christ is the Key to creation, who, being Himself both Creator and creature, reveals the Creator to the creature and the creature to itself. Similarly his treatment of the doctrine of man is illuminated and controlled by the Pauline passages which speak of the "flesh," a word which he rightly understands to denote the whole man: body, soul, reason, and will.

When Johannes Bugenhagen preached Luther's funeral sermon he applied to him the description of the angel messenger in the Apocalypse, flying in midheaven, having the eternal Gospel to proclaim, and calling on all to fear God and give glory to Him, for the hour of His judgment is come. Judgment and grace, Law and Gospel — these, said the preacher, were the two themes of Dr. Martin Luther's teaching, whereby the whole of Scripture is opened out, and Christ is made known to us as our Righteousness and eternal Life. As a general rule, funeral panegyrics are a safer guide to the literary fashions of the age than to the character of the deceased. But this tribute, coming from one who stood so close to Luther, has an authentic ring, and its claims can be verified. Luther would have reckoned it the acme of praise, knowing that God commits no higher task to any of His messengers, angelic or mortal, than to display His Word and to make Christ known.

14. Cp. WA 33, 20 f.: John 6:27 is to govern the interpretation of Luke 6:37, 38 and Luke 16:9. Rather than do violence to this "clear, plain text," Luther professes his inability to account for Dan. 4:27.

IX.

PRINCIPLES OF BIBLICAL INTERPRETATION IN THE LUTHERAN CONFESSIONS

Ralph A. Bohlmann

The Lutheran Confessions suggest the following *Vorverständnis,* or presuppositions, for the Lutheran interpreter of Holy Scripture:

1. He regards the Scriptures as the Word spoken by God Himself; he knows that *God* is addressing him in every word of the Bible.
2. He knows that God Himself must enlighten his understanding in order for him to believe what God is saying in Holy Scripture; he reads the Scriptures as one who has the Spirit and expects the Spirit.
3. He knows that in Holy Scripture God speaks a condemnatory word (Law) and a forgiving word (Gospel), the former for the sake of the latter; he therefore seeks to distinguish rightly between the two words of God lest the word of Gospel become a word of Law.
4. He reads the Scriptures as one who has been justified by God's grace for Christ's sake through faith; he knows that Jesus Christ is the center of all the Scripture.

But we are here involved in a circle! The above statements are not merely *presuppositions for* Biblical interpretation but *products of* Biblical interpretation.[1] An awareness of the Confessional principles of Biblical interpretation, which we shall attempt to set forth in the first part of our article, becomes necessary both to evaluate the legitimacy of these presuppositions and to appreciate the exegesis of the Confessions, which was shaped by these presuppositions. In the second part of our presentation we shall ask whether some of the above presuppositions (Law-Gospel, justification) are in fact principles of interpretation and attempt to answer the question on the basis of samples of Confessional exegesis. We shall conclude with some implications of this study for the task of Biblical interpretation today.[2]

---

1. Here we are taking seriously the Confessions' claim to be expositions of Scripture.
2. In our investigation we are limiting ourselves to an examination of statements explicitly referring to Biblical interpretation and to examples of biblical interpretation within the Confessions that illustrate hermeneutical principles. We are not examining the non-Confessional writings of the Confessional authors (although this should be done to get a complete picture of their hermeneutical principles). We are also not investigating pre-Reformation hermeneutical principles in detail (something that also should be done in order to note the

139

I. The Holy Scriptures and Their Interpretation

A. *The Nature of Holy Scripture*

The principles for interpreting any piece of literature are to a large extent determined by the nature of the literature. That this maxim applies also to the Holy Scriptures is clearly evidenced in the Lutheran Confessions. At the risk of repeating accents made in H. J. A. Bouman's paper, let us examine some of the basic Confessional attitudes toward the nature of Holy Scripture.

1. *The author of Holy Scripture is God Himself.* The absence of a specific article on the nature of Biblical inspiration in the Confessions should not be overemphasized.[3] Whatever the reasons for such an omission may have been, it is obvious that from beginning to end the Confessions treat Holy Scripture as divinely authoritative. This divine authority is expressed in explicit statements as well as in the copious use of Scripture throughout the Book of Concord. The divine authority of Scripture rests substantially on its divine authorship. Melanchthon chides the Romanists for condemning "several articles in opposition to the clear Scriptures of the Holy Spirit" (Ap, Preface, 9). Amazed that they are "unmoved by the many passages in the Scriptures that clearly attribute justification to faith," he asks: "Do they suppose that these words fell from the Holy Spirit unawares?" (Ap IV 108).[4] The article of Christian liberty is "an article which the Holy Spirit through the mouth of the holy apostle so seriously commanded the church to preserve" (FC SD X 15). The frequent designation of Holy Scripture as the "Word of God" adds additional evidence that the confessors clearly regarded God as the *auctor primarius* of Scripture.[5]

---

continuity and discontinuity of Biblical hermeneutics in the Confessions). Nor are we attempting to pass judgment on the correctness of the exegesis of individual Bible passages in the Scriptures. Three studies on the Biblical exegesis of the Confessions are: Wilhelm C. Linss, "Biblical Interpretation in the Formula of Concord," in *The Symposium on Seventeenth Century Lutheranism,* I (St. Louis: The Symposium on Seventeenth Century Lutheranism, 1962), 118-135; Edmund Schlink, *Theology of the Lutheran Confessions,* trans. P. F. Koehneke and H. J. A. Bouman (Philadelphia: Muhlenberg Press, 1961), pp. 297-317; and Jürgen Roloff, "The Interpretation of Scripture in Article IV of Melanchthon's Apology of the Augsburg Confession," *Lutheran World,* VIII (1961), 47-63.

Within the Confessions we are limiting our study to the official texts of each document. Our citations are taken from *The Book of Concord,* ed. T. G. Tappert (Philadelphia: Muhlenberg Press, 1959).

3. For explanations, see Schlink, pp. 1 f., n. 1; Werner Elert, *The Structure of Lutheranism,* trans. Walter A. Hansen (St. Louis: Concordia Publishing House, 1962), pp. 182 ff.; and F. E. Mayer, *The Religious Bodies of America,* 2d ed. (St. Louis: Concordia Publishing House, 1956), pp. 142 ff. It should be remembered that *all* parties involved in the controversies treated in the Confessions accepted the divine authority of Scripture.

4. See AC XXVIII 49: "If, then, bishops have the power to burden the churches with countless requirements and thus ensnare consciences, why does the divine Scripture so frequently forbid the making and keeping of human regulations? Why does it call them doctrines of the devil? Is it possible that the Holy Spirit warned against them for nothing?"

5. The Preface to the Book of Concord calls them the "Holy Scriptures of God" (p. 12), as does FC SD V, 3.

The divine authorship of Scripture is the basic reason for its absolute reliability. We know "that God does not lie" and that "God's Word cannot err" (LC IV 57). Therefore Luther advises: ". . . believe the Scriptures. They will not lie to you" (LC V 76). Our position is based "on the Word of God as the eternal truth" (FC SD, Rule and Norm, 13). The Formula rejects an opinion as wrong because: "In this way it would be taught that God, who is the eternal Truth, contradicts himself" (SD XI 35). The Preface to the Book of Concord describes the Scriptures as the "pure, infallible, and unalterable Word of God" (p. 8). The divine authorship of all Scripture gives it a unity and infallibility not found in other writings.[6]

2. *Holy Scripture is Christocentric.* Its content from beginning to end deals with the justification of the sinner by God's grace for Christ's sake through faith. Scripture presents "the promise of Christ . . . either when it promises that the Messiah will come and promises forgiveness of sins, justification, and eternal life for his sake, or when, in the New Testament, the Christ who came promises forgiveness for sins, justification, and eternal life" (Ap IV 5). The "promise [of grace in Christ] is repeated continually throughout Scripture; first it was given to Adam, later to the patriarchs, then illumined by the prophets, and finally proclaimed and revealed by Christ among the Jews, and spread by the apostles throughout the world." (XII 53)[7]

Because of the conviction that the entire Scripture testifies of Christ, it is not surprising that Christological interpretations are frequently given to Old Testament texts. Dan. 4:27 is thus explained: "Daniel knew that the forgiveness of sins in the Christ was promised not only to the Israelites but to all nations. Otherwise he could not have promised the king forgiveness of sins" (Ap IV 262). That the death of Christ is a satisfaction not only for guilt but also for eternal death is proved from Hos. 13:14 (Ap XII 140). Passages from Is. 53 are used directly of Christ (XX 5; XXIV 23; SA-II I 2, 5). The burning of the lamb, the drink offering, and the offering of flour mentioned in Num. 28:4 ff. "depicted Christ and the whole worship of the New Testament" (Ap XXIV 36). The Levitical propitiatory sacrifices are symbols of Christ's future offering (Ap XXIV 24, 53). The Old Testament is used frequently for support throughout Melanchthon's detailed treatment of justification in the fourth article of the Apology. Ps. 8:6; 93:1 and Zech. 9:10 are cited to show that the prophets foretell that Christ, the God-man, is everywhere present to rule (FC SD VIII 27). These and similar examples demonstrate that for the Confessions the unity of Scripture is grounded not

---

6. For an excellent treatment of the authority, use, and interpretation of the Bible in the Lutheran Confessions, see the recently published work of Holsten Fagerberg. *Die Theologie der lutherischen Bekenntnisschriften von 1529 bis 1537*, trans. Gerhard Klose (Göttingen: Vandenhoeck & Ruprecht, 1965), pp. 14-44. Fagerberg writes: "Die BK betrachten Gottes Wort als eine in der Bibel geoffenbarte Wahrheit. Da nur sie eine sichere Kenntnis von Gottes Willen vermitteln kann, wird die Schrift, ein einzelnes Bibelwort oder andere bibelnahen Worte Gottes Wort genannt," p. 18 f.
7. See also Ap 24 55 and FC SD VI 23.

only on the fact that it has but one Author but on the fact that it has but one basic message, Jesus Christ.[8]

3. *The Holy Scriptures, God's Word centering in Jesus Christ, speak directly to the reader.* This is not to suggest that they are "suprahistorical" or that the original context and setting of the words of Scripture are unimportant. It is rather to affirm that they are "omnihistorical"; they speak to the reader and his age, whatever that may be. One is struck by the frequency with which the Confessions apply passages directly to contemporaneous situations without a discussion of the original purpose or context of the passage. A few examples will have to suffice.

Emperor Charles V is implored not to "agree to the violent counsels of our opponents but to find other ways of establishing harmony" because God "honors kings with his own name and calls them gods (Ps. 82:6), 'I say, You are gods'" (Ap XXI 44). Matt. 23:2, "The Pharisees sit on Moses' seat," is used in support of the doctrine that "the sacraments are efficacious even if the priests who administer them are wicked men" (AC VIII). John the Baptist's preaching of repentance is applied directly (SA-III III 30-32). Both Acts 5:29 and Gal. 1:8 are applied to the pontiffs "who defend godless forms of worship, idolatry, and doctrines which conflict with the Gospel" (Treatise, 38). "Beware of false prophets" (Matt. 7:15) and "Do not be mismated with unbelievers" (II Cor. 6:14) are used in support of the statement that all Christians ought to "abandon and execrate the pope and his adherents as the kingdom of the Antichrist" (Treatise 41). The words "for you" in the words of institution of the Lord's Supper "are not preached to wood or stone but to you and me" (LC V 65). Christ's words over Jerusalem in Matt. 23:37: "How often would I have gathered your children together as a hen gathers her brood under her wings, and you would not!" are used to show that no injustice is done when the Holy Spirit does not illuminate a man who despises the instruments of the Holy Spirit (FC SD II 58). Examples of this direct application of Scripture abound in the Book of Concord. They suggest that the Confessions' interest in Scripture is both existential and historical. The Confessional exegete asks not only, "What did God through the human author say to His audience then?" but also, "What is God saying to us now?" He is convinced that the answer to both questions is the same.[9] In short, the Confessions approach the Scriptures under the conviction that "everything in Scripture, as St. Paul testifies, was written *for*

---

8. Confessional statements reflecting the Christological interpretation of the New Testament have not been cited because they are more obvious, and in order to conserve space. We have spoken of "Christocentricity" here to epitomize what is elsewhere more completely described as the Law-Gospel content of Scripture, or the centrality in Scripture of the doctrine of justification by grace for Christ's sake through faith.
   See H. J. A. Bouman, "Some Thoughts on the Theological Presuppositions for a Lutheran Approach to the Scriptures," pp. 2-20, for a more complete treatment of this point.
9. This is not to suggest that the Confessions are unaware that the ordinances under the Old Covenant and certain other prescriptions do not bind the Christian today, e.g., Ap XXIII 41; XXIV 27, 37; XXVIII 16.

our instruction that by steadfastness and by the encouragement of the Scriptures we might have hope." (FC Ep XI 16, 16, italics added; see SD XI 12)[10]

4. *Holy Scripture, God's Word to us about Jesus Christ, is clear and understandable (allgemeinverständlich).* The perspicuity of Scripture was one of the most important assertions of the Lutheran Reformation. For centuries the Scriptures had been regarded as a dark and mysterious book requiring the interpretation of the church and the utilization of allegorical exegesis to understand its mysteries. Through his understanding of the Christocentric and revelational nature of the Scriptures, as well as from Scripture's own claim to clarity, Luther came to emphasize the perspicuity and general understandability of the Bible. Luther maintained both the "external clarity" of the text and the "internal clarity" of the Christocentric subject matter of Scripture gained through the Holy Spirit.[11] This does not mean that there are no difficult or obscure passages in Scripture. But such passages can be interpreted through clearer passages or through philological and grammatical studies. If such passages still remain unclear after such investigation, Luther suggests that the reason lies not in the obscurity of the text but in the mind of the reader. The importance of this emphasis on the clarity of Scripture cannot be overestimated: it freed the Bible from the need for official interpretation by the church, helped place the Book of Life into the hands of anyone who could read, and stimulated exegetes to search the Scriptures.[12]

---

10. This reference to Rom. 15:4 includes the New Testament within the scope of "Scripture," as the context makes clear.
11. See Martin Luther, *The Bondage of the Will*, trans. J. I. Packer and O. R. Johnston (Westwood, N.J.: Fleming H. Revell Company, 1957), pp. 70-74, 123-134, et passim.
12. For an excellent treatment of the *claritas Scripturae* and Luther's major hermeneutical rules in relationship to pre-Lutheran exegesis, see Gerhard Krause. *Studien zu Luthers Auslegung der Kleinen Propheten* (Tübingen: J. C. B. Mohr, 1962), pp. 171-281. Krause states: "Es ist nun sehr bezeichnend für Luthers Gesamtauffassung von der Bibelexegese, dass er sich nicht begnügt mit der dogmatischen Behauptung einer 'claritas scripturae' in Christus" (p. 268) but spoke "von der grundsätzlichen Klarheit der Schrift in sprachlicher Hinsicht und in der Glaubens-Summa ihrer Botschaft" (p. 281). The most complete study of Luther's concept of the clarity of Scripture is Rudolf Hermann, *Von der Klarheit der Heiligen Schrift* (Berlin: Evangelische Verlagsanstalt, 1958).
    Peter Fraenkel describes Melanchthon's views on Scriptural clarity in a similar way: "Just as Melanchthon had a high regard for the Scriptures as a text and connected this closely with their saving import and force, so also he thought that both the text as such and the entire matter of the Christian faith are 'clear', in the sense that God has clearly revealed these mysteries for us and thus given them to us and has not left anything to our initiative to find out. . . . This is not affected by the fact that some passages are obscure and that we may have to resort to commentaries, dictionaries or gifted exegetes to find out what they mean. For hand in hand with the perspicuity of the document goes, as we saw, the perspicuity of its subject matter, the Law and Gospel of God, the salvation offered in Christ." In *Testimonia Patrum: The Function of the Patristic Argument in the Theology of Philip Melanchthon* (Geneva: Libraire E. Droz, 1961), pp. 209 f.

It is not surprising that the belief in the *claritas Scripturae* should permeate the Lutheran Confessions. To be sure, this truth is not set forth in a systematic way nor defined as carefully as we might like. But it is evident in several ways.

Perhaps the most obvious and compelling Confessional evidence for the clarity of Scripture is the manner in which Scripture is cited as the basis of Confessional doctrine. Again and again passages are simply quoted without any explanation. Of the more than 1,700 Scripture citations in the Confessions, the preponderant majority are simply direct quotations of the sacred text without explanation or extended commentary. At times several paragraphs in succession present the Confessional argument simply by quoting passage after passage almost without comment (e.g., FC SD II 10 ff.; XI 28 ff.; SA-II I 1 ff.). Melanchthon almost tires of citing so much evidence: ". . . since it is obvious throughout the Scriptures" (Ap VII 37). Again he states: "We would cite more passages if they were not obvious to every devout reader of Scripture, and we want to avoid being lengthy in order to make our case more easily understood" (XII 83). The use of Scripture in this unadorned way in documents that at least in part were intended for a nonclerical audience indicates the Confessional belief in the general understandability of Scripture.

There are explicit statements on the clarity of Scripture as well. The prophetic and apostolic writings of the Old and New Testaments are described as "the pure and clear fountain of Israel" (FC SD, Rule and Norm, 3).[13] This description of the Scriptures, the source of all doctrine, as *lauter*, or *limpidissimus*, is an affirmation of their clarity. In the Preface to the Apology (9) Melanchthon says the authors of the Confutation "have condemned several articles in opposition to the clear Scripture of the Holy Spirit." In the matter of transferring the Lord's Supper to the dead *ex opere operato*, the Romanists could claim support from Gregory and later medieval theologians, but "we set against them the clearest and surest passages of Scripture (*nos opponimus clarissimas et certissimas Scriptura*)" (Ap XXIV 94). A highly significant passage appears in the Formula's treatment of the Lord's Supper:

> In the institution of his last will and testament and of his abiding covenant and union, he uses no flowery language but the most appropriate, simple, indubitable, and clear words (*ganz eigentliche, einfältige, unzweifelhaftige und klare Wort gebraucht*), just as he does in all the

---

With reference to the Confessional understanding of the clarity of Scripture. Fagerberg states: "Die hl. Schrift ist ihrem Inhalt nach grundsätzlich klar, so dass das, was sie sagen will, in begreifbare Sätze gefasst werden kann. Wenn Zweifel über den Gehalt einer Schriftstelle herrschen, dann haben die deutlichen Stellen die undeutlichen zu erklären," p. 41 f.

13. ". . . zu dem reinen, lautern Brunnen Israels . . ."; ". . . ut limpidissimos purissimosque Israelis fontes . . .," *Die Bekenntnisschriften der evangelisch-lutherischen Kirche*, 5th rev. ed. (Göttingen: Vandenhoeck & Ruprecht, 1963), p. 834. With reference to Scripture as the source of doctrine, Fraenkel states: "The 16th century, like its ancient models and ourselves, used *fons* as a technical term for literary origins or intellectual and spiritual presuppositions," p. 190, n. 83.

articles of faith and in the institution of other covenant-signs and signs of grace or sacraments, such as circumcision, the many kinds of sacrifice in the Old Testament, and holy Baptism. (SD VII 50; italics added)

The Confessions maintain in article after article that their argument rests on "clear passages" of Scripture. The following are examples of teachings for which the Confessions claim clear Scripture: Communion in both kinds (AC XXII 2), the institution of marriage to avoid immorality (XXIII 3), no humanly established regulations merit God's grace (XXVIII 43), lust is sin (Ap II 40), justification through faith (IV 314), the distinction between human and spiritual righteousness (XVIII 10), the Eucharistic words of institution (LC V 45; FC Ep VII 15; SD VII 50), and that conversion is to be attributed to God alone. (SD II 87)

5. *The Holy Scriptures are literary documents.* The point is not stated as such in the Confessions but is assumed throughout. The Scriptures were written by God through human authors in particular languages and times. This fact, while obvious, has important implications for the interpretation of Scripture, as we shall see below.

B. *Principles of Biblical Interpretation*

The Holy Scriptures are God's clear literary Word to us about Jesus Christ. How do I get at the meaning of this Word? How do I hear what God is saying to me in His Law and in His Gospel? The Confessions give basically one answer (with many aspects) to these questions: *through grammatical-historical exegesis.* To enthusiasts of every kind "who boast that they possess the Spirit without and before the Word and who therefore judge, interpret, and twist the Scriptures or spoken Word according to their pleasure" (SA-III VIII 3), the Confessions assert that God's message does not lie behind or above or apart from the Word but *in* the Word.[14]

1. *"Derive the meaning from the text"* may thus be regarded as the basic Confessional principle of Biblical interpretation. This principle is especially evident in the Apology's criticism of the exegesis of the Roman Confutation. This criticism is of three kinds:

a. The Romanists are selective in their use of Scripture. They select "passages about law and works but omit passages about the promises." (IV 183; see also IV 107, 221, 284, 286; XII 34)

b. They twist and distort the Scriptures to suit their own non-Scriptural opinions. "Our opponents twist many texts because they read their own opinions into them instead of deriving the meaning from the texts themselves" (IV 224; see also IV 244, 253, 255, 260, 286; XII 123; XXIV, 14). While this "eisegesis" usually takes the form of imposing a false human opinion about justification on the text of Scripture, the Romanists also read later inventions, such as canonical satisfactions or monasticism, into the Scriptures. (XII 131; XXVII 29)

---

14. Note that Luther regards "enthusiasm" as "the source, strength, and power of all heresy" (SA-III VIII 9).

c. Their actual exegesis is careless, slovenly, illogical, and often dishonest. They add words to the text (IV 264) or omit a word and the central thought as well (IV 357). They quote passages in a garbled form (IV 286) or out of context (XXIV 15). They are guilty of bad grammar (by applying a universal particle to a single part [IV 283]), of neglecting grammar (XII 163), or even of despising grammar (XII 106). Their use of logic in understanding the text is sophistic or 'wrong (IV 222, 335, 360 f). They "make the effect the cause" (XX 13). Melanchthon laments: "Who ever taught these asses such logic? This is not logic or even sophistry, but sheer dishonesty" (XII 123). Such "exegesis" had indeed obscured "important teachings of the Scriptures and the Fathers." (II 32)

In short, the Romanists "do violence not only to Scripture but also to the very usage of the language" (IV 357; see also IV 286, where Melanchthon summarizes the above criticisms of Roman exegesis). The criticisms of the Apology make it very clear that the Romanists held wrong presuppositions for their interpretation of Scripture. They were wrong in the first instance because they were not derived from the Scriptures through careful and objective literary exegesis. Implicit in the above criticisms is the contention that sober exegesis will lead not only to proper presuppositions but also to correct conclusions.

The actual exegesis in the Confessions makes it clear how seriously they took the principle of deriving the meaning from the text of Scripture. Statements like the following are frequent: "we shall simply present Paul's meaning" (Ap IV 231); "the text does not say this" (264); "as the narrative in the text shows" (267); "what we have said is what Paul really and truly means" (XII 84); "Where does Scripture say this?" (138); "the prophet's own words give us his meaning" (XXIV 32). The appeal throughout is to what God is actually saying through His holy penmen.

The Confessions evidence a careful concern for many of the aspects of grammatical exegesis. They know the importance of word study and usage. We note how carefully the word "to be justified" and "justification" are explained (Ap IV 72; see FC Ep III 7: "according to the usage of Scripture," and SD III 17: "And this is the usual usage and meaning of the word in the Holy Scriptures of the Old and the New Testaments"). Particular attention is given to understanding "faith in the true sense, as the Scriptures use the word" (Ap IV 112; see IV 304). Similar attention is given to deriving the meaning of the word "Gospel" from the Biblical usage, and it is noted: "The word 'Gospel' is not used in a single sense in Holy Scripture" (FC Ep V 6; see SD V 3-6). The Biblical meaning of the word "necessity" is studied (SD IV 14, 17), and the Biblical usage of the word "repentance" is analyzed. (V 7-8)

Sometimes extra-Biblical data are helpful for the understanding of a word used in Scripture. Commenting on the meaning of "sin offering" in Is. 53:10 and Rom. 8:3, Melanchthon writes:

> We can understand the meaning of the word more readily if we look at the customs which the heathen adopted from their misinterpretation of the patriarchal tradition. The Latins offered a sacrificial victim to placate the wrath of God when, amid great calamities, it seemed to be

unusually severe; this they called a trespass offering. Sometimes they offered up human sacrifices, perhaps because they had heard that a human victim was going to placate God for the whole human race. The Greeks called them either "refuse" or "offscouring." (Ap XXIV 23)

Later in the same article Melanchthon discusses the use of the word "liturgy" by the Greeks. He quotes Demosthenes, the rescript of Pertinax, and Ulpian, a commentator on Demosthenes, and concludes:

> But further proofs are unnecessary since anyone who reads the Greek authors can find examples everywhere of their use of "liturgy" to mean public duties or ministrations. Because of the diphthong, philologists do not derive it from *lite*, which means prayers, but from *leita*, which means public goods; thus the verb means to care for or to administer public goods. (81-83)

Readers of the Large Catechism will also remember that Luther explains the Greek and Latin background of the word "Kirche." (II 48)[15]

Particular weight is often laid on one word in a passage. Melanchthon carefully explains the force of the word "judge" in I Cor. 11:31 (Ap XII 163). The word "bread" in I Cor. 11:28 and 10:16 is enough Biblical basis to oppose transubstantiation (SA-III VI 5). Much importance is attached to the exclusive particles ("alone," "freely," "not of works," "it is a gift") in passages dealing with justification (Ap IV 73; FC SD III 52). Melanchthon feels no compulsion to do so but offers a distinction between the words "faith" and "hope" (Ap IV 312). The Greek text is appealed to for a deeper understanding of key words (e.g., LC III 113: "In the Greek this petition reads, 'Deliver or keep us from the Evil One, or the Wicked One' "; or FC SD II 12, which explains that the Greek expression "does not receive" in I Cor. 2:14 actually means "does not grasp, take hold of, or apprehend").

Grammar is of the utmost importance, as the general exegesis of the Confessions from beginning to end makes very clear. The Treatise, for example, can argue that the plural form of the word "you" in Matt. 16:15; 18:19; John 20:23 shows that "the keys were given equally to all the apostles and that all the apostles were sent out as equals." (Treatise, 23)

The literary context and historical setting must also be carefully considered. Luke 7:47 is interpreted on the basis of its context, especially verse 50 (Ap IV 152). I Peter 4:8 is explained on the basis of its closer context and its wider context, 2:4, 5, and 6 (238). James 2:24 is explained on the basis of its context, especially 1:18 (246 f.). Tobit 4:11 is interpreted by vv. 5, 19 (277-280). I Tim. 5:8, 9, 14 help us understand vv. 11, 12. That the word "Gospel" in Mark 1:1 is to be interpreted in the wider sense is based on Mark 1:4 (FC SD V 4). Not only the context of the words of institution but also the circumstances of the Last Supper help us to understand our Lord's words (VII 44, 48). The "purpose and context of St. Paul's entire discourse" in I Cor. 10 help us explain his words in v. 16 (VII 57). Such

---

15. Luther's derivation of *Kirche* from the Greek is generally held to be correct, although his attempt to associate it with the Latin "curia" is probably faulty. See *Bekenntnisschriften*, p. 656, n. 7.

examples could be multiplied. Confessional exegesis practices what Melanchthon preaches:

> It is necessary to consider passages in their context, because according to the common rule it is improper in an argument to judge or reply to a single passage without taking the whole law into account. When passages are considered in their own context, they often yield their own interpretation. (Ap IV 280)

2. *"Seek the native sense of the text"* may be posited as a second principle of Confessional hermeneutics, and it is closely related to the first. The insistence of the Lutheran Reformation that every passage of Holy Scripture has but one simple sense constituted a major breakthrough in the history of Biblical interpretation.[16] In medieval times Scripture was expounded by means of the *Quadriga*, or fourfold rule, according to which Bible passages could have a literal, moral, allegorical, and anagogical sense. The moral, or tropological, sense applied to the individual believer, the allegorical to the church, and the anagogical to the future. This type of exegesis made of the Scriptures a "waxen nose," a book filled with obscurity and mystery which only the church could interpret.[17] It might be observed, however, that throughout the Middle Ages and into the period of the Reformation only the literal sense was valid in disputations and the exegete was not compelled to search for all four senses in every verse.[18] Over against this view of Scripture, Luther asserted: "The literal sense of Scripture alone is the whole essence of faith and Christian theology"; and again: "If we wish to handle Scripture aright, our sole effort will be to obtain the one, simple, seminal and certain sense."[19] Or again: "The Holy Spirit is the plainest writer and speaker in heaven and earth and therefore His words cannot have more than one, and that the very simplest sense, which we call the literal, ordinary, natural sense."[20]

Once again this principle of Confessional hermeneutics can be seen most clearly in the consistent exegetical practice of setting forth the simple, literal,

---

16. For the prior history of this rule and its significance in Luther's thought, see F. W. Farrar, *History of Interpretation*, (Grand Rapids: Baker Book House, 1961). See also Krause, pp. 174 f., n. 6.
17. Farrar states: "He [Luther] saw as clearly as Melanchthon that the pretense of a *multiplex intelligentia* destroyed the whole meaning of Scripture and deprived it of any *certain* sense at all, while it left room for the most extravagant perversions, and became a subtle method for transferring to human fallibility what belonged exclusively to the domain of revelation" (Pp. 327 f.).
18. A. Skevington Wood, *Luther's Principles of Biblical Interpretation* (London: The Tyndale Press, 1960), pp. 24 f. This 36-page booklet gives a clear and basically accurate overview of Luther's hermeneutics.
19. Quoted by Farrar. p. 327.
20. Martin Luther, *Dr. M. Luther's Answer to the Superchristian, Superspiritual, and Superlearned Book of Goat Emser of Leipzig, with a Glance at His Comrade Murner*, 1521, trans. A. Steimle, *Works of Martin Luther*, III (Philadelphia: A. J. Holman Company, 1930), 350. This writing is particularly useful for understanding Luther's exegetical principles.
    For Luther's distinction between *sententia generalis et specialis* and his understanding of the *scopus* of the text, see Krause, pp. 213-223, 241-260.

or native sense intended by the author as the meaning of passages. A few examples may serve to illustrate this fact. We note Melanchthon's disregard for allegories: "Our opponents will really achieve something if we let them defeat us with allegories, but it is evident that allegory does not prove or establish anything" (Ap XXIV 35). Melanchthon ridicules such an example of Roman exegesis. Commenting on the Roman use of Prov. 27:23, "Know well the condition of your flocks," to justify a priest's investigating the sins of a penitent, Melachthon observes:

> By a marvelous transformation, our opponents make passages of Scripture mean whatever they want them to mean. According to their interpretation, "know" here means to hear confessions, "condition" means the secrets of conscience and not outward conduct, and "flocks" means men. The interpretation surely is a neat one, worthy of these men who despise grammar. (Ap XII 106)

Melanchthon counters by pointing out that Solomon is not talking about confession but merely giving a bit of domestic advice to the head of a household. He does not, however, rule out the possibility of applying this passage to a pastor "by analogy." Again, commenting on the Confutation's use of I Sam. 2:36 to justify distributing only the bread to the laity, Melanchthon comments: "Our opponents are obviously clowning when they apply the story of Eli's sons to the sacrament." (Ap XXII 10)

Nowhere is the Confessions' appeal to the native sense of the text more evident than in their interpretation of the Eucharistic words of institution. We remember Luther's words in the Large Catechism: "Here we shall take our stand and see who dares to instruct Christ and alter what he has spoken. . . . For as we have it from the lips of Christ, so it is; he cannot lie or deceive" (V 13 f.). Again: "Mark this and remember it well. For upon these words rest our whole argument, protection, and defense against all errors and deceptions that have ever arisen or may yet arise." (V 19)

The Formula of Concord deals with the interpretation of these words explicitly and in great detail. At the risk of belaboring the obvious, we shall cite the Formula in some detail. After setting forth the Sacramentarian position, the Formula quotes at length from earlier Lutheran confessions and the writings of Luther to indicate the true Lutheran position on the Real Presence. Commenting on the Wittenberg Concord of 1536, the Formula remarks:

> Thereby they wished to indicate that, even though they also use these different formulas, "in the bread, under the bread, with the bread," they still accept the words of Christ in their strict sense and as they read (*eigentlich und wie sie lauten*), and they do not consider that in the proposition (that is, the words of Christ's testament), "This is my body," we have to do with a figurative predication, but with an unusual one (that is, it is not to be understood as a figurative, flowery formula or quibble about words). (SD VII 38)

The Formula asserts that the Lutheran position set forth above

> rests on a unique, firm, immovable, and indubitable rock of truth in the words of institution recorded in the holy Word of God and so under-

stood, taught, and transmitted by the holy evangelists and apostles, and by their disciples and hearers in turn. (42)

The article then turns to an interpretation of Christ's words, pointing out that Christ speaks not as a mere man or angel but as the one who is "himself the eternal truth and wisdom and the almighty God" (43). Noting the great care and deliberation with which our Lord chose His words "as he was about to begin his bitter passion and death for our sin" (44), the Formula concludes:

> We are therefore bound to interpret and explain these words to the eternal, truthful, and almighty Son of God, Jesus Christ, our Lord, Creator, and Redeemer, not as flowery, figurative, or metaphorical expressions, as they appear to our reason, but we must accept them in simple faith and due obedience in their strict and clear sense, just as they read (*wie sie lauten, in ihrem eigentlichen, klaren Verstand*). Nor dare we permit any objection or human contradiction, spun out of human reason, to turn us away from these words, no matter how appealing our reason may find it. (45)

The article cites the example of Abraham as one who did not ask for a "tolerable and loose interpretation" of God's command to sacrifice his son Isaac but "understood the words and command of God plainly and simply, as the words read" (46). Then it returns to the words of institution.

> All circumstances of the institution of this Supper testify that these words of our Lord Jesus Christ, which in themselves are simple, clear, manifest, certain, and indubitable, can and should be understood only in their usual, strict, and commonly accepted meaning. (48)[21]

The next paragraphs show how the context of the Last Supper indicates that there can be no metaphor or metonymy (change in meaning) in Christ's words. We must remain with the simple meaning of the words.

> In the institution of his last will and testament and of his abiding covenant and union, he uses no flowery language but the most appropriate, simple, indubitable and clear words, just as he does in all the articles of faith and in the institution of other covenant-signs and signs of grace or sacraments, such as circumcision, the many kinds of sacrifice in the Old Testament, and holy Baptism. And so that no misunderstanding could creep in, he explained things more clearly by adding the words, "given for you, shed for you." He let his disciples keep this simple and strict understanding and commanded them to teach all nations to observe all that he had commanded them (that is, the apostles). (50 f.)

After a number of pages dealing with further explanations of the doctrine of the Lord's Supper, the article returns to the matter of interpretation.

---

21. "Nun zeugen alle Umstände der Einsetzung dieses Abendmahls, dass diese Wort unsers Herrn und Heilands Jesus Christi, so an sich selbst einfältig, deutlich, klar, fest und unzweifelhaftig sein, anders nicht dann in ihrer gewöhnlichen, eigentlichen und gemeinen Deutung können und sollen verstanden werden." (*Bekenntnisschriften*, p. 987)

We shall not, can not, and should not permit any clever human opinions, no matter what appearance or prestige they may have, to lead us away from the simple, explicit, and clear understanding (*von dem einfältigen, deutlichen und klaren Verstand*) of Christ's word and testament to a strange meaning different from the way the letters read, but, as stated above, we shall understand and believe them in the simple sense. (92)

It is not surprising, then, that the Formula explicitly condemns those who hold that the words of institution "through tropes or a figurative interpretation are to be given a different, new, and strange sense." (113)

The native or proper sense of a passage, however, is the sense intended by the author, and the Biblical authors do not always speak in literalistic terms. This fact is also evident in the Confessions. The Scriptures can employ figures of speech, e.g., synechdoche (Ap IV 152) or perhaps hyperbole (277). In the same article we have been quoting above, the Formula asserts that John 6:48-58 refers to a "spiritual" eating of the flesh of Christ (SD VII 61). In the following article the Formula adopts Luther's explanation that the right hand of God "is not a specific place in heaven, as the Sacramentarians maintain without proof from the Holy Scriptures. The right hand of God is precisely the almighty power of God which fills heaven and earth . . ." (VIII 28). Our Lord's statement in Matt. 16:18: "On this rock I will build my church," does not have reference to a literal rock but to the "ministry of the confession which Peter made when he declared Jesus to be the Christ, the Son of God." (Treatise, 25)[22]

Luther's interpretation of the Ten Commandments should be studied carefully in this connection. With regard to the Third Commandment he says:

> Therefore, according to its literal, outward sense (*nach dem groben Verstand*), this commandment does not concern us Christians. It is an entirely external matter, like the other ordinances of the Old Testament connected with particular customs, persons, times, and places, from all of which we are now set free through Christ. (LC I 82)

Luther then proceeds to offer "ordinary people a Christian interpretation of what God requires in this commandment" (83). At first glance it would appear that Luther interprets the Third Commandment as having a double sense, the one "literal" and the other "Christian." But as Luther's context makes clear, the true and proper sense of the commandment is its "Christian" sense, and it was also this for the Old Testament Jews. Its proper sense, then and now, is "that we should sanctify the holy day or day of rest" (81). True: "As far as outward observance is concerned, the commandment was given to

---

22. Luther gives this advice for postulating figures of speech in Holy Scripture: "Rather let this be our conviction: that no 'implication' or 'figure' may be allowed to exist in any passage of Scripture unless such be required by some obvious feature of the words and the absurdity of their plain sense, as offending against an article of faith. Everywhere we should stick to just the simple, natural meaning of the words, as yielded by the rules of grammar and the habits of speech that God has created among men. . . . All 'figures' should rather be avoided, as being the quickest poison, when Scripture itself does not absolutely require them." (*Bondage of the Will*, pp. 191 f.)

the Jews alone" (80), but this "outward observance" for Luther is not the real, proper meaning of the text. Much the same explanation should be given to Luther's remarks on the last two commandments: "These two commandments, taken literally, were given exclusively to the Jews; nevertheless, in part they also apply to us." (293)[23]

A related problem greets us in Melanchthon's comments on the Levitical sacrifices in Apology XXIV. All Levitical sacrifices can be classified under two heads, propitiatory or eucharistic (21). Yet there has really been only one propitiatory sacrifice in the world, the death of Christ (22). What, then, were the Levitical "propitiatory" sacrifices? They were so called only as "symbols of a future offering (*ad significandum futurum piaculum*)" (24). That is, they were "merely a picture (*imago*) of the sacrifice of Christ which was to be the one propitiatory sacrifice" (53). However: "By analogy (*similitudine*) they were satisfactions since they gained the righteousness of the ceremonial law and prevented the exclusion of the sinner from the commonwealth" (24).[24] For the Apology it would appear that there is but one proper meaning of the Levitical "propitiatory" sacrifices: they are symbols of the coming sacrifice of Christ. The New Testament (in this case, Hebrews) has not added "another" meaning to their "original" meaning. In fact, it is only by way of "similitude" to what they signify that they are called "propitiatory" in terms of their civil function in the Israelite community.

3. *"Let Scripture interpret itself"* is a third major Confessional principle of Biblical interpretation. The classic formulation *Scriptura Sacra sui ipsius interpres* is evident in Luther's writings as early as 1519.[25] The same principle is sometimes expressed as "Scriptura Scripturam interpretatur," the "analogy of Scripture," or the "analogy of faith."[26] Although the Lutheran Reformation gave this principle classic expression and meaning, it cannot be said to be a new discovery of Luther's.[27] In fact, the principle is in a general

---

23. "Diese zwei Gebot sind fast den Jüden sonderlich gegeben wiewohl sie uns dennoch auch zum Teil betreffen." (*Bekenntnisschriften*, p. 633)
24. See paragraph 56, where it is stated that "by analogy (*similitudine*)" Old Testament sacrifices can be said to have "merited civil reconciliation."
25. Karl Holl, "Luthers Bedeutung für den Fortschritt der Auslegungskunst," *Gesammelte Aufsätze zur Kirchengeschichte*, I, *Luther* (Tübingen: J. C. B. Mohr, 1927), 569. Holl explains: "Luther weist mit ihm zunächst den Anspruch ab, den die kirchliche Auktorität bezüglich des Rechts der Schrifterklärung für sich erhob. Aber wichtiger noch war das darin liegende Positive, die Hervorhebung des Eigenrechts der Urkunde. Nach dieser Seite hin war Luthers Satz ein Ereignis für die ganze Geisteswissenschaft. Und vielleicht konnte die Erkenntnis, dass jede Urkunde *aus sich selbst verstanden* werden muss, nur an einem religiösen Denkmal gewonnen werden." (p. 559 f.)
26. While some have understood the "analogy of faith" to refer to the creeds or other fixed summary formulations of belief, Lutherans have generally defined it as the clear passages of Holy Scripture. Wood says of Luther: "For him the rule of faith is the Scripture itself. No extraneous canon is invoked. He finds his sufficient criterion within the Word of God" (p. 22). The "analogy of faith" suggests, however, that the *whole* of Scripture should be kept in mind in the interpretation of any of its parts.
27. See F. Kropatscheck, *Das Schriftprinzip der lutherischen Kirche*, I, *Die Vorgeschichte: Das Erbe des Mittelalters* (Leipzig: 1905), 448f., for the use of this principle by Luther's predecessors.

way applicable to any piece of literature. Because this principle presupposes the fundamental clarity of Scripture, it is not surprising that some observers regard Luther's emphasis on the clarity and self-interpreting nature of the Scriptures to have been motivated primarily by his desire to free Scripture from the need of ecclesiastical interpretation.[28] That these two factors are closely related to the *sola Scriptura* principle cannot be denied. However, that this principle was more a historical necessity than a theological deduction cannot be granted. For the principle follows not only from the revelatory nature of the Word but especially from its unity of authorship, content, and purpose. That the Scriptures were authored by God suggests that the principle *Scriptura Sacra sui ipsius interpres* is simply an extension of the general hermeneutical principle of grammatical interpretation that any passage must be considered and explained in terms of its context; thus the context of any Bible passage is ultimately the entire Scripture. That the "context" of Scripture can give a *true* explanation of any passage rests on the fact of its *divine* authorship, by virtue of which Scripture is held to be in agreement with itself.[29] Likewise the Christological content and soteriological purpose of the entire Scriptures can never be divorced from this principle.

In the practice of exegesis this principle means that passages dealing with the same matter (*parallelismus realis*) can be used to explain and corroborate each other. More importantly (and this has been its chief use in Lutheran circles), the principle means that the less clear or plain passages are to be considered in the light of the clearer passages. Ludwig Fuerbringer comments: "In accordance with this general rule, we must expound the Old Testament in the light of the New Testament, the New Testament being the clearer portion of Holy Writ." And again: "In like manner figurative passages or metaphorical expressions touching upon a certain matter must be expounded in the light of such passages as speak of the same matter plainly and in proper terms."[30]

This principle is consistently followed in the Confessions. It is in evidence in the many places where long lists of passages are cited as being in agreement with one another and therefore expressing the same truth. A few examples will illustrate this. Passages from Paul and John are used side by side (Ap IV 29-33), as are citations from Paul, John, Acts, Habbakuk, and Isaiah (88-99). I Corinthians, Ephesians, Matthew, Acts, John, and Colossians are cited in the same paragraph (FC SD II 10). The host of citations in SD II 26 is taken from 15 different Biblical books, three of them from the

---

28. This is suggested by Fr. Torm, *Hermeneutik des Neuen Testaments* (Göttingen: Vandenhoeck & Ruprecht, 1930), p. 229.

29. Cf. FC SD Rule and Norm 13; FC SD XI 35; LC IV 57. Ludwig Fuerbringer wrote: "The complete agreement of Scripture with itself must be accepted *a priori* as a basis in its interpretation. This claim must under no circumstances be surrendered, because the divine origin of the Scriptures makes impossible any inconsistency of thought or speech, any contradiction, or even the smallest error." (*Theological Hermeneutics* [St. Louis: Concordia Publishing House, 1924], p. 14).

30. *Ibid.*, p. 16. To Fuerbringer's first point we might add that New Testament interpretations of the Old Testament are the Holy Spirit's and therefore authoritative.

Old Testament. Passages from Romans, Genesis, and Hebrews are cited together to explain how Abraham was justified before God through faith alone (III 33). These samples could be multiplied. The mutually explanatory nature of Scripture passages is further evidenced not only by the use of New Testament passages to explain Old Testament references (as we shall illustrate below) but correspondingly by using Old Testament passages with reference to New Testament Christians. For example, Old Testament references are used to describe the voluntary nature of the works done by "the people of the New Testament" (FC SD IV 17). A passage from Deut. 12 is used as the basis for the assertion that believers should not "set up a self-elected service of God without his Word and command." (VI 20).

Moreover, the hermeneutical principle that Scripture should interpret itself is stated rather explicitly in the Confessions. In his article on monastic vows Melanchthon deals with the Romanists' interpretation of the vows of the Nazarites and Rechabites. He states:

> Besides, examples ought to be interpreted according to the rule (*juxta regulam*), that is, according to sure and clear passages of Scripture, not against the rule or the passages. It is a sure thing that our observances do not merit the forgiveness of sins or justification. When the Rechabites are praised, therefore, we must note that they did not observe their way of life out of the belief that they would merit forgiveness of sins by it. . . . (Ap XXVII 60 f.)[31]

It is to be noted that Melanchthon's use of the doctrine of justification to clarify the nature of Rechabite vows is based on the rule that sure and clear Scripture passages interpret those that are unclear; he is not using justification by grace as an independent hermeneutical principle. Melanchthon has much the same point in mind when he says with reference to Luke 11:41 ("Give alms; and behold, everything is clean for you"): "A study of the whole passage shows its agreement with the rest of Scripture." (Ap IV 281, 284).

Sometimes a passage is cited simply to corroborate the interpretation given to another passage. Thus the meaning of "remembrance" in I Cor. 11:24 is illustrated by the citation of Ps. 111:4-5 (Ap XXIV 72). That Matt. 26:27 indicates that *all* communicants should receive the wine is corroborated by the evidence of I Cor. 11:23-28 (AC XXII 2-3). I Cor. 10:16 is cited and discussed to show that the words of institution teach the real presence of Christ's body and blood in the Lord's Supper. (FC SD VII 54-60)

The principle that Scripture is to interpret itself is particularly helpful in finding the meaning of a passage that is somewhat obscure or difficult to interpret. Of key significance for understanding the interpretation of the Law in Apology IV are the following statements:

> In the preaching of the law there are two things we must always keep in mind. First, we cannot keep the law unless we have been reborn by

---

31. It seems likely that *regula* here is a reference to the *regula fidei* or *analogia fidei*, although this cannot be proved.

faith in Christ, as Christ says (John 15:5), "Apart from me you can do nothing." Secondly, though men can at most do certain outward works, this universal statement must be permitted to interpret the entire law (Heb. 11:6), "Without faith it is impossible to please God." (256)

Whenever law and works are mentioned, we must know that Christ, the mediator, should not be excluded. He is the end of the law (Rom. 10:4), and he himself says, "Apart from me you can do nothing" (John 15:5). By this rule, as we have said earlier, all passages on works can be interpreted. (372)

We should note that the Apology's "rule" here again consists of clear passages of Holy Scripture.

Other examples of the use of this principle in the Confessions should be noted, first of all within the New Testament. That Paul in Rom. 3:28 is talking about the whole Law and not just Levitical ceremonies is proved not only from Rom. 7:7 and 4:1-6 but also from Eph. 2:8 (Ap IV 87). The scope of Matt. 23:3 ("Observe whatever they tell you") is limited by Acts 5:29 ("We must obey God rather than men") (XXVIII 21). The plural form of "you" in John 20:23 (as well as in two Matthean passages) indicates that in Matt. 16:15 Christ was addressing not only Peter but Peter as representative of the entire company of apostles (Treatise 23). Luke 24:46-47, a passage which does not contain the word "Gospel," is used to explain the word "Gospel" in Mark 16:15 (FC SD V 4). The reason that some of those who receive the Word with joy fall away again (Luke 8:13) is not that "God does not want to impart the grace of perseverance to those in whom he has 'begun the good work.' This would contradict St. Paul in Phil. 1:6" (XI 42). The Second Commandment, which enjoins the *proper* use of God's name, explains the question "that has tormented so many teachers: why swearing is forbidden in the Gospel [Matt. 5:33-37], and yet Christ, St. Paul [Matt. 26:63 f., Gal. 1:20, II Cor. 2:23], and other saints took oaths." (LC I 65)[32]

Of particular interest is the Confessional use of New Testament passages to interpret Old Testament ones. Eph. 5:9 and Col. 3:10 are used to interpret "image of God" in Gen. 1:27 (Ap II 18, 20). Abraham's faith and Abel's sacrifice are explained on the basis of Rom. 4:9-22 and Hebrews 11:4 (IV 201-202). "Purify yourselves, you who bear the vessels of the Lord" (Is. 52:11) is interpreted by Titus 1:15: "To the pure all things are pure" (XXIII 64). The Levitical sacrifices are interpreted as symbolical of Christ's death on the basis of the Epistle to the Hebrews (XXIV 20, 22, 53). That the drink offering referred to in Num. 28:4 ff. has reference to the sanctifying of believers throughout the world with the blood of Christ is proved by I Peter 1:2 (36). In an extremely interesting use of Scripture the Formula cites Gen. 17:4-8, 19-21 against the Anabaptist denial of infant Baptism (SD XII 13; Ep XII 8). Paul's words in Rom. 8:7 and Gal. 5:17 explain

---

32. The Confessions use the principle of the self-interpreting Scripture also within the Old Testament. E.g., Ap XXIV 28—31, where several Old Testament texts are used side by side to show that also the Old Testament condemns *ex opere operato* worship.

Gen. 8:21; "The imagination of man's heart is evil from his youth." (SD II 17) [33]

An important aspect of the principle that Scripture interprets itself is the legitimacy of using deductions, inferences, or analogies *based on Scripture* (see FC SD XI 55, which cautions against making deductions on the basis of *our own speculations*). Faith is necessary to receive the benefits of the sacraments because the sacraments are signs of the promises, and a promise is useless unless faith accepts it, as Paul teaches in Rom. 4:16 (Ap XII 61). One of the chief Confessional arguments for infant Baptism is this: The promise of salvation also applies to little children; Christ regenerates through the means of grace administered by the church; therefore it is necessary to baptize children so that the promise of salvation might be applied to them (Ap IX 2; see SA-III V 4). Over against the contention of Flacius that original sin is man's *substantia*, the Formula argues that a distinction must be made between our nature as it was created by God and original sin, which dwells in the nature. Why? "The chief articles of our Christian faith compel us to maintain such a distinction" (SD I 34). The article goes on to show how the articles of Creation, Redemption, Sanctification, and Resurrection are opposed to the Flacian position (34-47). That "articles of faith" in the above citation means nothing other than the teaching of Holy Scripture is evident (a) from the parallel statement: "According to the Holy Scriptures we must and can consider, discuss, and believe these two as distinct from each other" (33); and (b) from the explicit demonstration or claim of Scriptural basis apparent in each of the four articles.

Several Scriptural deductions are evident in Formula VII and VIII, dealing with the Lord's Supper and the person of Christ respectively. Because all four accounts of the words of institution use "the same words and syllables" in saying, "This is My body," and "apply them in one and the same manner . . . without any interpretation and change," there can be no doubt that the words of Paul and Luke: "This cup is the new covenant in My blood," have no other meaning than the words of Matthew and Mark: "This is My blood of the new covenant" (SD VII 52-53). Several non-Eucharistic passages of the New Testament (e.g., Matt. 11:28: "Come unto Me, all who labor and are heavy laden, and I will give you rest") are used to illustrate that the Lord's Supper is intended also for those whose faith is weak (70-71); this

---

33. In light of the many ways in which the Confessions apply the principle that Scripture interprets Scripture, it would appear that my colleague Norman Habel has not accurately defined this principle and has limited the meaning of the clarity of Scripture. He writes: "In applying this principle ['relate all of Scripture to its center, viz., *solus Christus*'] the Lutheran exegete must follow the rule that 'Scripture interprets Scripture' (*Scriptura Scripturam interpretatur*). Understood in its primary sense, this rule means that the clear passages of Scripture, namely those which display the teaching of justification by grace through faith in all its force and glory, must be used to interpret and evaluate those portions of Scripture where this truth is obscure. In short, the right distinction between Law and Gospel must be rigorously maintained in all biblical exegesis (Apology IV 5)." In *The Form and Meaning of the Fall Narrative, A Detailed Analysis of Genesis* 3 (St. Louis: Concordia Seminary Print Shop, 1965), p. 1.

inference is possible because of the Confessional belief that the Lord's Supper is Gospel. The rule: "Nothing has the character of a sacrament apart from the use instituted by Christ," which is used in discussing several aspects of the Supper, is "derived from the words of institution" (85). Article VIII accepts the Christological rule (inferred from the Scriptures) that whatever the Scriptures say that Christ received in time He received according to His human nature and not according to His divine nature (VIII 57). The personal union of the two natures in Christ is used as an analogy to help us understand the sacramental union of Christ's body and blood (VII 36 f.). The doctrine of the exchange of properties in Christ (which was so crucial in the debate against the Sacramentarians) is derived from the personal union and the communion of natures (VIII 31). Furthermore, the Formula argues inferentially that since there is no variation with God (James 1:17), "nothing was added to or detracted from the essence and properites of the divine nature in Christ through the incarnation" (49). Finally let us note a deduction from Scripture that is also related to the interpretation of Scripture. Because everything in the Word of God is written that we might have hope, "it is beyond all doubt" that the true understanding of God's foreknowledge will not cause or support either impenitence or despair. (SD XI 12)

C. *The Testimony of the Fathers*

The *sola Scriptura* principle is sometimes taken to mean that Lutherans must have a total disregard for the tradition of the church. It could very easily have meant that for Luther and the Lutheran Confessions in the light of their circumstances. But it did not. The *sola Scriptura* principle, with its closely related emphases on the clarity and self-interpreting nature of Scripture, means that "the prophetic and apostolic writings of the Old and New Testaments are the only rule and norm according to which all doctrines and teachers alike must be appraised and judged" (FC Ep, Rule and Norm, 1). But the *sola Scriptura* principle does not rule out a respectful listening to the testimony of the fathers, and this has implication for the interpretation of Scripture.

The Lutheran Symbols reflect a high regard for the fathers of the church and the testimony of the church in general, for they are convinced that the church of the Augsburg Confession is in direct historical continuity with the true church of all ages. They did not see their movement as a revolution, but as a restoration and re-formation of the church. Melanchthon claims: "They [our preachers] have not introduced any innovations, but have set forth the Holy Scriptures and the teachings of the holy Fathers" (Ap II 50). Again: "Let no one think that we are teaching anything new in this regard when the Church Fathers have so clearly handed down the doctrine that we need mercy even in our good works" (IV 325; see 389). The Conclusion of the Augsburg Confession maintains that we have "introduced nothing, either in doctrine or in ceremonies, that is contrary to Holy Scripture or the universal Christian church." (5)

The Confessions cite a great many fathers in support of their exegesis. You need only check the 11-page "Verzeichnis der Zitate aus kirchlichen und

Profanschriftstellern" in the back of the *Bekenntnisschriften* to see the truth of this statement. What the Apology says about the doctrine of justification ("We have proof for this position of ours not only in the Scriptures, but also in the Fathers" [IV 29]) is something they say often, not only about entire doctrines and confessions but about the interpretation of individual passages as well. For example, Melanchthon claims that his interpretation of "on this rock" in Matt. 16:18 has the support of "most of the holy Fathers" (Treatise, 27 to 29). Or there is the claim that the doctrine of the real presence has been "the unanimous teaching of the leading Church Fathers." (FC Ep VII 15)

Neither the Confessions nor we are suggesting that the testimony of the fathers is a source or norm of doctrine or even a hermeneutical principle. We and they recognize: "It will not do to make articles of faith out of the holy Fathers' words or works" (SA-II II 15). The principle is:

> Other writings of ancient and modern teachers, whatever their names, should not be put on a par with Holy Scripture. Every single one of them should be subordinated to the Scriptures and should be received in no other way and no further than as witnesses to the fashion in which the doctrine of the prophets and apostles was preserved in post-apostolic times. (FC Ep, Rule and Norm, 2)[34]

The Confessional use of the testimony of the fathers has two things to say to us as expositors of the Scriptures today. One is the constant reminder that the exegesis of the fathers — whether they be fathers of the ancient church, the Reformation church, or The Lutheran Church — Missouri Synod — cannot determine our doctrine; only Holy Scripture can do that. In a day when traditional interpretations are being questioned, we need to beware of a *real* "Romanizing tendency" — that of using tradition as a source and norm of doctrine.

The testimony of the fathers says something else. It suggests that we listen carefully and respectfully and humbly to the past interpretations of Scripture. It suggests that we think at least twice before advocating radically different interpretations from the traditional ones. It implies that the interpretations of Scripture which men under the Spirit have held to be true for hundreds of years may well be true today. In this process of appreciative, yet critical listening, the testimony of the fathers can serve as a hermeneutical guide.

II. Soteriological Presuppositions and Hermeneutical Principles

At this point we should raise the question: Do the Lutheran Confessions employ their soteriological presuppositions as hermeneutical principles? More precisely, can we say that the Law-Gospel distinction and the doctrine of justification by grace are actually used as principles for deriving the meaning from the text of Scripture?

---

34. For an excellent study of the role of the testimony of the fathers in Melanchthon's theology see Fraenkel.

Those who would answer these questions affirmatively often cite the following passages from the Confessions:

> The distinction between Law and Gospel is an especially brilliant light which serves the purpose that the Word of God may be rightly divided and the writings of the holy prophets and apostles may be explained and understood correctly (*eigentlich erkläret und verstanden*). (FC SD V 1)
>
> [The article of justification] is of especial service for the clear, correct understanding of the entire Holy Scriptures, and alone shows the way to the unspeakable treasure and right knowledge of Christ, and alone opens the door to the entire Bible. . . . (Ap IV 2 [German])

A few comments on each of these passages may be helpful.

The citation from the Formula quite obviously states a basic Lutheran perspective or presupposition for explaining and understanding the Scriptures. But what does it mean to distinguish Law and Gospel? The immediate context answers: that we do not "confuse the two doctrines and change the Gospel into Law." Confusing the doctrines of Law and Gospel means that "what belongs to one doctrine is ascribed to the other"; thus "the two doctrines would be tangled together and made into one doctrine" (SD V 27). In effect the Formula is saying: What is Law in Scripture must be explained and understood as Law, and what is Gospel in Scripture must be explained and understood as Gospel. If all Scripture is understood and explained as Law, there will be no instrument for the Spirit to create faith and as a result no comfort against the terrors of the Law. If all Scripture is explained and understood as Gospel, there will be no instrument for the Spirit to convict man of his sin and show him his need for a Savior, thereby weakening also the force of the Gospel. But the citation from the Formula does not answer these questions directly: How do I determine whether a passage in Scripture is Law or Gospel or both? When I have determined whether it is Law or Gospel, how do I derive the specific Law message or specific Gospel message from the passage?[35] The Formula, judging from its own methodology, would answer: Through the illumination of the Holy Spirit in the practice of careful grammatical-historical exegesis. This passage does *not* suggest that the distinction between Law and Gospel is a hermeneutical *principle*.[36]

---

35. The distinction between Law and Gospel is both quantitative and functional. In some passages God is clearly speaking Law ("Thou shalt not steal"); in others He is clearly speaking Gospel ("Believe on the Lord Jesus Christ, and thou shalt be saved and thy house"). Still others can be both Law and Gospel, depending on the emphasis; e.g.: "Christ died for our sins" is Law because it emphasizes the enormity of our sins, and Gospel because it shows the extent of God's redeeming love in Jesus Christ. See FC Ep V 9 f.

36. For an excellent discussion of the relationship of the Law-Gospel distinction to the interpretation of Scripture, see C. F. W. Walther, *The Proper Distinction Between Law and Gospel*, trans. W. H. T. Dau (St. Louis: Concordia Publishing House, 1929), pp. 60-67.
   With regard to "die Regel von Gesetz und Evangelium," Fagerberg states: "Niemals wird diese Regel als ein übergreifendes, hermeneutischs Prinzip

The citation from Justus Jonas' unofficial and paraphrastic translation of the Apology likewise expresses a most important Lutheran presupposition for understanding the Scriptures. We might well ask, however, what it means to have a clear and correct "understanding of the entire Holy Scriptures." To understand the Scriptures correctly is to know and believe their message of salvation in Jesus Christ! To have the door opened "to the entire Bible" means to read the Bible as a believing Christian, knowing that in it and through it God speaks to me about my Savior and through His Spirit makes me His son. In short, Jonas is here expressing the conviction of the Confessions that the Scriptures are Christocentric and that their central purpose is to make men wise unto salvation. The man who believes the doctrine of justification by grace will understand this; he will see that everything in the Bible is directly or indirectly related to this center. As one who knows himself to be justified by God's grace, he will expect and find nothing in the divine Scriptures to be contrary to this doctrine; he will have his eyes opened by the Spirit to the wonders of God's grace throughout the Scriptures. All of this Jonas is saying; but he is not advocating a hermeneutical *principle*.[37]

But are there not passages in the Confessions where the doctrine of justification and the distinction between Law and Gospel are used as hermeneutical principles? Let us note some passages where this seems likely. Commenting on the work-righteous interpretation given by the Romanists to two passages, Melanchthon comments:

> . . . in the preaching of penitence the preaching of the law is not enough because the law works wrath and continually accuses. The preaching of the Gospel must be added, that is, that the forgiveness of sins is granted to us if we believe that our sins are forgiven for Christ's sake. Otherwise what need would there be of Christ, what need of the Gospel? We must always keep this important teaching in view. In this way we can oppose those who reject Christ, destroy the Gospel, and maliciously twist the Scriptures to suit the man-made theory that by our works we purchase the forgiveness of sins. (Ap IV 260)

With reference to the Confutation's suggestion that there are sacrifices in the New Testament besides the death of Christ which are valid for the sins of others, Melanchthon states:

> This notion completely negates the merit of Christ's suffering and the righteousness of faith, it corrupts the teaching of both the Old and the New Testament, and it replaces Christ as our mediator and propitiator with priests and sacrificers who daily peddle their wares in the churches. (Ap XXIV 57)

---

verwandt oder gar als höhere Instanz uber die hl. Schrift gesetzt. Sie will dem Bibelleser vielmehr dazu verhelfen, sich in den Aussagen der hl. Schrift über die guten Werke zurecht zu finden und ihnen einen guten und eindeutigen Sinn zu geben," p. 38.

37. "Hermeneutical principle" is used here in the sense of a rule applied by the interpreter to the text in order to discover its meaning.

Similar references are found frequently in the Apology, e.g., IV 231, 277; XXVII 64-65. In the Smalcald Articles Luther argues similarly that the Mass as a means for meriting God's favor (II II 7), purgatory (12), indulgences (24), the invocation of saints (25) and monastic vows to achieve God's favor (III 2; III XIV) must all be opposed as contradictory to the fundamental article.

To be sure, the above references (and many others too) argue from the doctrine of justification. But two things should be noted: (1) all such arguments deal with passages or practices where the doctrine of justification itself is at stake; and (2) the doctrine of justification is derived from the Scriptures.[38] To argue from the doctrine of justification in such contexts is in reality to employ the principle *Scriptura Sacra sui ipsius interpres*. For this principle means not only that a single passage may shed light on another one but also that an *article of faith*, derived as it is from Scripture, may be used to clarify individual passages.[39]

Are the doctrine of justification and the distinction between Law and Gospel then used as hermeneutical principles by the Confessions? Yes, in the sense that Law-Gospel and justification as clearly enunciated Scriptural doctrines are used to interpret other passages where the Law-Gospel distinction or the doctrine of justification is at stake. *In such passages* (and there are many of them, for this is indeed the fundamental article of Scripture) the distinction between the Law and the Gospel and the doctrine of justification by grace function not only as hermeneutical presuppositions but as applications of the hermeneutical principle that Scripture interprets itself.

The Lutheran Confessions never arbitrarily impose the doctrine of justification by grace on any passage where it is not in fact taught. This would violate the principle of deriving the meaning from the text itself through grammatical-historical exegesis. Let us look at an example of Confessional exegesis where the doctrine of justification is clearly the issue: the interpretation of James 2:24: "You see that a man is justified by works and not by faith alone," in Ap IV 244-253. How does the Apology reach the conclusion that this passage does not violate the Pauline doctrine of justification by grace? Not by imposing Paul's teaching *on* the passage but by deriving it *from* the passage by careful exegesis. The Apology is interested in "what James meant" (244). It carefully reads the text, noting that James "does not omit faith nor exalt love in preference to it" (245). It takes the context seriously by pointing out that in James 1:18[40] "regeneration takes place through the Gospel" (247). Thus "the context demonstrates that the works spoken of here are those that follow faith" (246). In short, "James says

---

38. See. e.g.. Ap IV 117, 89-101, 213. Note also that Luther's formulation of the "fundamental article" is made up almost entirely of Bible passages (SA-II I).
39. Some would prefer to call this hermeneutical principle the "analogy of faith" because it employs an *article* rather than an individual passage. This is certainly legitimate, provided it is recognized that articles of faith, no less than individual passages, are derived from Scripture.
40. "Of his own will he brought us forth by the word of truth that we should be a kind of first fruits of his creatures."

none of this, which our opponents shamelessly infer from his words" (253). Nowhere in the whole chain of argumentation is a Law-Gospel hermeneutical principle applied, nor is there any evidence that the Confessions considered this an "obscure" passage requiring interpretation by a clearer one. James *teaches* — he is not *made* to teach — justification by grace.

In interpreting passages where the doctrine of justification or the distinction between Law and Gospel is not the issue (and there *are* such instances), the Confessions likewise make it very evident that their exposition is based on the principles outlined above (I, B). For example, in the lengthy discussion of the meaning of "This is My body" in Formula VII,[41] the appeal is consistently made to deriving the meaning from the text itself, using the context and setting of the Supper and noting parallel passages. Neither the doctrine of justification nor the Law-Gospel distinction was an issue in this controversy, both sides regarding the passage in question as Gospel. Does not this example suggest that it is rather pointless to regard the distinction between Law and Gospel and the doctrine of justification by grace as independent hermeneutical principles of general applicability?

We have dealt with this point at some length because of the current tendency to confuse soteriological presuppositions with hermeneutical principles. May I cite two examples?

The recent essay "The Lutheran Confessions and *Sola Scriptura*" presents a "summary of the confessional views regarding the purpose, content, and interpretation of the Scriptures."[42] The essay does an excellent job of setting forth the soteriological purpose and Christological content of the Scriptures on the basis of the Confessions. It likewise documents very well the Confessional commitment to the sole authority of Scripture. It offers the proper perspective for Biblical interpretation from the vantage point of the doctrine of justification by grace. There can be no question about the validity of these accents. But as a "summary of the confessional views regarding the . . . interpretation of Scripture" it is remarkably quiet about the principles outlined above (I, B). Granted the need for interpreting the Scriptures "in conformity with the purpose of God expressed in the Scriptures" (p. 17) — and I agree with this statement completely — can we really derive hermeneutical *principles* from this purpose alone, apart from the nature of Holy Scriptures as God's inspired Word? Is it correct to state: "The doctrine of the forgiveness of sins through faith in Christ is not only the *praecipuus locus doctrinae christianae* ("main doctrine of Christianity"), but it also *determines the interpretation of all Scripture*" (p. 18; italics added)? Is "soteriological concern" enough of a basis to assert that exegesis will lead to basically the same application?[43] Is this statement accurately

---

41. Cited at length above, pp. 37 ff.
42. *Essays Adopted by the Commissioners of the American Lutheran Church and The Lutheran Church — Missouri Synod*, Nov. 22 and 23, 1964; April 19 and 20, 1965, p. 3.
43. "Where this soteriological concern is present, exegesis, whether it deals with a single article of faith or with Scripture as a whole, will lead to basically the same application" (*ibid.*, p. 18).

formulated: "All theology that receives its dimensions and contours from this guiding principle is pure and true" (p. 11)? As I understand the document (and *my understanding* may well be at fault), I would have to answer "No" to all of the above questions.[44]

Another item that raises some similar questions is "A Response to Questions Raised by Memorial 331, Propositions 1 and 2," submitted by the Commission on Theology and Church Relations to the Detroit convention of The Lutheran Church — Missouri Synod.[45] Both "A Response" and the synodical resolution (*Proceedings*, p. 101) recommend that the first two propositions of Memorial 331[46] be studied "in the light of the approach to the Scriptures that is enunciated in the Lutheran Confessions which we all subscribe" (p. 296). "A Response" then gives considerable emphasis to the doctrine of justification and the proper distinction between Law and Gospel as the proper perspectives from which to interpret the Scriptures. Furthermore, "A Response" speaks very relevantly and correctly in insisting that the interpreter is not "free to disregard *any* of the hard facts of the Scripture -" and that he can determine the form in which the Scriptures speak "by observing it in each case in its Biblical context as it presents itself to him" (p. 297). There can be no quarrel with these accents; they are Biblical and Confessional. My questions deal merely with the *emphasis and relevance of the document to the issues raised in Propositions 1 and 2.* In the final analysis, how does the doctrine of justification or the proper distinction between Law and Gospel help to determine the length of the days in Genesis 1 (Proposition 1) or whether the Genesis account of the Creation and Fall is literal, factual history (Proposition 2)? Is it not possible that the differences of opinion among us on these questions come from men who, on *both* sides of the argument, proceed from the doctrine of justification by grace and properly distinguish Law and Gospel in these accounts? Granted that:

> To interpret the Scriptures in terms of Law and Gospel, as the Lutheran Confessions do, does not mean that the interpreter is free to disregard *any* of the hard facts of the Scripture, whether these are the creation and the fall or the cross and the resurrection (p. 297),

how does the doctrine of justification or the Law-Gospel distinction help us to determine which *are* the "hard facts" of Scripture and which are not? Can this last question be answered in any other way than by clarifying the hermeneutical principles of grammatical-historical exegesis as it deals with literary forms (as "A Response" itself begins to do when it emphasizes

---

44. These questions are asked in keeping with the spirit of the Preface, which states: "The first two of these study documents are herewith presented to members of the churches for study and discussion, with the suggestion that joint conferences be arranged at the local level for this purpose" (*ibid.*, p. 3).

45. *Proceedings of the 46th Regular Convention of The Lutheran Church — Missouri Synod*, Detroit. Michigan, June 16-26, 1965, pp. 296 to 298.

46. The first proposition asks whether the six days of Creation described in Genesis and Exodus are ordinary, calendar days; the second proposition asks whether the Genesis account of the Creation and Fall is literal. factual history.

the importance of the "Biblical context" for determining the form, p. 297)?

The doctrine of justification by grace and the proper distinction between Law and Gospel are indeed vital presuppositions for the proper interpretation of Holy Scripture. These presuppositions, moreover, are derived from the Scriptures themselves and epitomize the content of the entire Bible. As such they serve as controls over against interpretations of Scripture that weaken or destroy the doctrine of justification by grace for Christ's sake through faith or confuse the condemning Law with the saving Gospel. But they are not principles for interpreting the message of Scripture; they *are* the message of Scripture.[47] What God is saying in His Law and in His Gospel can be heard only through the ears of a grammatical-historical exegesis that operates with principles of interpretation consistent with the nature of the Scriptures. *Sola Scriptura* and *solus Christus* are inseparably joined together; let no man put them asunder!

III. Some Conclusions and Implications

1. The Confessions want to be understood and accepted as expositions and summaries of Holy Scripture, which remains "the only rule and norm according to which all doctrines and teachers alike must be judged and appraised" (FC Ep, Rule and Norm, 1).[48] Subscription to the Confessions is thus our affirmation that the doctrinal content of the Confessions is a correct explanation and summary of Holy Scripture, and our pledge to God and to one another that we will preach, teach, and administer the sacraments accordingly.[49]

---

47. Fagerberg states: "Die Rechtfertigung ist wichtig auf Grund ihrer biblischen Verwurzelung und sie gibt den Aussagen der hl. Schrift in bezug auf das Heil ihren guten Sinn. Ein genereller Schlüssel zur hl. Schrift ist sie jedoch nicht. . . . Statt das einzige Prinzip für die Deutung der hl. Schrift zu sein ist sie die wichtigste Regel, die das Verständnis der hl. Schrift das Verhältnis von Glauben und guten Werken betreffend klarlegt," p. 36. Gerhard Gloege reaches a similar conclusion: "Das bedeutet nun nicht, dass die Rechtfertigungslehre in dem Sinne ein hermeneutisches 'Prinzip' wäre, dass mit ihrer Hilfe jedweder Text des AT oder NT von der Rechtfertigung zu reden hätte, bzw. auf die Rechtfertigung entfaltet oder angewendet werden müszte. Im Gegenteil!" "Die Rechtfertigungslehre als hermeneutische Kategorie," *Theologische Literaturzeitung*, 89 (1964), 163.

48. Helmut Echernacht puts it well: "Was ist Bekenntnis? Das Bekenntnis steht der Schrift gegenüber als die Antwort der Kirche auf die Rede Gottes. In ihm sagt die Kirche anbetend und gelobend ihrem Herrn das wieder, was Er ihr zuvor in der Bibel gesagt hat. Es ist damit Dialog and Liturgie" ("Schriftprinzip und Bekenntnis," *Evangelisch-lutherische Kirchenzeitung*, V [Feb. 15, 1951], 38).

49. In view of the Confessions' self-understanding as expositions of Holy Scripture, it is not entirely accurate to say that confessional subscription does not "bind" us to the exegesis of the Confessions. C. F. W. Walther wrote:

"If, for instance, an exegete does not reach the specific sense of a Bible passage and yet interprets it in such a manner that his interpretation rests on other clear Bible passages, he is indeed mistaken in supposing that a certain teaching is contained in this specific Bible passage, but he is not erring in doctrine. In like manner, he who unconditionally subscribes to the Symbolical

2. In subscribing to the Lutheran Confessions we bind ourselves to the Confessional doctrine of the nature, content, and purpose of Holy Scripture (namely, that Holy Scripture is God's literary Word about Jesus Christ for man's salvation) and to all hermeneutical presuppositions and principles implicit in this doctrine. Agreement on proper hermeneutical principles cannot be expected without prior agreement on the nature of Holy Scripture as God's own Word.

3. The soteriological presuppositions of the Confessions give direction and purpose to the exegetical application of Confessional hermeneutical principles. As a result, the Lutheran interpreter will utilize grammatical-historical exegesis to explain the Scriptures of both the Old and the New Testaments from the center of all Scripture, Jesus Christ.[50] In deriving the meaning from the text, seeking the native sense of the text, and permitting Scripture to interpret itself, the Lutheran interpreter of Scripture continues to hear God speaking Law and Gospel for the gracious justification of all men through faith in Jesus Christ. He hears this message throughout the Scriptures, not because he has manipulated the text or practiced eisegesis but because that is precisely what God is saying in the text of Scripture.

4. Because God is their author and Jesus Christ their chief content, the Scriptures are a literary and theological unit and must be interpreted as such. Because God's authorship was accomplished through human authors living and writing at various times as men of their times, the Scriptures must also be read as historical literary documents. Because of the theanthropic nature of every word of Scripture, the interpreter is obliged to utilize — and be judged by — the canons of both theological and historical interpretation, with the latter clearly in the service of the former.

5. Because of the interrelationship of the *sola Scriptura* and *solus Christus* principles, the church should be rightfully concerned with any interpretation or interpretive technique that is contrary to these principles or creates uncertainty about them. In employing nontraditional techniques or advancing nontraditional interpretations the Lutheran interpreter, out of love

---

Books declares that the interpretations which are contained in the Symbols are 'according to the analogy of faith.' "

Walther summarized the meaning of Confessional subscription thus:

"A subscription to the confessions is the church's assurance that its teachers have recognized the interpretation and understanding of Scripture which is embodied in the Symbols as correct and will therefore interpret Scripture as the Church interprets it."

"Why Should Our Pastors, Teachers, and Professors Subscribe Unconditionally to the Symbolical Writings of Our Church," translated and condensed by Alex Wm. C. Guebert, *Concordia Theological Monthly*, XVIII (April 1947), 242, 246.

50. Nils Alstrup Dahl comments: "For the person who allows the church's confession to direct him to biblical exegesis, the elementary task of exegesis remains the most important and the most authentic one: the precise reading of what is written. . . . The actual goal of his work remains to arrive at an understanding of the gospel attested in the Scriptures in its significance for the total life of the church and the world." The Lutheran Exegete and the Confessions of His Church," *Lutheran World*, VI [June 1959], 10).

for the people he serves, should clearly demonstrate that he has not violated either the *sola Scriptura* or the *solus Christus* principle.[51]

6. The Confessional presuppositions and principles of Biblical interpretation are not a set of neatly formulated rules and guidelines, which, if followed consistently, will yield guaranteed and unanimous results in every exegetical detail. On the other hand they are prescriptive enough to measure the validity of every exegetical approach to the Scriptures. The Lutheran interpreter of Scripture who follows these principles carries out his task with the confidence that the Holy Spirit will open his eyes to behold "the things of the Spirit of God." (I Cor. 2:14)

> And after God, through the Holy Spirit in Baptism, has kindled and wrought a beginning of true knowledge of God and faith, we ought to petition him incessantly that by the same Spirit and grace, through daily exercise in reading his Word and putting it into practice, he would preserve faith and his heavenly gifts in us and strengthen us daily until our end. Unless God himself is our teacher, we cannot study and learn anything pleasing to him and beneficial to us and others. (FC SD II, 16)

Bibliography

A. *Primary Sources*

Die Bekenntnisschriften der evangelisch-lutherischen Kirche. 5th rev. ed. Göttingen: Vandenhoeck & Ruprecht, 1965.

The Book of Concord. Ed. T. G. Tappert. Philadelphia: Muhlenberg Press, 1959.

B. *Secondary Sources*

Commission on Theology and Church Relations. "A Response to Questions Raised by Memorial 331, Propositions 1 and 2," *Proceedings of the 46th Regular Convention of The Lutheran Church — Missouri Synod* (St. Louis: Concordia Publishing House, 1965), pp. 296-298.

Dahl, Nils A. "The Lutheran Exegete and the Confessions of His Church," *Lutheran World,* VI (June 1959), 2-10.

---

51. Some of the "minor" problems confronting the church are not so minor as they appear at first glance. Many people are concerned about matters like the authorship of the Pentateuch. Isaiah. and Ps. 110 or the historicity of Jonah, not because of the intrinsic importance of these questions but because they feel that some current answers to these questions are contrary to what they understand Christ and the New Testament to be saying. They are thus concerned for the *sola Scriptura* principle: Do these "new" interpretations suggest that the Bible is unreliable? If the Bible is unreliable in these points. may I trust it when it tells me about my Savior? These people are also concerned about the *solus Christus* principle: Do these "new" interpretations imply that Christ was wrong? And if Christ was wrong, then He was not omniscient; and if He was not omniscient. then He was not God. and if He wasn't God. how could He be my Savior? If I cannot trust Christ's words on such matters. can I trust them on *any* matter? Perhaps such people have an unclear understanding of what Christ and the New Testament are actually saying on such matters, but for their sake this needs to be demonstrated with all love and patience.

Echternacht, Helmut. "Schriftprinzip und Bekenntnis," *Evangelisch-lutherische Kirchenzeitung*, V (Feb. 15, 1951), 38 ff.

Elert, Werner. *The Structure of Lutheranism*, trans. Walter A. Hansen (St. Louis: Concordia Publishing House, 1962), pp. 179-200.

Fagerberg, Holsten. *Die Theologie der lutherischen Bekenntnisschriften von 1529 bis 1537*. Trans. Gerhard Klose. Göttingen: Vandenhoeck & Ruprecht, 1965.

Farrar, F. W. *History of Interpretation*. Grand Rapids: Baker Book House, 1961.

Fraenkel, Peter. *Testimonia Patrum: The Function of the Patristic Argument in the Theology of Philip Melanchthon*. Geneva: Libraire E. Droz, 1961.

Fuerbringer, Ludwig. *Theological Hermeneutics*. St. Louis: Concordia Publishing House Print, 1924.

Gloege, Gerhard. "Die Rechtfertigungslehre als hermeneutische Kategorie." *Theologische Literaturzeitung*, 89 (1964), 161 – 176.

Habel, Norman. *The Form and Meaning of the Fall Narrative, A Detailed Analysis of Genesis 3*. St. Louis: Concordia Seminary Print Shop, 1965.

Hermann, Rudolf. *Von der Klarheit der Heiligen Schrift: Untersuchungen und Erörterungen über Luthers Lehre von der Schrift in De servo arbitrio*. Berlin: Evangelische Verlagsanstalt, 1958.

Holl, Karl. "Luthers Bedeutung für den Fortschritt der Auslegungskunst," *Gesammelte Aufsätze zur Kirchengeschichte*, I, *Luther* (Tübingen: J. C. B. Mohr, 1927) pp. 544-582.

Krause, Gerhard. *Studien zu Luthers Auslegung der Kleinen Propheten*. Beiträge zur historischen Theologie, 33, ed. Gerhard Ebeling. Tübingen: J. C. B. Mohr, 1962.

Kropatscheck, Friedrich. *Das Schriftprinzip der lutherischen Kirche*. I. *Die Vorgeschichte: Das Erbe des Mittelalters*. Leipzig: A. Deichert, 1904.

Linss, Wilhelm C. "Biblical Interpretation in the Formula of Concord," *The Symposium on Seventeenth Century Lutheranism*, I (St. Louis: The Symposium on Seventeenth Century Lutheranism, 1962), 118-135.

Luther, Martin. *The Bondage of the Will*. Trans. J. I. Packer and O. R. Johnston. Westwood, N. J.: Fleming H. Revell Company, 1957.

.... *Dr. M. Luther's Answer to the Superchristian, Superspiritual, and Superlearned Book of Goat Emser of Leipzig, with a Glance at His Comrade Murner*. 1521. *Works of Martin Luther*, Vol. III, trans. A. Steimle (Philadelphia: A. J. Holman Company, 1930), 307-401.

"The Lutheran Confessions and *Sola Scriptura*," in *Essays Adopted by the Commissioners of the American Lutheran Church and The Lutheran Church – Missouri Synod*, Nov. 22-23, 1964; April 19-20, 1965, pp. 11-19.

Mayer, F. E. *The Religious Bodies of America*. 2d ed. (St. Louis: Concordia Publishing House, 1956), pp. 142-144.

Roloff, Jürgen. "The Interpretation of Scripture in Article IV of Melanchthon's Apology of the Augsburg Confession," *Lutheran World*, VIII (June 1961), 47-63.

Schlink, Edmund. *Theology of the Lutheran Confessions*. Trans. P. F. Koehneke and H. J. A. Bouman. Philadelphia: Muhlenberg Press, 1961.

Torm, Fr. *Hermeneutik des Neuen Testaments.* Göttingen: Vandenhoeck und Ruprecht, 1930.

Walther, C. F. W. *The Proper Distinction Between Law and Gospel.* Trans. W. H. T. Dau. St. Louis: Concordia Publishing House, 1929.

————. "Why Should Our Pastors, Teachers, and Professors Subscribe Unconditionally to the Symbolical Writings of Our Church." Translated and condensed by Alex Wm. C. Guebert. *Concordia Theological Monthly,* XVIII (April 1947), 241-253.

Wood, A. Skevington. *Luther's Principles of Biblical Interpretation.* London: The Tyndale Press, 1960.

X.

THE WORD OF GOD AND "PROPOSITIONAL TRUTH"

H. Daniel Friberg

For some decades now it has been a vogue to disparage the confession that the Scriptures are the very Word of God with the claim that since the Bible is made up of "propositional truth" it cannot constitute the living, dynamic, existential, and therefore real Word of God — which is, it may be added when this claim is made, exclusively Jesus Christ himself. The claim has a certain plausibility, the line of reasoning being apparently something like the following: the Bible is full of statements; there is something fixed about a statement; much that is fixed is inert and dead; but the real Word of God is "living and active." The claim has also notable conveniences. No particular assertion need be faithfully adhered to as a word of God. It is also fraught with fearful liabilities. For instance, even in regard to Jesus Christ, what single definite promise can he be said with assurance ever to have made? Or, for that matter, how can we be sure that even he deserves to be called the Word of God? It is a cardinal truth that the Scriptures cannot be known apart from Christ. But it is just as true that Christ cannot be known apart from the Scriptures. Fantastically presumptive is the readiness of the past one hundred years and more to delineate Christ, both popularly and academically, right out of the blue of fancy and prejudice.

The claim is also sophistical, and it is its sophistry that I would like to expose.

Actually, better words than "propositional" can be used in this connection. By common usage, that is "propositional" which can be entertained for assent or denial, such as a list of resolutions for debate. But though interminable lists of propositions for debate can be formulated out of biblical material, the Bible itself is no such list; it consists of assertions made simply in order that all men might believe them to be true. Thus when the reader of the Scriptures comes to the words, "And it came to pass that. . . ," the intention is that he should believe that "it came to pass that. . . ." I shall therefore speak of "assertions," "statements," and "predications" rather than "propositions." My argument is with those who claim that the Bible cannot be the true Word of God since it is made up of definite and repeatable statements.

It is to be observed that one implication of this claim is that no utterance of the Incarnate Logos made in the presence of his disciples or the multitudes was the Word of God except perhaps the syntactically amorphous groans that he emitted before the grave of Lazarus.

The metaphysics corresponding to this claim is the view that reality is not truly comprehended by predication. But this is fallacious. Surely there is no part of reality that does not have its true account as opposed to false accounts. Indeed, even he who disputes the possibility of covering all reality by predication rejects the predicationist's account only by assuming that there is a better account — but any account is only assertion or predication. Nor need we be troubled over the adequacy of the account that is possible for any part of reality, the whole of which has been seen to be accountable, for if no part of reality is without its true account, no part of any part of reality is without accountability. The possibility of predication thus covers indeed all being. For cognitive purposes it is all a matter of associating all subjects with all their proper predicates, and in the nature of the case there is nothing that cannot be known.

But the association of all subjects with all their proper predicates is a work of God. With him, however, speech is more than reporting. It is itself causative of its object, creative, for before he spake there was nothing, and when he speaks it is neither a lie nor futility. "For He spake, and it came to be" (Ps. 33:9a).

God's "I AM" is a speech particularly pregnant with marvel. The case is not that God at the commissioning of Moses said, "I am, and I send you to the people of Israel to deliver them from Pharoah." It is that He in response to Moses' request for the Commissioner's self-identification directed him, "Say to the people of Israel, 'I AM has sent me to you.' " This "I AM" is the preeminent characteristic of God. God does not utter it only when addressing an inquirer like Moses; it is God's eternal speech, Moses or no Moses, the eternal soliloquy apart from which there is no God. Of the manner of its utterance as divine monologue we can form no just notion; by consideration of its meaning we soon plunge ourselves into the dizziness of a mental fainting spell; but of it we can nevertheless affirm nothing less than that it is true speech, apart from which God is not God, and by which he is what he is. His "I AM" is his essence. So far is God from indulging in anything anthropomorphic when he says, "I AM," that we should rather say that man, reflecting on his wholly derivative being, is faintly theomorphic when he weakly and falteringly echoes, "I am." There is no cause to be condescending when talking about assertion and predication!

Patently much of God's speech besides his soliloquizing "I AM" is transcendent. How his Son is his Logos is a mystery. Even much of what he addresses directly to our hearing is beyond our full comprehension. If he works and creates by speech, consider how thoroughly all our existence and sustenance and every movement are taken up in his speech and to how much of it we are totally deaf!

Speech from the Transcendent

But not all God's speech is transcendent. Capacity to speak transcendentally does not imply incapacity to speak untranscendentally, nor is it beyond God to say something that is not beyond our hearing and understanding. A biochemist can talk for days entirely beyond the comprehension of his little son, but he can also say, "Johnny, when we get to the park you shall have a sandwich." Nor are the to-Johnny-understandable words about the sandwich unworthy of his biochemist father. To love children is to want communication with them. He who can speak exclusively over the heads of angels would be a poor father of men and a poor communicator to them if his speech to them were such that even those who prayed for his help to understand what he said would have to say that though it was all very vibrantly over-whelming, not a single assertion could be captured by man for exact retention and repetition. In view of our obtuseness and fickleness we need words of God that can be gone over again and again in the mind, and in view of the dark silence as regards divine truth that prevails over the majority of mankind we need words of God that can be repeated to the ends of the earth with assurance that we know exactly what God has said. Therefore God has to speak to us as to men. Speech to men need not be restricted in such a way that in its upper reaches of meaning it does not far outdistance man's grasp, but unless in its lower levels of intention it makes such sense to man that he can distinguish it from variant speech and repeat it, it is not beamed to man's kind of receptivity nor can it be a speech to man. But if the kind of hearer man is places a limitation of a kind — the presence of a reachable nearer boundary — upon the transcendency of God's word to him, the kind of speaker God is places the necessity of being unreservedly true and good upon all his word to man. Even talk about sandwiches must be true to be his talk. After all, claiming for something that it is the Word of God in the normative and authoritative sense is claiming for it something more than that it is the word of godly men, even men most thoroughly instructed, for instance, in the facts and meaning of the whole course of God's saving work in Christ for man and most sensitively participant in the Christian community. We have whole libraries of the latter category of words.

God's Word and the Time Barrier

Another point about which there is confusion that has led some to reject the possibility of definite Scripture statements' being the real Word of God is the relation of statement to time. It is asked, "How can statements two and more thousand years old be the contemporary Word of God?"

Whatever the time of the making of a statement, that statement is of course repeatable as true for as long a time as the fact to which it gives expression remains a fact. If anything ever was true, it will obviously always be true that it was true, and thus true history will always be true history. But of ongoing situations it may always be said not only that at one time the situation did obtain, but also that for as long a time as the situation obtains, a statement of it as current situation is repeatable as true. The continuing force of once-made statements of continuing situations underlies the principle that laws once gazetted are deemed binding until repealed, without the need of repeated gazetting. Nor do we require that the sign "30,000 Volts!" be painted freshly every morning in order that its deterrence may have a current force. Written words have a particular character in this regard. Though the act of writing is definitely dated, the words have a quality of being uttered afresh every time they are read. Thus written words have a peculiar fitness for the indefinitely repeated expression of definite and unaltered statement. Where the speaker has veracity and adequate knowledge, including, where it is relevant, knowledge of his own power, whatever he says is true for whatever time he says it, regardless of the time he says it.

Take the case of a well-operated airline. The published schedules of services and tariffs are conclusive for the period concerned regardless of date of printing. One learns as much from these printed schedules as from the *viva voce* proclamations of the announcer, or indeed from the very roar of the jets warming up on the apron. If fussy travelers with a light opinion of printed timetables insist on face-to-face encounter with the executive, they may be admitted to the inner office or they may not. If they are, it may well be only to be told: "It's all in the published schedules. Let's see what they say. . . . I wish you a very pleasant flight." In fact, reading a timetable is a true encounter with the executive as regards his present will in all the essentials of the services as far as they concern the prospective traveler. If the latter will conform to the announcements, he will find the executive and his organization doing everything that was said in the printed word.

Misapprehension may also exist in regard to the motive potential of the indicative mood. It may be asked, "How can a book so largely written in the inert story-telling mood have a dynamic appropriate to the true Word of God?" But consider, for instance, that in the former British colonies of Africa — as, presumably, elsewhere in the Commonwealth — a large "L" (for "Learner") displayed on the front and back of a car actually means, "Give this driver a lot of room." So imperative is this indicative that it is printed in bright red. I have read somewhere that in the Chinese Revolution of 1911 the wells of the great Manchu garrison cities were stopped with the bodies of Manchu women and girl suicides. It is probable that the stimulus to this tragic wave of self-destruction was — perhaps next to example itself — more often the plain but terrible indicatives, "The Revolutionaries are now in the next compound," or, "They are breaking down the gate," than the formal imperative, "Go, jump in the well!" The difference between "30,000 Volts" and "Beware of High Tension Cables" is entirely formal; one is as deterrent from careless action as the other. Indeed, imperatives are powerless apart from sanctions that can be directly described only in the indicative. Hearing the cry "Jump in the well!" no one will comply unless he is ready to put this (mistaken) evaluation on his case: "Something worse than perishing by my own leap is overtaking me." The dynamics of words therefore depends on the hearer's view of the relation between the matter they indicate, or seem to indicate, and his own well-being, not on grammatical mood, nor on the actual time of enunciation, nor yet on decibles, except insofar as these bear upon the attention-getting property of the words. Did men and women not fade so quickly, a marriage proposal of forty years past might be reread with more inclination to acceptance now than when first received. "You are beautiful, my beloved, truly lovely" (Cant. 1:16) —

these are probably the most consistently moving words of courtship ever expressed. And of course no wooer uses a megaphone.

Not only does the dynamics of words depend upon the hearer's estimate of their bearing on his own welfare: their motive power will be in proportion to the degree of such bearing. The things that the Scriptures say make them the most dynamic words ever addressed to men. In fact, no more powerfully moving words are conceivable than those of the Bible. *By way of warning they threaten the ultimate in woe*: everlasting destruction of man's being, body and soul, through eternal separation from the Source of life and bliss, and this plight consciously sustained forever with the self-judgment that it has been justly imposed by the holy and perfect wrath of God in retribution for breaking his holy and perfect law and for spurning his offer of full and free forgiveness through Jesus Christ. *By way of heart-lifting assurance they offer the ultimate in weal and bliss*: everlasting salvation of man's entire being through the forgiveness of sins, the imputation of Christ's righteousness, and the imparting of the life of God which is victorious over the flesh, the world, Satan, sin, and death, the enjoyment of this life of God and with God to begin right now, to be consummated at the end of the world and at Christ's return in fullness of glory, and to endure ages without end, all for the sake of Jesus, who through the eternal appointment of God's love died on the cross in payment of the penalty of sin and in appeasement of God's righteous wrath — all this to be had for the mere taking in faith, the very faith for acceptance being offered with the object to be accepted! Surely these are words to raise the dead. If any heart is stonily deaf and impassive to such words, what kind of words could it possibly hear? Were the rejecters of the possibility of definite statements' constituting the true Word of God not spared from compliance by the very terms of their rejection, we should certainly press them for a sample of what they consider a more dynamic word, a true Word of God.

But we face the enigma that these most powerful words that can be conceived do in fact bring only the minority of men to repentance and faith. In further definition of the dynamics of words we may distinguish between the estimate hearers actually make of the bearing of the words in question on their own welfare and the estimate which that bearing ought to lead them to make, for as far as most men are concerned the motive power of the words of the Scriptures can be said to be the greatest possible only with the latter estimate in mind. This distinction may help one to see how it is true both that the Word of God is always efficacious unto salvation — God has said things that should always move men to repentance and faith and with such words he offers the grace to be so moved — and that nevertheless it does not always accomplish the effect of salvation. But the distinction does nothing to solve the mystery of men's various responses to God's saving Word. Why some are alerted by repeated flashings of timetable particulars on the closed-circuit screens of their innermost consciences or by the solicitous tap of an attendant's hand and so come to with a start and a dash for the ramp, while others doze glassily on right through their whole day at the airport — this is one of the abiding mysteries of theology, one of the most baffling and most inscrutable. The management has offered no explanation.

Outer or Inner Word?

An explanation has been attempted by distinguishing between an inner and an outer word: the outer word fails to effect a hearing; the inner word, on the contrary, or the word that reverberates in the innermost tympanum of the ear of the soul, *that* gets through and awakens a man from the sleep of death and brings him to spiritual response. Those who are saved have all heard the inner word; those who are lost have heard nothing but the outer word.

This explanation implies one of the strangest confusions in theology and if consistently followed through is seen to embrace the most pernicious tenets, for it involves a transfer of the blame for man's monstrous unresponsiveness from himself to the Word of God. Actually it is compounded confusion. In regard to man, while recognizing his deafness, it locates this affliction not in the inner ear, where it belongs, but in the outer ear, where his hearing is quite perceptive. Market reports, political forecasts, lascivious stories, prudential ethics, even Red Cross appeals and formal religion — these all get through and move to appropriate action. It is the inner ear, an ear for the things of the Spirit, or rather for things spiritually reported, that is utterly deformed in natural man. Further confusion lies in a division of God's Word that that Word will not bear. It is true of God's Word that it has an aspect which is naturally, not supernaturally, grasped, and to which no man is deaf. Thus a devoted Buddhist might make political and ethical observations of considerable penetration on reading the biblical account of the Jewish monarchy — he might even make religious observations of some truth and insight. But the same Word, even that relating to the history of the Jewish monarchy, has another aspect by which it calls unto a thorough brokenness of heart and a living confidence in God, which aspect is spiritually perceived and to which natural man is totally deaf. But there are also words of God of which the former aspect is so largely swallowed up by the latter that one is driven to ask: If they are not addressed to man as intended for the most spiritual communion with God, how else could they be addressed to him? Such words are, "Thou shalt love the Lord thy God with all thy heart, and with all thy soul, and with all thy mind, and with all thy strength," and "God so loved the world that he gave his only begotten Son, that whosoever believeth on him should not perish, but have everlasting life." These words touch a man only at a point where he is dealing with his Creator, Judge, and Saviour, and if words which resound through that location do not deserve to be called "inner," what words would? Even if a man rejects them, that is where he does so. And if God would have all men be saved, why should he first employ a word which has no chance to get in where the critically important hearing must take place if it is to take place? Why should he not immediately have recourse to the only suitable medium, a better word? The doctrine of the inner word exalts man and degrades both God and his Word.

174

But a turning from the Scriptures to the chimera of a better Word of God that is more dynamic, more penetrating, more compulsive, is inveterate with man. God, however, has denied the existence of such a word. In answer to Dives, who in his post-mortem missionary interest distrusted the Scriptures and showed strong existentialist leanings, our Lord puts into the mouth of Abraham the categorical dictum that where Moses and the prophets are not heard, nothing will be heard even if it comes straight from the other side.

A True Means of Grace

Where God does get Himself a hearing, it is not apart from Moses, the prophets, and the evangelists, but by them as a true means of grace. Why some remain deaf when others do not is a mystery, but why any at all hear is simply because the Scriptures, like the voice that cried, "Lazarus, come forth!," themselves confer upon the dead and the deaf the hearing by which they are heard, and this hearing God is always pressing to confer by them. The Word accomplishes its own hearing and reception. Luther's preface by attention to the reading of which Wesley's heart was strangely and determinatively warmed was to the Epistle to the Galatians. The words the great saint and doctor of Tagaste read at the personalized command, "Take up and read" — by which words he was introduced to the City of God — were from Romans 13, verses 13 and 14: "Not in reveling and drunkenness, not in debauchery and licentiousness, not in quarreling and jealousy. But put on the Lord Jesus Christ, and make no provision for the flesh." Even our Lord, Jesus Christ, whose word was directly and authoritatively God's without his quoting the Scriptures, nevertheless deigned to use the Scriptures. The matter he "opened" by his talk to the Emmaus-walkers was *the Scriptures.* Indeed, he, the Personal Word, by whose opening of the written Word they were brought to such a pleasurably burning state, charges their whole befuddlement and sadness to the folly of being slow of heart to believe all that the prophets had spoken.

There is an existentiality without being smitten by which the soul goes on in death, but it is an existentiality of the Scriptures, an overpowering aliveness of the continuing relevance of what the Bible says, a peremptory self-assertion of the Scriptures as the speaking of God, as God's talking to me, as His calling for my trustful obedience to what He tells me, and that in the moment that now is, and with the momentous issue of eternal life or eternal death.

XI.

FOUND TOO LATE: THE WORD OF GOD

A pilgrimage to faith in the integrity of Scripture

Donald R. Neiswender

Enough things are lost in the average church to make some sort of lost-and-found department necessary, even if it is only a drawer in a desk somewhere. Church coatrooms often contain an interesting selection of old hats, overshoes, umbrellas, and gloves. Human memory being what it is, this is not surprising.

But what a shock it would be if the minister and his people gradually misplaced the Bibles until finally there were none left. In time, the memory of God's word would grow dim, and no doubt some departure from the biblical norms would occur.

Apparently this very thing, this unspeakable and absurd thing, happened at the temple in Jerusalem during the latter years of the kings of Judah. Second Kings tells how the high priest "found the book of the law in the house of the Lord" (22:8, RSV). Righteous King Josiah, hearing the law read for the first time, tore his garments in horror at the thought of the wrath of God that must be directed against a people who so despised His words. Josiah did not try to shift all the blame to former generations, the ones who had let the Word of God slip away. He saw that the wrath of God was kindled against his generation, even though this wrath was rooted in the disobedience of their forefathers.

Chapter 23 then shows two things: the great idolatry and corruption that had followed the neglect and loss of God's Word, and the vigorous reforms instituted by Judah's horrified king. Vessels and priests had been consecrated to the service of Baal and other gods. Cult prostitutes had been plying their trade within the temple itself. The people had given their sons and daughters as burnt offerings to Molech. Josiah's predecessors on the throne had dedicated horses and chariots to the worship of the sun. Even great Solomon had erected temples to heathen gods. Josiah rooted out all the worship of false gods, including the pretended altar to Yahweh that Jeroboam, son of Nebat, had erected at Bethel.

When this destruction of the worship of false gods was finished, there still remained the vast job of teaching the people about even such basic elements of the worship of the true God as the Passover. Josiah did all that could be done: "Before him there was no king like him, who turned to the Lord with *all* his heart and with *all* his soul and with *all* his might, according to *all* the laws of Moses . . ." (23:25). And his greatness included this, that he gave everyone a chance to share in the work of reform and return to the Word of God: "Then the king sent, and *all* the elders of Judah and Jerusalem were gathered to him. And the king went up to the house of the Lord, and with him *all* the men of Judah and *all* the inhabitants of Jerusalem, and the priests and the prophets, *all* the people, both small and great; and he read in their hearing *all* the words of the book of the covenant which had been found in the house of the Lord" (23:1, 2).

The people must have responded with great zeal, for the return to the ways of God was sweeping. Yet when all this thrilling story is finished, *"still the Lord did not turn from the fierceness of his great wrath,* by which his anger was kindled against Judah. . . . And the Lord said, 'I will remove Judah out of my sight, as I have removed Israel, and I will cast off this city which I have chosen, Jerusalem, and the house of which I said, My name shall be there'" (23:26, 27). This was a case, not of "too little," but rather of "too late"!

I believe that these things "happened to them as a warning but . . . were written down for our instruction, upon whom the end of the ages has come" (I Cor. 10:11). If God's chosen people, dwelling in the promised land, could lose the Word he had given them — and lost it right in his temple — then surely any Christian congregation or denomination can do the same.

And it seems to me that many *are* doing it. Not that we can now find prostitutes operating openly on church premises; we have not yet come that far. We seem to be on our way, though, for now within the church we hear about a "new morality" in which biblical standards are ignored or distorted. We do not yet hear of teachers of non-Christian religions being allowed to use the facilities of Christian churches; but whenever universalism raises its head within a church, whenever "Christians" claim that God is not so narrow-minded as to insist that men approach him only through Christ, whenever (and here almost every major denomination in America is indicted) a church shows by its allocation of manpower and money that it has relatively little interest in bringing the Gospel to the unevangelized — whenever these occur, the Church has taken another step toward acknowledging Muslim, Buddhist, Jew, Mormon, or Taoist as the spiritual brother of the Christian.

The whole issue hinges on our attitude toward the Bible. Dare we neglect, lose, or in any way mishandle the Word that God caused to be written? Is the Bible authoritative or not? If it is, is its authority limited or not? If limited, where are the bounds? What higher authority is the basis for the judgment that the authority of the Bible is limited?

More and more theologians of our day are saying that the Bible is both inspired and errant. Many of these theologians insist that the virgin birth, the physical resurrection, and other supernatural elements in the life of Jesus Christ are factual. They staunchly defend the deity of Christ, with all its implications for his personal authority. Yet they say that the proclamation of Christ needs no protective doctrine like biblical inerrancy. In this way they posit a strong dichotomy between the authority of the Bible and the Word made flesh.

I have listened to them and thought and prayed about their views. But somehow I keep remembering the days when I, as a young man just out of

177

high school, first learned why Christ was crucified. I learned it from the Bible. All of what I know about my Saviour I have learned from the Bible. I find there no hint that Christ was ever jealous of the attention men paid to Scripture. Rather, he made it plain that he accorded to Scripture the very highest authority, and he used the words of Scripture as the authoritative base of his own teaching.

From personal experience I well understand the theological attraction of an inspired yet errant Bible. Some years ago, while studying at a seminary in the Black Forest of Germany, I sat under two men who had taken their degrees under Karl Barth at the University of Basel. I had largely neglected Barth in my previous studies, and what a thrill it was to revel in the big, white volumes of his *Die Kirchliche Dogmatik!* In what he said about Christ, how Barth nourished my soul! But though he often spoke highly of the Bible, Barth convinced me that there were errors, inaccuracies, and contradictions in the text. For the first time in my Christian life, I was faced with having to decide which verses of the Bible were authoritative for me and which were not.

I clearly remember the morning when in my devotional time I read the first chapter of Hebrews, where the writer addresses to Jesus the verse from Psalm 45, "Thy throne, O God, is for ever and ever. . . ." The thought came to me: How do I know that we ought to call Jesus *God?* Wasn't Hebrews written by an unknown author? And don't many theologians doubt whether it should even be in the Bible?

With deep shock I suddenly realized that, because I had come to limit the authority of the Bible, I no longer had any way to decide which verses were true. I had begun by believing that some records in the books of Kings contradict the book of Chronicles. I had gone on to wonder whether the Red Sea actually parted during the Exodus. I had doubted that Jonah could have lived for three days inside a fish. Now I was doubting whether or not Jesus was God.

For three days I struggled as the Christian Church struggled when it had to choose between the teachings of Arius and Athanasius. Like the Church, I chose to hold to the faith in the full deity of Christ. And also like the Church, I made this decision because that is what the Bible teaches. Since that day, the matter has been settled for me: To stick with the Bible is to stick with Christ. An inspired but errant Bible cannot teach me anything for certain, even about Christ. It cannot provide what I need more than life itself — assurance that my sins are forgiven.

As I see the theological landscape, those who hold to a fully authoritative Scripture are in a dwindling minority. Not long ago a pastoral intern came for a year of supervised parish work in the church I was attending. He came, not directly from the seminary, but from post-graduate work in the philosophy department of a large Eastern university. The transition to the world of the pastor — sick calls, Sunday school, preaching, visitation, funerals — was no doubt difficult.

Not long after this vicar had arrived, he assumed the duty of Sunday school teacher-training. There came a Sunday when the lesson was based on the Book of Daniel. For about an hour, the vicar presented the Sunday school staff with the latest word on Daniel, which adds up to the "assured finding of modern scholarship" that there never was any Daniel. One of the teachers then went right to the heart of the matter by asking whether the vicar wanted him to tell his students that there was no Daniel. The answer, of course, was no. That bit of enlightenment could wait until the children were older. And yet Jesus spoke to adults about Daniel as if he were an historical person.

If a minister, whether he is a Basel theologian or a seminarian, assumes the right to judge certain parts of Scripture erroneous, every person in the world should have the same "right." And when minister and people exercise that "right," we will move on toward a re-enactment of the apostasy spoken of in Second Kings. I worry that for us, as for Josiah's people, it might be too late.

But in hopes that it is not too late, let's imitate the faith of Josiah. If we evangelical Christians have a higher view of the Bible than some others, let our doctrine be demonstrated by the amount of time we spend studying the Bible. May *our* spiritual descendants not be able to say, "Great is the wrath of the Lord, because our fathers have not obeyed the words of this book."

XII.

THE LUTHERAN CHURCH AND THE
ECUMENICAL MOVEMENT

Robert D. Preus

A. The Lutheran Idea of Ecumenicity

The Lutheran Church has always been ecumenical in its outlook: it has been very conscious of its continuity with the church of former ages, and it has been most concerned about those denominations with whom for various reasons it has no outward fellowship. The spirit of the Reformation shows this. Roman Catholic historians have chosen of late to call this movement a revolt, but this is a misnomer. Luther was concerned to cleanse the Roman Church, not to revolt against it. He did not wish to break with any true teaching or good tradition of the Church. He learned much of his theology from the ancient Fathers of the Church; he drew from the ancient hymnody; he used the old liturgy which had developed in the Church through the years. And this spirit we see in the Lutheran Confessions. The Augsburg Confession makes it clear that it teaches and confesses only what has been drawn from the sacred Scriptures and what has been generally taught in the Church. It is significant to note that after Luther the three great Lutheran theologians in their respective generations were all the most serious and competent patristic scholars of their day, viz. Chemnitz, Gerhard and Calov. Such activity did not represent a morbid interest in the past but an ecumenical awareness of their oneness with the Church of former ages.

The Lutheran Church also has been concerned with the reunion of Christendom and the settlement of those differences which divide Christians. This was the concern behind Luther's desire for an ecumenical council, behind Melanchthon's correspondence with the Greek Church and his fruitless interest in the Council of Trent. The interest in communicating with the Greek Church is shown in a rather touching manner by the appearance of Jacob Heerbrand's *Compendium Theologiae* in a bilingual edition (Latin and Greek) in 1582. To these faint overtures the Greek Church responded with indifference. Throughout the 16th and 17th centuries, even after confessional lines were drawn between Reformed and Roman Catholic, colloquium were held between the groups (e.g. Ratisbon 1601, Leipzig 1631, Thorn 1645). The meetings were for the most part sponsored and called by political leaders, but each denomination was well in attendance and even the most rigid Lutherans took part. What usually soured many of the friendly relationships between the parties was political encroachment and pressure, particularly by the Romanists and Reformed when they had opportunity. However, no matter how far formal discussions and negotiations broke down, there was always a great interest among Lutheran theologians in the teachings and activities of those who were not within their fellowship. A literary dialogue was always carried on between the great confessions. A dozen Roman Catholics answered Chemnitz, and a dozen Lutherans answered Bellarmine. True, these discussions were often polemical, and from the very Lutheran idea of ecumenicity they should have been. But the use of each other's output was not always polemical. Gerhard quotes Aquinas approvingly more than disapprovingly. Calov and Quenstedt cite Reformed theologians favorably very often. There was no hardening of the lines dividing the great confessions between Luther and the Formula of Concord, and between the Formula and the rise of pietism. Channels for rapproachment were open throughout that era which, although never fully exploited, were as effective for achieving true ecumenicity as those methods employed generally today.

But today there is something quite different at hand, a new approach to the question of divided churches and ecumenicity. It is a movement so great among the churches that it includes almost all of the Protestant denominations. As one writer has said, this movement, good or bad, may have effects as far reaching as the Reformation. But what is the nature of the movement? And where is it going? The first question we can answer only in part. The second question I do not believe we can answer at all. That the movement is so indefinite, so unclear in many respects, and yet so attractive, is what makes it all so bewildering and even frightening to many of us.

The movement today may be correctly epitomized in the WCC. True, we Synodical Conference Lutherans, the Roman Church, and a small group which calls itself the ICC have programs for theological discussion and even union, but who outside our own circles is listening to us? The WCC has now gathered under its wings a large number of smaller missionary movements, denominational conferences, and ecumenical societies. At New Delhi it united with the International Missionary Council. At the same time it proposes to cooperate fully with the various national councils of churches. In other words this movement which is centered in the WCC is a dynamic and popular movement and must be reckoned with.

B. Background

One of the reasons for the surprising impact and appeal of the present movement is its different basic approach to the question of discussion, cooperation and reunion from the programs of the past. This leads us into a very brief review of the background of the present ecumenical movement. The programs of the past have always had as a definite goal unity of doctrine. Even the syncretists like Calixt, Lattermann, et al., wanted reunion and cooperation on the basis of doctrine; it was just that they narrowed the basis of union to the doctrinal consensus of the first five centuries. The same was true of the program of John Dury (1596-1689) who made the fundamental dogmas (which unfortunately he never clearly defined) a necessary basis for the union of Reformed and Lutheran confessions which he envisioned.

181

In other words the older movements for union and cooperation among the churches assumed that a doctrinal basis was necessary for such cooperation, although the basis might well have been some sort of compromise. The present ecumenical movement appears to spring from different concerns, concerns which are mostly practical.

What are the origins of the present ecumenical movement as centered in the WCC? And what can they tell us about the movement today and its basic approach? They are many and varied, and perhaps no one would venture to delineate them all. Sasse and others (*CTM*, 31 [1960], p. 92) are convinced that Schmucker with his *Definite Platform* is a true father of the movement in the USA. For the most part, however, the roots of the movement lie in: 1) youth agencies such as the YMCA, YWCA, The Student Christian Movement, and the World's Student Christian Federation (Europe), 2) in the many foreign missionary organizations which for practical purposes were cooperative ventures of different denominations (London Missionary Society, The Layman's Missionary Movement, 1906, Foreign Mission Conference of North America, the Conference for Foreign Mission Societies [British] and many other German, Scandinavian, American and British Mission Societies). The most important of these became The International Missionary Council which has met periodically from 1910 and which included many of the prior national councils. None of these societies or Conferences attempted to discuss doctrine or come to any doctrinal agreement. Their purpose was purely cooperation in the practical work of the Church. 3) A third source of our present movement might be found in evangelical movements, typified by the Evangelical Alliance, founded by Thomas Chalmers (1846). This was an attempt, not to achieve union, but to bring about closer fellowship between Christians. Here a doctrinal platform was involved. Evangelical zeal was behind such a movement. But it was a zeal which was interdenominational and unionistic. 4) The Social Gospel — the concern for combating social evils of the day — was a factor behind the present Ecumenical Movement. It was agreed that if the ideas envisioned by Walter Rauschenbusch, Josiah Strong, and others were to be carried out, a new and united strategy was necessary. The influence of the Social Gospel was perhaps more indirect than direct. William Adams Brown says (*Toward a United Church*, p. 40): "While this association [in the work of the Social Gospel] helped ultimately to prepare the way for the Ecumenical Movement, its contribution at first was only indirect."

Now admittedly the purposes behind these pre-WCC movements and societies are good. The Church must serve its young people and students. It must do mission work as effectively as possible without unnecessary overlap and with as little offense to the heathen as possible. Certainly to bring Christians to a greater appreciation of the Gospel is most desirable. And the Church is concerned with society and its betterment. But can these noble purposes be achieved effectively, can they be achieved in a manner pleasing to God, can they be achieved at all, by a group so heterogeneous that there is no unanimity as to what the Church is, the Gospel is, or the Sacraments are? My question may seem to prejudge the WCC which is the cloth woven from the various strands mentioned above. And perhaps it is now too early to make any a posteriori judgment of WCC's success to date. I would simply ask: Does not the WCC *as the agency* for carrying out these purposes at the very outset condemn it to failure? My affirmative answer to the question will be brought out in the following resumé and analysis of the expressed purposes of the present WCC. But first a little more data must be given by way of review of the immediate progenitors of the WCC.

The father of the WCC is the movement called Faith and Order, a series of conferences which began at Edinburgh in 1910. The first meeting was composed mainly of missionary societies, especially from the U.S.A. However, since these societies were generally in the control of denominations, we find the respective denominations represented. "Faith and Order" describes what the purpose of these conferences was. The question of Faith asked about the doctrinal basis of the denominations and their differences from each other. The question of Order addressed itself to the ministry, the Sacraments, authority — all those matters which pertain to the ordering of the life of the Church. Not much was accomplished at this first meeting in settling these important matters. A great deal of emphasis was placed upon unity in the Church, even though little doctrinal unity was displayed. However, an optimistic note prevailed and most of those present looked forward to a "higher unity" in the future. And it was determined that some of the subjects tabooed at Edinburgh would be taken up in great seriousness at the next conference. Only two further meetings of Faith and Order were held prior to the founding of the WCC, one in Lausanne in 1927 and one in Edinburgh in 1937. These meetings discussed doctrine at some length. Not much was settled, but greater understanding between the denominations resulted. They learned to know each other better. This meant that the representatives present saw more clearly the great cleavages between their denominations and at the same time went away feeling that some sort of unity was behind it all (Normann Goodall, *The Ecumenical Movement*, p. 54).

The mother of the WCC was a movement known as the Life and Work Movement. The guiding spirit in this movement was Nathan Söderblom, a theological liberal, who was concerned primarily in having the Church exert a salutary influence on society and politics. He was particularly interested that the Church help in negotiations for a just and lasting peace after the First World War. In 1925 the first meeting of this movement took place in Stockholm with Söderblom as chairman. The purpose of the conference was "to concentrate the mind of Christendom on the mind of Christ as revealed in the Gospels towards those great social, industrial and international questions which are so acutely urgent in our civilization" (*ibid.*, p. 60). The movement was unionistic and dominated by the spirit of the Social Gospel (*ibid.*, p. 59). In 1938 a second meeting was held at Oxford a few days before the Edinburgh Conference on Faith and Order. Thus, preparations were made for a union of the two movements into the WCC. Again Söderblom was a leading figure. "What I advocate," he said, "is an Ecumenical Council of Churches. This should not be given external authority but would make its influence felt in so far as it can act with *spiritual authority*. It would not speak *ex cathedra*, but from the depth of the Christian conscience" (*ibid.*, p. 64). What he advocated came about: in Amsterdam in 1948 the WCC was established.

C. Purposes of the WCC

The basis and purposes of the WCC might best be shown by quoting from its constitution. (*Findings and Decisions — WCC 1st Assembly*, pp. 91-92):

I. BASIS

The World Council of Churches is a fellowship of Churches which accepts our Lord Jesus Christ as God and Savior. It is constituted for the discharge of the functions set out below.

II. MEMBERSHIP

Those Churches shall be eligible for membership in the World Council of Churches which express their agreement with the basis upon which the Council is founded and satisfy such Criteria as the Assembly or the Central Committee may prescribe.

Election to membership shall be by a two-thirds vote of the member Churches represented at the Assembly, each member Church having one vote. Any application for membership between meetings of the Assembly may be considered by the Central Committee; if the application is supported by a two-thirds majority of the members of the Committee present and voting; this action shall be communicated to the Churches that are members of the World Council of Churches, and unless objection is received from more than one-third of the member Churches within six months the applicant shall be declared elected.

III. FUNCTIONS

The functions of the World Council shall be:
- i To carry on the work of the world movements for Faith and Order and for Life and Work.
- ii To facilitate common action by the Churches.
- iii To promote cooperation in study.
- iv To promote the growth of ecumenical consciousness in the members of all Churches.
- v To establish relations with denominational federations of world-wide scope and with other ecumenical movements.
- vi To call world conferences on specific subjects as occasion may require, such conferences being empowered to publish their own findings.
- vii To support the Churches in their task of evangelism.

A few comments concerning this program might be made at this point.

1. The WCC has as its function to carry out the work of its parent movements, Faith and Order, and Life and Work. This means that it has primarily missionary and social interests. And it wishes to do something in these areas.

2. When stating as its function "to facilitate common action by the Churches" the WCC envisions joint Church work among the so-called member Churches.

3. When stating as its function the promotion of cooperation in study the WCC envisions more than mere discussion. At first in the parent movements public declarations were not proposed. But declarations did come out. The "Message" of Lausanne on the subject of the Gospel and the "Affirmation" of Edinburgh on the question of the Church were issued by these respective conferences. Following in this pattern the WCC will speak with authority on doctrinal and social questions, and minority opinions will only be buried in the official report. From the declarations which have been issued so far we may see how doctrinal differences are glossed over.

4. Following the spirit of the Edinburgh Conference the WCC starts with a given unity (*op. cit.*, p. 14) and from there proceeds to attempt to achieve agreement. The present differences are described as "varieties of emphasis," "schools of thought," etc. Any concept of heresy or false doctrine is totally lacking in the WCC.

In the light of the above observations — and more could be made — it is clear that from our Lutheran position the WCC is unionistic.

I now proceed to some questions which I believe confront us as we face this great movement and try to establish some position toward it. The questions are my own, and I hope that they will accomplish more than merely to raise problems. The questions center in the main in the purposes and functions of the WCC. There is great lack of clarity here, as I shall show. It would almost seem as though this great movement is groping about in the dark, not knowing what its purpose or functions are. And it seems very strange that confessional groups like the ALC and ELC in our country joined the WCC when so little can be really known about the movement.

Question 1. Is the WCC directed toward a reunited Church in the future or are its purposes more modest? At Lausanne a united Church was envisioned with open communion and full fellowship, but with each constituent holding its own doctrine, liturgy and tradition. This seems to be an impossible program (*Lausanne Report,* p. 339). At Edinburgh, Archbishop Temple stated that all division in the Church is sin, and implied that the Body of Christ will exist only when all denominations are finally brought together. And, following the platform of the Faith and Order Movement, the Edinburgh Report (p. 250) urges "the organic union of all Christendom in one, undivided church." The Evanston Report is much more cautious. It recognizes that God "in his mercy has used divisions to save souls" (p. 87) and that divisions are prompted by a sincere regard for the gospel. But it asks the question whether "we do not sin when we deny the sole lordship of Christ over the Church by claiming the vineyard for our own, by possessing our 'church' for ourselves, by regarding our theology, order, history, nationality etc. as our 'valued treasures,' thus involving ourselves more and more in the separation of sin." This gives an idea of how questions are sometimes loaded. But apart from this, Evanston makes us no longer sure whether the WCC wants a united Church which ignores doctrinal differences, a united Church which includes differences and sees an advantage in them, or a united Church which has settled differences.

185

Certain crucial things we missed at Evanston: There was no mention of heresy, of the fact that the Church must exclude from her midst false teachers. Evanston, although many Lutherans were represented there, showed no awareness of the marks of the Church (*AC*, VII), which means there is no way of coping with false doctrine. It speaks of one Church as the body of Christ, but then confuses this *Una Sancta Ecclesia* with the totality of visible Churches (Henry Van Dusen, *World Christianity*, p. 235). That the Church, properly speaking, "is nothing else than the assembly of all believers and saints," and therefore an *ecclesia abscondita*, is simply not understood. The only conclusion to be drawn from all this is that the WCC either wants the wrong thing in a united Church or does not know what it wants.

Question 2. Does the WCC seek to achieve doctrinal unity or not? From the Official Decisions of the First Assembly of the WCC (p. 16), it would appear that some unity of doctrine is a desirable and sought after goal. The following confession is made: "We all believe that the Church is God's gift to men for the salvation of the world; that the saving acts of God in Jesus Christ brought the Church into being; that the Church persists in continuity throughout history through the presence and power of the Holy Spirit. Within this agreement, we should continue, in obedience to God, to try to come to a deeper understanding of our differences in order that they may be overcome." Here a goal seems to be the resolving of differences. But how they are to be resolved and the means of overcoming them is never set forth. Scripture as a unifying principle is not mentioned. This is as strong a statement as I have found on the desire for doctrinal unity. And yet we cannot be sure that the statement has *doctrinal* differences in mind.

There is, however, much evidence that the WCC, or at least a large element therein, does not believe doctrinal unity is desirable or even God-pleasing, even if it could be achieved. William Adams Brown (*op. cit.*, p. 4) has this to say on the matter:

> Those who have united in the Movement have recognized that when finite and imperfect men are dealing with matters as high and deep as those which concern the Christian faith, one cannot expect complete agreement as to their meaning and implications. In any unity worthy of the name there must be room for honest difference of conviction, not merely in unimportant matters of habit and preference, but even in matters of vital belief. The aim of the Ecumenical Movement, therefore, is to commit the Churches to a form of unity which is consistent with the recognition of honest difference, in the hope that when this has been done, the Spirit of God will lead those who make their start at this point into ever-expanding areas of common insight.

And modern Lutherans are of the same opinion. Anders Nygren says (*Lutheran World Review*, January, 1949):

> At an earlier stage in the ecumenical movement, it was sometimes thought that the various churches must move out from their respective traditional positions and meet one another halfway, as it were. If they seem to hold varying convictions, each one must give up what is

most unacceptable to the others. Each one must surrender something in order to reach a common result. It must be clear at once that for such a conception of ecumenicity a strong confessional consciousness is indeed a threat.

But, as a matter of fact, that is really a caricature of ecumenicity. We shall never reach unity among Christians by the route of mutual concessions. The most that could be attained that way would be a syncretistic mass that would have neither unity nor truth nor power. As Christians we must pray to be delivered from that kind of ecumenicity. Just as we Lutherans cannot give up any of the truth which has been given to us and recognized by us, so we hope that other Christian churches will hold to their convictions.

In view of the above it is difficult to see why confessionalism remains any problem in the WCC; but apparently many do not go along with Nygren. At least Henry Van Dusen is sufficiently disturbed to say: "The relation of the 'world-wide confessionalism' . . . to world interdenominationalism is one of the most baffling and urgent problems of current ecumenical discussion" (see Norman Hope, *One Christ, One World, One Church*, p. 83). As of now the fact seems to be that the WCC desires unity but has not yet spelled out the nature of the unity it seeks (cf. *Ecumenical Review*, October, 1960, pp. 61ff.). From what I have been able to make out, the unity sought is one already existing in the *Una Sancta*, but the WCC by equating the *Una Sancta* with the sum of outward denominations and churches does not realize this.

Question 3. Is the basis of the WCC clear? Is it sufficient? Perhaps it is unnecessary to make comment on this matter which has been stressed so often. Suffice it to say that some denominations belonging to the WCC (e.g., certain branches of the Quakers) and leading figures in the movement have equivocated on the true deity of Christ as well as on other fundamental doctrines. Can a confessional Church on such a basis join a non-confessional organization like the WCC which engages in church work?

Question 4. Are the purposes of the WCC really clear? I am particularly concerned about the entry into economics, social ethics, and even politics. The whole Life and Work movement as sponsored by Söderblom seems to be orientated to this world, to activities which, though laudable in themselves, are not the central work of the Church. The things of Caesar are being confused with the things of God. Many of the *Findings and Decisions of the First Assembly of the WCC* read like a discussion on sociology (cf. also the Report of the First Assembly of the WCC, p. 73), and reflect a spirit of social-gospelism. Our Confessions have stated clearly that the Church must remain in its own sphere of influence; listen to *AC*, XXVIII, 5-6, 11-17):

> Our teachers assert that according to the Gospel the power of keys or the power of bishops is a power and command of God to preach the Gospel, to forgive and retain sins, and to administer and distribute the sacraments. . . . Temporal authority is concerned with matters altogether different from the Gospel. Temporal power does not protect the soul, but with the sword and physical penalties it protects body and goods from the power of others.

Therefore, the two authorities, the spiritual and the temporal, are not to be mingled or confused, for the spiritual power has its commission to preach the Gospel and administer the sacraments. Hence it should not invade the function of the other, should not set up and depose kings, should not annul temporal laws or undermine obedience to government, should not make or prescribe to the temporal power laws concerning worldly matters. Christ himself said, "My kingship is not of this world," and again, "Who made me a judge or divider over you?" Paul also wrote in Phil. 3:20, "Our commonwealth is in heaven," and in II Cor. 10:4, 5, "The weapons of our warfare are not worldly but have divine power to destroy strongholds and every proud obstacle to the knowledge of God."

Question 5. Can doctrinal discussions be carried out in the WCC on a sort of *de novo* basis which tends to ignore past differences and confessions? Is not the present posture of the WCC — which never speaks of false doctrine — incapable of arriving at doctrinal unity, even if such unity were desired? Are we being narrow and picayunish when we demand antitheses in doctrinal statements (cf. the Augsburg Confession, the Formula of Concord — and Holy Scripture itself)? Doctrinal discussion cannot be carried on under the general assumption that there are no heresies. We Lutherans must insist that confessionalism and ecumenicity belong together, as was the case in the ancient Church which regarded its ecumenical synods as orthodox. There is a free and embracing side to ecumenicity, but there has always been an exclusive side as well. What I have just said is certainly the historic position of the Lutheran Church. And this leads me to a comment regarding the LWF. By and large, the LWF emerged from just such a Lutheran position, from a platform which said a) that Christians of like faith belong together in outward fellowship, b) that careful, thorough and patient discussions should determine whether such like faith exists, and c) that Scripture will be the basis of discussion, and this discussion will be doctrinal discussion. But when the LWF states as one of its purposes, "to foster Lutheran participation in [present] ecumenical movements," it has denied this element of its birthright.

I would like to make one final remark in regard to our Synod's joining the WCC. This matter has often been broached by asking the wrong question first. The first question we must ask ourselves is: Can we with a good conscience and in obedience to God's Word join the WCC? The second question is: Is it wise for us to join the organization? If we believe that the first question must be answered negatively we have no good reason to go on to the second question. And I do not believe we should let ourselves be drawn into a discussion of it. For the second question speaks primarily concerning our opportunity to witness in the WCC and the very lack of opportunity to witness is one of the chief reasons why we must answer the first question negatively.

My conclusions are that the present Ecumenical Movement as typified by the WCC is unsound, unclear in its purpose, and as presently orientated incapable of achieving truly ecumenical results. Our negative reaction to the WCC is in no way to be construed as a rejection of ecumenicity as such.

We all want as much cooperation and coordination among Christians as is possible and right, especially in these difficult days when the Christian Church is fighting for its life in many areas. We all desire a restoration of the unity which has been lost. Our earnest desire in this matter has never changed since 1530. This is the reason we sent observers to Oberlin and New Delhi. This is the reason we read with interest and concern the literature which in great quantity is emanating from Geneva. And we do not condemn it all: we have in fact praised some of the doctrinal material coming from WCC study groups. But as much as we desire to witness to the truth and give a reason of the hope that is in us, we cannot without confessional compromise place our Church under the aegis of the WCC.

THE CONTRIBUTORS

Ralph A. Bohlmann, Ph.D. (Yale), a member of the faculty of the Concordia Seminary, St. Louis, currently serves as Executive Secretary of the Commission on Theology and Church Relations of the Lutheran Church-Missouri Synod.

The Rev. Douglas Carter is a clergyman of the Church of England and a renowned Luther scholar.

Dr. H. Daniel Friberg teaches theology at Lutheran Theological College, Makumira, Tanganyika, Africa.

The Rev. Donald R. Neiswender is a missionary of the Lutheran Church-Missouri Synod in Japan.

Robert D. Preus, Ph.D., Th.D., is professor of systematic theology at the Concordia Seminary, St. Louis, Missouri. He is best known for his book, *The Inspiration of the Scripture; A Study of the Theology of the Seventeenth Century Lutheran Dogmaticians* (2d ed.; Edinburgh: Oliver & Boyd, 1957), and has published two other related works in this field.

Dr. Hermann Sasse is a member of the faculty of the Immanuel Theological Seminary in Adelaide, Australia. He was formerly Professor of Church History at University of Erlangen. For many years active in the World Conference on Faith and Order, he was one of the founders of the "Confessing Church" in Germany.

Dr. Lewis W. Spitz, Sr., is professor of systematic theology at the Concordia Seminary, St. Louis.

Raymond Surburg, Ph.D., Th.D., is professor of Old Testament at Concordia Theological Seminary, Springfield, Illinois.

● ● ●

John Warwick Montgomery, the editor of *Crisis in Lutheran Theology,* is professor and chairman of the division of church history at Trinity Evangelical Divinity School, Deerfield, Illinois, and director of the Divinity School's European program at the University of Strasbourg, France. He is a graduate of Cornell University (A.B.), the University of California at Berkeley (B.L.S., M.A.), Wittenberg University (B.D., S.T.M.), University of Chicago (Ph.D.), and the University of Strasbourg, France (Th.D.).

In addition to his present post, Dr. Montgomery has taught at Wittenberg University, University of Chicago, and Waterloo Lutheran University (Ontario, Canada), and has served as head librarian of the Swift Library of the University of Chicago. He is an ordained Lutheran minister.

Dr. Montgomery has written many books in the areas of theology, philosophy, and church history. His most recent volumes include *Damned Through the Church, The Suicide of Christian Theology, Situation Ethics: True or False, The Quest for Noah's Ark,* and *Principalities and Powers.* He is a member of numerous professional organizations and learned societies, and is included in *Who's Who* both in this country and in France.

INDEX OF NAMES

191

Las Cases, 90
Lattermann, 181
Lefèvre, Jacques, 131
Lehmann, Helmut T., 84
Lehrmann, J. M., 43
Lessing, 52
Leupold, H. C., 96, 97
Levie, J., 46
Lightfoot, R. H., 105
Lilje, Hanns, 17
Linss, Wilhelm C., 140, 167
Loehr, Max, 54
Loetscher, Lefferts A., 53
Lofgren, David, 128
Lohr, 55
Lohse, Bernhard, 124
Losen, Carl, 97
Loyola, Ignatius, 136
Ludolf, 136
Lueker, Erwin, 48
Luthardt, 18
Luther, Martin, 23, 35, 51, 82, 84,
   85, 87, 88, 98, 116, 123-128, 130-
   138, 141, 143, 145, 147-149, 151-
   153, 157, 161, 167, 175, 180, 181
Lyra, Nicholas, 128

Mack, Edward, 70
Maier, Walter, 118
Manley, G. T., 52
Mann, C. S., 111-113
Martin, 27
Marty, Martin E., 55
Maurice, F. D., 19
Mayer, F. E., 140, 167
McKenzie, John L., 58
Melanchthon, Phillip, 98, 140, 141,
   143, 144, 146-149, 152, 154, 157,
   158, 160, 180
Mendenhall, 54
Menius, Justus, 133
Mill, John Stuart, 19
Moeller, H., 96, 97
Möller, Wilhelm, 55, 61
Montgomery, John Warwick, 6, 110,
   189, 190
Morgenstern, 54
Moriarity, Frederick J., 58
Mowinckel, Sigmund, 53, 55, 73
Muilenberg, James, 68

Neale, John Mason, 131
Neil, William, 66, 68

Neiswender, Donald R., 7, 176, 189
Nestle, 48
Nicolau, M., 37
Niebuhr, Reinhold, 28, 67
North, C. R., 55
Nyberg, 55
Nygren, Anders, 20, 21, 186, 187
Nyss, S. Gregory, 42

Occam, William, 123, 131
Oesterley, 53
Oestreicher, Th., 54
Ogden, Schubert M., 27, 100
Origen, 135
Orr, James, 55

Packer, J. I., 45, 143
Pascal, 51
Pelikan, Jaroslav, 84
Peterson, Erick, 17
Peyrerius, Isaac, 90
Pfeiffer, R. H., 50, 54, 62, 63
Pfleiderer, Otto, 52
Philo, 133
Phythian-Adams, W. J., 27
Pieper, 118
Piepkorn, Arthur Carl, 34
Pieters, Albertus, 69
Porporato, F., 42
Pourrat, P., 136
Preus, Robert D., 7, 8, 18, 34, 52,
   74, 81, 126, 180, 189
Prideaux, H., 19
Prierias, Silvester, 124
Procksch, Otto, 96

Quanbeck, Warren, 103, 106, 115
Quenstedt, 39, 181

Randolf, Julien L., 96
Rauschenbusch, Walter, 182
Reich, Max, 70
Reid, 20
Rethpath, 55
Reu, M., 62, 123, 127
Reuchlin, John, 131
Reuss, 53
Richardson, Alan, 64, 68, 69, 70, 72
Riehm, 70
Ringgren, Helmer, 72
Ritschl, A., 18, 21, 29
Robinson, Edward, 53, 54
Robinson, H. Wheeler, 77

193

Robinson, James M., 55
Roehrs, Walter R., 50
Roloff, Jürgen, 140, 167
Rowley, H. H., 55, 56, 59, 60, 64
Rust, Eric C., 58
Rylaarsdam, Coert, 68

Saint-Blancat, Louis, 132
Salaverri, I., 37
Sampey, John R., 58, 70
Sasse, Hermann, 7, 13, 81, 109, 182, 189
Scharlemann, Robert, 114
Schleiermacher, 18, 19, 21
Schlier, Heinrich, 17, 26
Schlink, Edmund, 140, 167
Schmucker, 182
Schweitzer, A., 26
Seeberg, Reinhold, 126, 127
Selnecker, Nicholas, 126
Semler, Johann, 52
Shakespeare, William, 41
Shelley, Percy, 41
Simon, Richard, 51
Smalley, B., 131
Smart, James D., 74
Smend, 53
Söderblom, Nathan, 183, 187
Spinoza, Benedict, 51, 52
Spitz, Lewis W., Sr., 7, 123, 189
Steinmann, Jean, 48, 49
Stephens-Hodge, Lionel E. H., 80
Stoeckhardt, George, 70, 82, 118
Strauss, 52, 69
Strong, Josiah, 182
Surburg, Raymond, 7, 48, 189
Sweet, L. M., 74
Szikszai, Stephen, 65

Tappert, T. G., 140
Tavard, George H., 125, 132
Taylor, Vincent, 102
Temple, 23, 24, 26, 27, 185

Terrien, Samuel, 51
Thimme, Karl, 124, 127
Tidwell, Josiah Blake, 58
Tillich, Paul, 17
Tischendorf, 48
Torm, Fr., 153, 168
Trithemius, Johannes, 131
Tromp, 36, 37
Turrettin, 36

Ulpian, 147
Unger, Merrill F., 56, 65, 71, 79

Van Dusen, Henry, 186, 187
Vatke, 52
Volz, Paul, 54, 55
Von Rad, Gerhard, 54, 55, 92, 94, 95, 97
Vriezen, T. C. 93

Wade, G. W., 62
Wallis, Charles L., 64
Walther, C. F. W., 36, 81, 82, 118, 127, 159, 164, 165, 168
Walther, Wilhelm, 124
Walwoord, John F., 56
Weiss, 48
Welch, A. C., 54
Wellhausen, Julius, 51-55
Wernle, Hans, 128
Wesley, 175
Westcott, 48
Whitehead, Alfred, 18
Wiener, 55
Wiseman, Donald, 105
Wolf, C. Unhau, 58
Wolff, 52
Wood, A. Skevington, 148, 168
Wright, G. Ernest, 21-23, 28, 54, 64, 77

Young, Edward J., 53, 76, 96, 97

Zerbolt, Gerhard, 131